TABLE OF CONTENTS

Top 20 Test Taking Tips 4
Mathematics 5
Science 37
Mathematics Practice Test 76
- Number Sense and Operations 76
- Algebra and Functions 80
- Measurement and Geometry 99
- Statistics, Probability, and Discrete Mathematics 112
- Constructed Response 119
- Answers and Explanations 121
- Number Sense and Operations 121
- Algebra and Functions 122
- Measurement and Geometry 126
- Statistics, Probability, and Discrete Mathematics 130

Science Practice Test 135
- Practice Questions 135
- Constructed Response 148
- Answers and Explanations 149

Secret Key #1 - Time is Your Greatest Enemy 162
- Pace Yourself 162

Secret Key #2 - Guessing is not Guesswork 162
- Monkeys Take the Test 162
- $5 Challenge 163

Secret Key #3 - Practice Smarter, Not Harder 164
- Success Strategy 164

Secret Key #4 - Prepare, Don't Procrastinate 164
Secret Key #5 - Test Yourself 165
General Strategies 165
Special Report: How to Overcome Test Anxiety 170
- Lack of Preparation 170
- Physical Signals 170
- Nervousness 171
- Study Steps 173
- Helpful Techniques 174

Additional Bonus Material 178

Top 20 Test Taking Tips

1. Carefully follow all the test registration procedures
2. Know the test directions, duration, topics, question types, how many questions
3. Setup a flexible study schedule at least 3-4 weeks before test day
4. Study during the time of day you are most alert, relaxed, and stress free
5. Maximize your learning style; visual learner use visual study aids, auditory learner use auditory study aids
6. Focus on your weakest knowledge base
7. Find a study partner to review with and help clarify questions
8. Practice, practice, practice
9. Get a good night's sleep; don't try to cram the night before the test
10. Eat a well balanced meal
11. Know the exact physical location of the testing site; drive the route to the site prior to test day
12. Bring a set of ear plugs; the testing center could be noisy
13. Wear comfortable, loose fitting, layered clothing to the testing center; prepare for it to be either cold or hot during the test
14. Bring at least 2 current forms of ID to the testing center
15. Arrive to the test early; be prepared to wait and be patient
16. Eliminate the obviously wrong answer choices, then guess the first remaining choice
17. Pace yourself; don't rush, but keep working and move on if you get stuck
18. Maintain a positive attitude even if the test is going poorly
19. Keep your first answer unless you are positive it is wrong
20. Check your work, don't make a careless mistake

Mathematics

Representation in mathematical processes

Representations are the tools of symbols and materials. They are used to help students understand mathematics by giving them visual guides in their thinking. For example, the conventional symbols that indicate addition, subtraction, equality, and so on (into the higher realms of symbols used in geometry, algebra, and calculus) tell students, at a glance, the process that is being calculated.

Materials that are used as representations are called manipulatives. These can be small plastic objects or pictures for the students to count, line up, or otherwise use to solve a problem. Representations make abstract concepts become concrete. They put mathematics into the students,' hands as well as heads, and the result is improved learning. Using familiar manipulatives with new problems helps the student to make connections and feel more confident and capable of expanding their skills.

Kindergarten concepts

In kindergarten, children can be prepared for the study of mathematics by practicing certain concepts such as:

- position – top, middle, bottom, above, below, before, after, between, under, inside, outside, left, and right
- visual attributes – same and different colors, shapes, and sizes; identifying items that are out-of-place or don't belong
- sorting – by size, color, type, or shape; identifying an equal number, more, or fewer of a given item
- graphing – the use of picture graphs and using data from graphs
- patterns – identifying, copying, extending, and making patterns; finding patterns that are different or alike, making predictions from patterns
- measurements – longer and shorter; how much they weigh, heavier and lighter; how much an item can hold

Mathematical properties

The properties of mathematical operations include:

- Commutative property – The product is the same regardless of the order of the factors. For example: 2 * 5 = 5 * 2.
- Associative property – The product is the same regardless of grouping. For example: (2 * 5) * 3 = 2 * (5 * 3).
- Distributive property – Multiplying a sum by a number is the same as multiplying each addend by the number and then adding the products. For example, 2 * (3 + 4) = (2 * 3) + (2 * 4) = 14.
- Zero property – The sum of a number and 0 is that number. In multiplication, the product of a number and 0 is 0. For example, 3 + 0 = 3 and 3 * 0 = 0.

Arithmetic terms specific to numbers

Numbers are the basic building blocks of mathematics. Specific features of numbers are identified by the following terms:

- Integers – The set of positive and negative numbers, including zero. Integers do not include fractions (1/3), decimals (0.56), or mixed numbers (7¾).
- Prime number – A whole number greater than 1 that has only two factors, itself and 1; that is, a number that can be divided evenly only by 1 and itself.
- Composite number – A whole number greater than 1 that has more than two different factors. In other words, any number that is not a prime number. For example: The composite number 8 has the factors of 1, 2, 4, and 8.
- Even number – Any integer that can be divided by 2 without leaving a remainder. For example: 2, 4, 6, 8, and so on.
- Odd number – Any integer that cannot be divided evenly by 2. For example: 3, 5, 7, 9, and so on.

Rational, irrational, and real numbers

Rational, irrational, and real numbers can be described as follows:

- Rational numbers are the set of whole numbers, integers, decimals, and fractions. Rational numbers can be expressed as either a negative or positive value. Any terminating decimal that can be expressed as a fraction is a rational number. For example, 45.6 can be written as 456/10.
- Irrational numbers are numbers that are not rational. That is, like the square root of 2, they cannot be written as fractions or decimals because the number of decimal places is infinite and a recurring pattern does not exist within the number. For example, Pi (π) begins with 3.141592653 and continues without end, so Pi is an irrational number.
- Real numbers are the set of all rational and irrational numbers and are used in all applications of measuring, comparing, counting, or determining quantities.

Factors

Factors are numbers that are multiplied together to obtain a product. For example, in the equation 2 * 3 = 6, the numbers 2 and 3 are factors. A prime number has only two factors (1 and itself), but other numbers can have many factors.

A "common" factor is a number that divides exactly into two or more other numbers. For example, the factors of 12 are 1, 2, 3, 4, 6, and 12, while the factors of 15 are 1, 3, 5, and 15. The common factors of 12 and 15 are 1 and 3.

A "prime" factor is also a prime number. Therefore, the prime factors of 12 are 2 and 3. For 15, the prime factors are 3 and 5.

Fractions, numerators, and denominators

A fraction is a way to compare equal parts with a whole. For example, the fraction 5/8 shows there are 5 equal parts out of 8 equal parts. A fraction is expressed as one integer written above another, with a dividing line between them (x/y).

The top number of a fraction is called the numerator, and it represents the number of parts under consideration. For example, ¼ means that 1 part out of 4 is being considered in the calculation.

The bottom number of a fraction is called the denominator, and it represents the total number of equal parts. For example, ¼ means that the whole consists of 4 parts.

Note: A fraction with zero in the denominator is called "undefined."

Decimal system

The decimal system is a number system that uses ten digits to help us with counting (0, 1, 2, 3, 4, 5, 6, 7, 8, 9), as opposed to the binary or base two number system, used by computers, that uses only the numbers 0 and 1. It is thought that the base ten (i.e. decimal) system originated when people had only their 10 fingers and 10 toes for counting.

Decimal – a number that uses a decimal point to show tenths, hundredths, thousandths, and so on. For example: 1.234

Decimal point – a symbol used, in the United States, to separate the ones place from the tenths place in decimals or dollars from cents in currency. Many countries use the decimal point to separate the one thousands place from the hundreds place.

Decimal place – the position of a number to the right of the decimal point. In the decimal 0.123, the 1 is in the first decimal place indicating tenths, the 2 is in the second decimal place indicating hundredths, and the 3 is in the third decimal place indicating thousandths.

Basic mathematical operations

The four basic mathematical operations are:

- Addition – increasing one number by adding one or more other numbers to attain a sum. For example: 2 + 4 = 6 or 8 + 9 + 10 = 27. Addition is the opposite operation to subtraction. Addition follows the associative and commutative laws.
- Subtraction – finding the difference between two numbers or reducing one number by another. For example: 6 – 4 =2. Subtraction is the opposite operation to addition. Subtraction does not follow the associative or commutative laws.
- Multiplication – a form of repeated addition in which two numbers are combined to give a product. For example: 3 * 2 = 6. In other words, add 2 three times: 2 + 2 + 2 = 6. Multiplication is the opposite operation to division. Multiplication follows the associative and commutative laws.
- Division – a form of repeated subtraction achieved by dividing one number by another number. For example: 20 ÷ 4 = 5. Division is the opposite operation to multiplication. Division does not follow the associative and commutative laws.

PEMDAS

PEMDAS stands for the order in which mathematical operations should be performed in an expression involving multiple operations. Some teachers use the phrase "Please Excuse My Dear Aunt Sally" to help the students remember PEMDAS, which stands for

Parentheses, **E**xponents, **M**ultiplication, **D**ivision, **A**ddition, **S**ubtraction.

For example, to solve the problem $5 + 20 \div 4 * (2 + 3)^2 - 6$ using PEMDAS:

P: First, perform the operations inside the parentheses, $(2 + 3) = 5$.

E: Then, solve the exponents, $(5)^2 = 25$.
At this point, the equation looks like this: $5 + 20 \div 4 * 25 - 6$.

M & D: Next, perform the multiplication and division from left to right, $20 \div 4 = 5$; then $5 * 25 = 125$.
A & S: Finally, do the addition and subtraction from left to right, $5 + 125 = 130$; then $130 - 6 = 124$.

Cardinal and ordinal numbers

Cardinal numbers are the numbers we use for counting. They are, therefore, also called counting numbers or natural numbers.

Ordinal numbers are used to show position, 1st, 2nd, 3rd, 10th, 25th, and so on.

There is more to the concept of numbers than just sequence and order. There is also magnitude to consider. For example, two is not only the number after one in order, but it is also twice as big as one. Order and magnitude are the two essential properties of numbers.

In the place value system, a number represents a quantity, a numeral is the written representation of that number, and a digit is a single-place numeral (0, 1, 2, 3, 4, 5, 6, 7, 8, 9). A digit has value based not only upon its magnitude but also on its place or position in the numeral (units, tens, hundreds, and so on). Elementary school students should be able to read numbers into the billions (12 digits).

Least common denominator, greatest common factor, and least common multiple

Least or lowest common denominator (LCD) – the lowest multiple of one or more denominators of a fraction. For example, the lowest common denominator for 2/3 and 4/9 is 9, so the fractions can be expressed as 6/9 and 4/9 for easier computation or comparison.

Greatest common factor (GCF) – the largest number that is a factor of two or more numbers. For example, the factors of 15 are 1, 3, 5, and 15; the factors of 35 are 1, 5, 7, and 35. Therefore, the greatest common factor of 15 and 35 is 5.

Least or lowest common multiple (LCM) – the smallest number that is a multiple of two or more numbers. For example, the multiples of 3 include 3, 6, 9, 12, 15, etc.; the multiples of 5 include 5, 10, 15, 20, etc. Therefore, the least common multiple of 3 and 5 is 15.

Equivalent fractions, common or simple fraction, and mixed number

Equivalent fractions – two fractions that have the same value, but are expressed differently. For example, 1/5 = 20/100 = 2/10 = 4/20.

Simplifying a fraction – the numerator and denominator of a fraction are reduced to the smallest possible integers. For example, 4/8 simplified equals 1/2.

Common or simple fraction – a fraction that has integers for both its numerator and denominator; this is the most commonly seen type of fraction. For example, 1/2, 4/3, 5/7.
Mixed number – a number containing both an integer and a fraction. For example, 5¼.

Bar graph, line graph, and pictograph

A bar graph is a graph that uses bars to compare data, as if each bar were a ruler being used to measure the data. The graph is made on grid paper and includes a scale of numbers that identify the units being measured.

A line graph is a graph that connects points to show how data increases or decreases over time. The time line is the horizontal axis. The connecting lines between data points on the graph are a way to more clearly show how the data changes.

A pictograph is a graph that uses pictures or symbols to show data. The pictograph will have a key to identify what each symbol represents. Each symbol stands for one or more objects.

The data in these types of graphs are the information that will be used in calculations.

Problem-solving strategies

For any problem, the following strategies can be used according to their appropriateness to the type of problem or calculation: i) Use manipulatives or act out the problem, ii) draw a picture, iii) look for a pattern, iv) guess and check, v) use logical reasoning, vi) make an organized list, vii) make a table, viii) solve a simpler problem, and ix) work backward.

In order to solve a word problem, the following steps can be used:

- Achieve an understanding of the problem by reading it carefully, finding and separating the information needed to solve the problem, and discerning the ultimate question in the problem.
- Make a plan as to what needs to be done to solve the problem.
- Solve the problem using the plan from step 2.
- Review the word problem to make sure that the answer is the correct solution to the problem and makes sense.

Relationship of fractions and decimals

Decimals are fractions that are based on a whole of 100 instead of a whole of 1; that is, one whole is equal to 100%. The word "percent" means "for every hundred."

Fractions can be expressed as percents by finding equivalent fractions with a denomination of 100. For example: 7/10 = 70/100 or 70%; 1/4 = 25/100 or 25%.

To express a fraction as a percent, use the formula % = 100 * (numerator/denominator). For example: 3/5 expressed as a percent would calculate as % = 100 * 3/5 = 300/5 = 60; therefore, 3/5 = 60%.

To express a percent as a common fraction, divide the percent number by 100 and reduce to lowest terms. For example: 96% = 96/100 = 24/25.

To convert decimals to fractions and fractions to decimals, just remember that percent means hundredths, that is, 0.23 = 23%, 5.34 = 534%, 0.007 = 0.7%, 700% = 7.0, 86% = 0.86, and so on.

Percentage

To find a percent of a number, the percent must first be changed to a decimal number. So 30% becomes 0.3. Then, 0.3 is multiplied by the number in question. For example: to find 30% of 33, multiply 0.3 * 33; the product is 9.9; that is, 9.9 is 30% of 33.

To find the percentage, you need to know the number of the part and the number of the whole. If you know only the separate numbers, you will have to add them to get the whole. For example: In the school cafeteria, 7 students from your class chose pizza, 9 chose hamburgers, and 4 chose tacos. To find any percentage, you first add 7 + 9 + 4 = 20. The percentages can be found by dividing 7, 9, and 4 each by the whole (20). Four out of 20 students chose tacos, and 4/20 = 1/5. Changing 1/5 to a percentage tells us that 20% of the students chose tacos.

Average, mean, median, and mode

Average is the overall term for the central tendencies of numbers that are found by determining the mean, median, and mode. An average is a single value used to represent a collection of data.

Mean is a measure of the general size of the data. The formula is: sum of values ÷ number of values. For example: given any six numbers that add up to 30, the mean of this distribution is 30 ÷ 6 = 5.

Median is the middle value of a distribution that is arranged in size order. The formula is: median = 1/2 (n + 1), where n is the number of values. However, if there is an even number of values, just add the two middle values and divide by two.

Mode is the value(s) that occur most often in a distribution. For example, in the list of 21, 23, 23, 25, 27, 27, 27, 28, 30, the value 27 occurs most often and is, therefore, the mode.

Absolute value and positive and negative integers

The Absolute Value of a number is its distance from zero. Therefore, -3 and +3 have the same absolute value of 3.

The addition of two positive quantities results in a positive quantity. For example: 4 + (+7) = +11. The addition of two negative quantities results in a negative quantity. For example: -6 + (-8) = -14.

The addition of a positive quantity and a negative quantity requires assessing which addend has the larger absolute value. Subtract the smaller absolute value from the larger one, and give to the answer the sign of the larger absolute value. For example: -8 + (+12) = (+4); 11 + (-15) = -4.

If there are three or more negative and positive numbers to be added, first combine all the like-signs, and then add the two groups. Then, determine the larger absolute value of the summed groups, and write the appropriate sign. Given the calculation -8 + (-9) + (-10) + (+12), group and add the three negative terms, leaving the positive term separated: -27 + (+12). Since the larger absolute value of the two terms is 27 (versus 15), give a negative sign to the sum, and the answer becomes -15.

Subtracting, multiplying, and dividing positive and negative integers

Subtracting a positive is the same as adding a negative and follows the rule of adding with two different signs: subtract the absolute value and give the sum the sign of the larger addend. For example: +7 – (+3) is the same as 7 – 3 = 4; or -5 – (+9) is the same as 9 – 5 = 4.

Subtracting a negative follows the same rule as the double negative in English: two negatives make a positive. Therefore, 9 – (-3) is the same as 9 + 3 or 12.

Multiplying and dividing integers with like signs follow the same rules as adding and subtracting integers: if both factors are positive, the product will be positive; if both factors are negative, the product will be positive. Multiplying or dividing a positive number by a negative one, or a negative number by a positive one, will result in a negative product; that is, multiplying or dividing integers with unlike signs always results in a negative.

Exponent

An exponent is the superscript number placed next to another number at the top right to indicate how many times the number is multiplied by itself. Exponents provide a shorthand way to write a mathematical problem.

If the exponent is 2, then the number is multiplied by itself twice, or squared; that is $a^2 = a * a$. For example: $2^2 = 2 * 2 = 4$; $3^2 = 3 * 3 = 9$

If the exponent is 3, then the number is multiplied by itself three times, or cubed, that is $a^3 = a * a * a$. For example: $2^3 = 2 * 2 * 2 = 8$; $3^3 = 3 * 3 * 3 = 27$.

The value of a number raised to an exponent is called its "power." So, 8^4 is said to be 8 to the 4th power, or 8 is raised to the power of 4.

Laws of exponents

The laws of exponents are:

- Any number to the power of 1 is equal to itself; that is, $a^1 = a$.
- The number 1 raised to any power is equal to 1; that is, $1^n = 1$.
- Any number raised to the power of 0 is equal to 1; that is $a^0 = 1$.
- Add exponents to multiply powers of the same base number; that is, $a^n * a^m = a^{n+m}$ with a as the base number and n and m representing any exponent value.
- Subtract the exponents to divide powers of the same number; that is $a^n \div a^m = a^{n-m}$.
- Multiply the exponent to raise a power to a power; that is $(a^n)^m = a^{n*m}$.
- Raise each number in the expression to the power to raise a multiplication or division expression to a power; that is, $(a * b)^n = a^n * b^m$ and $(a/b^m) = a^m / b^m$.
- Fractional exponents can be multiplied and divided like other exponents; for example, $5^{1/4} * 5^{3/4} = 5^{1/4 + 3/4} = 5^1 = 5$.

Building number sense

It is important to think flexibly to develop number sense. Therefore, it is imperative to impress upon students that there is more than one right way to solve a problem. Otherwise, students will try to learn only one method of computation, rather than think about what makes sense or contemplate the possibility of an easier way. Some strategies for helping students develop number sense include the following:

- Frequently asking students to make their calculations mentally and rely on their reasoning ability. Answers can be checked manually afterwards, if needed.
- Having a class discussion about solutions the students found using their minds only and comparing the different approaches to solving the problem. Have the students explain their reasoning in their own words.
- Modeling the different ideas by tracking them on the board as the discussion progresses.
- Presenting problems to the students that can have more than one answer.

Using manipulative materials

As with all classroom supplies, the students must understand that there are rules for their use, including how to store the materials when they are not in use.

In addition the teacher should discuss with the students the purpose of the manipulatives and how they will help the students to learn.

The students should understand that the manipulatives are intended for use with specific problems and activities; however, time for free exploration should be made available so students are less tempted to play when assigned specific tasks.

A chart posted in the classroom of the manipulatives with their names will help the students to gain familiarity with them and develop mathematical literacy skills, and loans of manipulatives for home use with a letter of explanation to the parents about the purpose and value of the manipulatives will encourage similar strategies with homework.

Square roots

A number multiplied by itself two times is squared, or raised to the power of 2; for example 4 * 4 = 16, 5 * 5 = 25, etc. The number that is squared is the square root; therefore, 4 is the square root of 16, 5 is the square root of 25. The square root of a number is indicated by a "radical" sign: √. For example: $2^2 = 4$; $\sqrt{4} = 2$ or the square root of 4 equals 2.

A perfect square is a number that has an integer for a square root. There are 10 perfect squares from 1 to 100: 1, 4, 9, 16, 25, 36, 49, 64, 81, 100 (the squares of integers 1, 2, 3, 4, 5, 6, 7, 8, 9, and 10).

Every number has both a positive and a negative square. For example, the square root of 9 is +3 and -3 because 3 * 3 = 9 and -3 * -3 = 9.

Algorithms and estimates

Algorithms result in an exact answer, while an estimate gives an approximation.

Algorithms are systematic, problem-solving procedures used to find the solution to a mathematical computation in a finite number of steps. Algorithms are used for recurring types of problems, thus saving mental time and energy because they provide a routine, unvaried method, like a standard set of instructions or a recipe. A computer program could be considered an elaborate algorithm.

An estimate attempts only to find a value that is close to an exact answer. A multidigit multiplication problem such as 345 * 12 can be calculated on paper or with a calculator but would be difficult to do mentally. However, an estimation of the answer based on something simpler *can* be done mentally, such as 350 * 10 = 3500 + 700 = 4200. This estimate is close to the actual answer of 4140. Students can practice their number sense by computing estimations.

Standard systems of measurements

There are two standard systems of measurement used for a variety of types of measurement:

- US customary units – A system used in many English-speaking countries, particularly the United States, although it has been replaced by the metric system in a number of areas. The units of measurement in this system are the inch, foot, yard, mile for length; fluid ounce, cup, pint, quart, gallon for capacity; and ounce, pound, and ton for mass.
- Metric system – A system used in many countries around the world that is based on decimals (e.g. tens, hundreds, thousands). The units of measurement in this system are the millimeter, centimeter, meter, kilometer for length; milligram, gram, kilogram, and metric tonne for mass; and milliliter, centiliter, and liter for capacity.

Length is the distance between two points. Mass is the amount of matter that an object contains, and capacity is the internal volume of an object or container.

Measures of motion

There are three measures of motion:

- Speed – the measure of distance moved over time. Speed is often measured in miles per hour, kilometers per hour, or meters per second. The formula for measuring the rate of speed is rate = distance ÷ time. Therefore, if 150 miles are traveled in 3 hours, the rate of speed is 150 ÷ 3 or 50 miles per hours.
- Velocity – the measure of distance moved in a particular direction over a period of time. Velocity is a vector quantity, meaning it has both magnitude (size) and direction. Often measured in mph or kph, velocity is expressed, for example, as 150 mph on a bearing of 45 degrees.
- Acceleration – the rate of change of velocity. Also a vector quantity, acceleration is most often measured in meters per second. The formula for calculating acceleration equals change of velocity divided by time taken. For example, a sports car is considered fast if it can accelerate from 0-100 kph in 4 seconds.

Measures of time

The standard measures of time are:

- Millisecond (ms) – there is 1,000 milliseconds in a second; this unit is useful for computing the rate of speed of computer processing.
- Second (s) – the smallest unit of time on a standard clock; there are 60 seconds in 1 minute.
- Minute (min) – 60 seconds; there are 60 minutes in one hour.
- Hour (hr) – 60 minutes; there are 24 hours in a day.
- Day – the time it takes the Earth to rotate once, or 24 hours.
- 12-hour clock – most time is expressed in two 12-hour groups: the time between midnight and noon or a.m. (**a**nte **m**eridian or before noon), and the time between noon and midnight,

or p.m. (**p**ost **m**eridian or after noon). Time on this system is written with the minutes after a colon, so 3:15 p.m. means fifteen minutes after 3 p.m.

- 24-hour clock – used by the military and on some digital clocks. There is no a.m. or p.m. since time, expressed in 4 figures, runs from 0000 h to 2359 h; for example 3:40 p.m. = 1540 h.

Scientific notation

Scientific notation, also known as exponential notation, is a way of writing large numbers in a shorter form. The form $a * 10^n$ is used in scientific notation, where a is greater than or equal to 1 and less than 10 and n is the number of places the decimal must move to obtain this form.

For example, the number 234,000,000 is cumbersome to write, with all those zeroes. So, to write the value in scientific notation, place a decimal point between the first and second numbers (2.34). Then, to find the appropriate power of 10, count the number of digits to the right of the decimal point (to the left if the number is less than one). Therefore, $234,000,000 = 2.34*10^8$ and $0.0000234 = 2.34*10^{-5}$. This method is also a quick way to compare very large and very small numbers. By comparing exponents, it is easy to see that $3.28 * 10^4$ is smaller than $1.51*10^7$ (because 4 is less than 7). Calculators often use scientific notation to express numbers that are too long to fit in the display.

Ratio and proportion

A ratio is a comparison of two quantities in a particular order. For example, if there are 14 computers in a lab, but the class has 20 students, there is a ratio of 14 to 20. Ratios can be written with a colon, so the ratio of students to computer would be 20:14, or as a fraction, 20/14.
A proportion is the relationship of change in two quantities. A direct proportion describes a quantity that increases with an increase in another quantity or decreases with a decrease in the other quantity. For example, if a sheet cake can be cut to serve 18 people and 2 sheet cakes can serve 36 people, the number served is directly proportional to the number of cakes.

Inverse proportion describes a quantity that increases as the other quantity decreases (or vice versa). For example, the time of a car trip decreases as the speed increases, so the time is inversely proportional to the speed.

Interest

Interest is the amount of money earned in savings (loaned to a bank) or paid for the use of borrowed money (bank gives loan). The rate of interest is set by the bank and varies according to economic conditions.

Principal is the amount originally loaned or borrowed.

Simple interest is the interest that is earned or paid only on the principal; it does not change.

Compound interest is the interest that is earned or paid on the principal and the interest already earned; thus, the amount of money that earns interest is cumulative and increases each year.

A multiplier is a number multiplied by the principal that gives the total amount earned or borrowed at the end of a given period, usually a year. The multiplier is 1 plus the rate of interest. So, an interest rate of 5% per annum results in a multiplier of 1.05.

Calculating interest

The following formula is used to calculate simple interest:

Simple interest = Principle * Rate of interest * Time ÷ 100.

For example, if a person invests $1,000 at an interest rate of 5% per annum, that would be 1,000 * 5 * 1 ÷ 100 or 5,000 ÷ 100 = $50.

The following formula is used to calculate compound interest:

- Compound interest = Principle * (1 + interest rate [i.e. the multiplier])^{Time} – Principle.

For example, $1,000 invested for 3 years at 5% interest would be 1,000 * (1.05)^{3} - $1,000 = 1157.63 – 1,000 = $157.63. Using simple interest, the same account would have earned only $150.

Probability

Probability is a branch of statistics that calculates the ratio of the number of ways an event can occur to the total number of possible outcomes; in other words, the calculation shows how likely something is to happen. The classic example is a coin toss. There are only two possible results: heads or tails. The likelihood that the coin will land as one or the other is 1 out of 2, or 1/2 (or 0.5, or 50%). When there are equally likely outcomes, such as in a coin toss, the events are called equiprobable.

Other terms used in probability include: Outcome – a possible result in an experiment or event; Sample – a selected part of a large group (large samples tend to be more accurate than smaller samples); Success – the desired result (for example, if you want the coin toss to come up heads and it does, you have had a successful outcome).

Probability scale

A probability scale is one that measures the likelihood of an outcome. Certainty is if something is certain to happen, such as growing older each minute, and has a probability of 1. Impossibility is if something has no possibility of happening (such as turning into a frog without an evil spell), and the probability assigned is 0. The values of 0 and 1 are the extremes of probability. Thus, the probability of an event happening between certainty and impossibility can be anything between 0 and 1. If the probability number is closer to 0, then the event is less likely to happen; if closer to 1, it is more likely to happen.

Probabilities are affected by the frequency of an event (2 out 3 tosses), how many items are involved (more than one coin), and whether the event can be altered by other factors (rain, loaded dice). Two or more events that cannot have a successful outcome at the same time are called mutually exclusive events.

Dividend, division, remainder, divisor, and quotient

Dividend is the number to be divided. For example, if 18 is divided by 6 (18 ÷ 6), then 18 is the dividend.

Division is the process that tells how many items are in a group, or how many groups exist.

Remainder is the surplus value when one number cannot be evenly divided by another; that is, the number less than the divisor that remains after dividing. For example, 36 divided by 5 is 7 with a remainder of 1.

Divisor is the number by which a dividend is divided. For example, if 18 is divided by 6 (18 ÷ 6), then 6 is the divisor.

Quotient is the number, other than the remainder, that is the result of the division operation. For example, if 18 is divided by 6, the outcome is 3 and is called the quotient.

Vertical axis, horizontal axis, scale, interval, and coordinates

Vertical Axis is the up-and-down number line on a graph.

Horizontal Axis is the left-to-right number line on a graph.

Scale is the marked intervals on the vertical or horizontal axis of a graph that represent the units being measured. For example, a common scale is from 1 to 10, with intervals of 1 (1, 2, 3, 4, 5, 6, 7, 8, 9, and 10).

Interval is the fixed distance between the numbers on the scale of a graph. For example, if the axis reads 2001, 2002, 2003, 2004, then the graph represents one year intervals of data.

Coordinates are the points on the graph that indicate the intersection of two data numbers. For example, a graph that shows 60% of a goal was reached in November would have a point placed where 60 and November meet on the graph.

Roman numerals

In ancient Rome, a system of numerals was devised that is still being used today. The system consists of 7 letters or symbols to represent numbers: I = 1, V = 5, X = 10, L = 50, C = 100, D = 500, and M = 1,000.

To represent numbers in between these 7 main numbers, a system of addition and subtraction was devised. If the symbol to the right is of equal or lesser value, add its value to the value of the symbol to the left; for example, VI = 5 + 1 = 6 or CC = 100 + 100 = 200. If the symbol to the right is of greater value, subtract the left symbol from the right one; for example, IV = 5 – 1 = 4 or XC = 100 – 10 = 90.

Rounding

Rounding is the approximation of a figure by reducing or increasing a number to the nearest integer (ten, hundred, etc.). The amount of approximation depends on the degree of accuracy of the number itself, and the amount of rounding often depends on what is being measured. For example, a person's height would be rounded to the nearest inch, but the national debt might be rounded to the nearest trillion.

To round a number, determine the digit place to which the number will be rounded, and then look at the digit to the right – if it is 5 or greater, increase the digit being rounded by 1. If it is less than 5, the digit being rounded remains the same. For example, 346 rounded to the nearest 10 would be 350, but 342 would be rounded to 340. The number 8,766 rounded to the nearest 1,000 would be 9,000 and to the nearest 100 would be 8800.

Temperature

Temperature is the measure of the degree of hotness or coldness of a substance according to a standard scale.

The Celsius temperature scale (once called Centigrade because the scale is divided into 100 parts) is one in which water boils at 100°C and freezes at 0°C. It was devised by Anders Celsius, a Swedish astronomer, in 1742.
The Fahrenheit temperature scale is one in which water boils at 212°F and freezes at 32°F. It was devised by Daniel Gabriel Fahrenheit, a German physicist who invented the alcohol thermometer in 1709 and the mercury thermometer in 1714. This scale is commonly used in the United States, but many other countries use the Celsius scale. To convert a temperature from Fahrenheit to Celsius, use the following formula: $F = 9/5C + 32$, where F is the temperature in Fahrenheit and C is the temperature in Celsius. If you are given the temperature in Fahrenheit, you can always rearrange the formula and solve for C.

Algebraic expressions and formulas

An algebraic expression is a mathematical statement written in a form that uses letters and symbols to represent numbers and the relationships between them. Letters from the beginning of the alphabet are used to represent known values (for example, $a^2 = a * a$), and letters from the end of the alphabet are used to represent unknown values (for example, $3x + 4y = 18$). An algebraic expression can contain any combination of letters or numbers and usually involves arithmetic operations, such as addition, subtraction, multiplication, or division.

A formula is the algebraic expression of a general rule. For example, the formula for finding the area of a parallelogram is $a = bh$ or area = base * height.

Variable, dependent variable, constant, and coefficient

A variable is an unknown number or quantity represented by a letter. Sometimes the letter will represent the word it is replacing (for example, d for distance, h for height, t for time), but ordinarily the variable is indicated by a general letter, like "x."

A dependent variable is a variable with a value that is calculated from other values. For example, the area of a parallelogram is dependent on the values of the base and the perpendicular height, that is, $a = bh$, with "a" as the dependent variable. Since the base and height are predetermined, they are independent variables.

A constant is a number with a value that is always the same. For example, in the algebraic expression $y = \frac{3}{4}x - 5$, 5 is the constant.

A coefficient is a constant that is placed before a variable in an algebraic expression. For example, in the expression $3y + 1$, 3 is the coefficient of y.

Term

A term can be a variable, a constant, or a coefficient separated from the rest of the mathematical expression by an algebraic sign, such as a "+" or "-" sign. For example, in the expression $\frac{3}{4}x - 5$, there are two terms: $\frac{3}{4}x$ and 5. The variable is "x," 5 is the constant, and ¾ is the coefficient.

Terms that contain the same letter or combination of letters and the same exponents are "like" terms (for example, xy and 2xy are like terms); terms that contain different letters or combinations of letters or different exponents are "unlike" terms (for example, 2y and y^2 are unlike terms).

Any algebraic expression containing two terms is called a binomial expression. An algebraic expression containing three terms is a trinomial expression (for example, $3x + y - xy$); however, any algebraic expression containing two or more terms can also be called a polynomial or multinomial expression (for example, $2 + 3y + 4x - 1$).

Parentheses, substitution, and simplification

Parentheses are used to group terms together. A term directly in front of a set of parentheses can be multiplied by each term in the parentheses; that is, $3(x - y) = 3x - 3y$.

Substitution is the replacement of the letters in an algebraic expression with known values. For example, given the formula for the area of a parallelogram, a = bh, if it is known that the base is 4 cm and the height is 5 cm, then these numbers can be substituted into the formula to calculate the area: $a = 4 * 5 = 20$ cm^2.

Simplification is the process of combining like terms in an algebraic expression to reduce the expression to the minimum number of terms.

Simplification

When like terms are added or subtracted, for example, $2x + 3y + 2y - x$ can be simplified to $(2x - x) + (3y + 2y) = x + 5y$.

When like terms are multiplied, simplification involves multiplying all terms; for example, $2a * 3b = 2 * a * 3 * b = 6 * a * b = 6ab$.

When like terms are divided, simplification involves canceling the common terms; for example, $6xy^3 \div 2y = 6 * x * y * y * y \div 2 \div y = 3xy^2$ ($6 \div 2 = 3$ and cancel out 1 y which is common in the numerator and denominator).
When like terms involve fractions, find a common denominator, collect like terms, and simplify as usual.

Factor an expression

An expression is factored when it is rewritten as a product of its factors. For example, to factor 4x – 16:

- Find the common factor of 4 and 16, and write it outside a set of parentheses 4 ( ).
- Divide each term by the common factor, 4x ÷ 4 = x and -16 ÷ 4 = -4.
- Write the result in the parentheses, 4(x – 4).
- Check the answer by applying the distributive property, 4(x-4) = 4x – 16.

Equation and solution

An algebraic equation is a mathematical statement that two expressions are equal. An equation is solved by finding the value of the unknown variable or variables.

A solution is any value of a variable that satisfies the equation; in other words, makes the equation true.

Rearranging an equation means moving around the terms until one of the terms is alone on one side of the equal sign. The equation can then be solved for that one term.
For example, to solve 3y = 6x - 9 for x:

- Rearrange the terms so that the *x* term will be separated on one side of the equation. This can be accomplished by adding 9 to both sides of the equation, resulting in 6y + 9 = 3x.
- Divide both sides by 3 to solve for the value of x, (6y + 9) ÷ 3 = 3x ÷3 = 2y + 3 = x.
- Therefore, the final answer is x = 2y + 3.

Quadratic equation

A quadratic equation includes a variable that is squared, and the standard form is $ax^2 + bx + c = 0$, where "a" does not equal 0.

The solutions of a quadratic equation are called its "roots."The following steps are used when a quadratic equation can be solved by factoring:

1. If not in standard form, rearrange the equation to equal zero.

2. Factor the left side of the equation to give two expressions in parentheses.

a) Find the factors of the "x^2" term, and place these terms first in each of the parentheses. If the factors were 2 and 1, we would have (2x +) (x +) = 0.

b) Now, find all factors of the "c" constant.

c) If the coefficient of x^2 is one, find two factors of "c" that, when multiplied, are equal to "c" and when added are equal to "b." For example, the equation $x^2 + 6x + 8 = 0$ factors to (x + 2) (x + 4) = 0. [If the coefficient of x^2 is not one, the terms in the parentheses will be a combination of the factors from x^2 and "c."]

3. Set each pair of parentheses equal to zero. That is, (x + 2) = 0 or (x + 4) = 0

4. Solve these two equations for x to obtain the roots of x = -2 or x = -4.

Completing the square

"Completing the square" means converting the left side of a quadratic equation into a perfect square: $(x + y)^2 = z$. This method can be used to solve any quadratic equation.

Starting with the standard quadratic form, $ax^2 + bx + c = 0$, move the number represented by c to the right side of the equation.
For example: $x^2 - 6x + 5 = 0$ becomes $x^2 - 6x = -5$.
To complete the square on the left, half the coefficient of x and square the result: $(6/2)^2 = 3^2 = 9$.
Then add the result to both sides: $x^2 - 6x + 9 = -5 + 9$.

Factor the left side using the form $(x + y)^2 = z$: $(x - 3)^2 = 4$

To solve for x, take the square root of both sides: $x - 3 = \pm 2$ or x = 5 or 1.

Note: Remember that there is a positive and negative value when taking a square root. If you only use the positive value, you will be missing one of the solutions of the quadratic.

Quadratic formula

The quadratic formula can be used to solve any quadratic equation in the form:
$ax^2 + bx + c = 0$.

The quadratic formula is:

$$x = \frac{-b \pm \sqrt{b^2 - 4ac}}{2a}$$

A, b, and c from the given equation.

If the equation is $2x^2 + 4x - 6 = 0$, then a = 2, b = 4, and c = -6.

Solve the equation by substituting the values for a, b, and c into the quadratic formula.

In our example above, the roots will be x = 1 and x = -3.

If your answer is correct, the sum of the roots should be equal to $-b \div a$. For example, the solutions summed equal 1 + (-3) = -2, which gives the same result as $-4 \div 2 = -2$.

Simultaneous equations

Simultaneous equations are pairs of equations in which the variables represent the same numbers in each equation. To solve, find a solution that makes both equations true.

One method to solve simultaneous equations is through the use of substitution. In this process, we substitute one of the expressions in the other equation to find the value of one variable. The value of this variable can then be substituted into the first equation to find the remaining variable. For example, given the two equations 5x – y =13 and 2x + y = 15, find the solution for x and y that makes both equations true.

First, solve one equation for the y variable: $y = 5x - 13$.

Substitute the re-written expression for the same variable in the other equation:
$2x + 5x - 13 = 15$.

Collect like terms and simplify: $7x - 13 = 15$, so $7x = 28$, and $x = 4$.

Substitute the known value into the other equation: $2(4) + y = 15$, so $y = 15 - 8$, and $y = 7$.

Therefore, the solution to this set of simultaneous equations is $x = 4$ and $y = 7$.

If the same or opposite terms appear in two equations, the method of elimination can easily be used to solve the simultaneous equations. If the terms are the same (for example 2x and 2x) subtract one equation from the other. If the terms are opposite (for example -2x and 2x), add the equations, then simplify.

To solve the equations $2x - 3y = 5$ and $x + 3y = 16$, add the two equations to eliminate the y term:
$3x = 21$, so $x = 7$.

Then substitute the value of the known variable into either equation to find the value of the unknown variable: $2(7) - 3y = 5$ or $3y = 14 - 5$ or $3y = 9$, and $y = 3$.

Therefore, the solution to this set of simultaneous equations is $x = 7$ and $y = 3$.

Eliminating terms

First, find the least common multiple of one pair of coefficients, and multiply one or both equations by the required number to make those coefficients equal. For example, given the equations $2x + 3y = 0$ and $3x + 2y = 5$, multiply the first equation by 2 and the second by 3 to get $4x + 6y = 0$ and $9x + 6y = 15$. (Don't forget to multiply through both sides of the equation!)

Now two terms are the same, and we can subtract one equation from the other. (If the terms had been opposite, we would have added the equations.) Subtracting the equations in the example...
$(4x + 6y) - (9x + 6y) = 0 - 15$ or $- 5x = -15$ or $5x = 15$, so $x = 3$.

Lastly, substitute the value of the known variable in either of the equations to find the value of the remaining variable. For example: $4(3) + 6y = 0$ or $12 + 6y = 0$ or $6y = -12$, so $y = -2$.
Therefore, the solution to these simultaneous equations is $x = 3$ and $y = -2$.

Inequalities

Opposite of an equation, an inequality is a mathematical statement that shows two algebraic expressions are not equal. An inequality, nonetheless, can be solved in a way similar to an equation.

The symbols for an inequality are given by the following:

a) $<$ means "less than"; b) $>$ means "greater than"; and c) $\neq$ means "not equal to."

A conditional inequality is one that is true only for certain values of the variable.

An unconditional inequality is one that is true for all values of the variables.

A double inequality is one in which a variable has to satisfy two inequalities.

Inequalities can be solved by rearranging the inequality and solving for an unknown variable. To keep the inequality true, any term added to or subtracted from one side of the inequality must be added to or subtracted from the other side. The same is true for multiplying or dividing. Although, if multiplying or dividing by a negative number, the inequality sign is reversed.

Domain, range, composite function, and inverse function

A function is a relationship in which two sets are linked by a rule that pairs each element of the first set with exactly one element of the second set. A function is represented by the letter "f." Functions are used in every-day situations. For example, the relationship between the cost of an item and the amount of sales tax is a function.

Result: a value that is obtained when a function is applied to a value x; represented as f(x) [pronounced "f of x"].

Domain: The set of values to which a function is applied.

Range: The set of values to which the results belong.

Composite function: a combination of two or more functions; the second and subsequent functions are represented by different letters. For example: $f \circ g(x)$ means "f of g of x;" g is calculated first and that answer is used in the function, f.

Inverse function: An operation or series of operations that reverses a function; usually written as $f^{-1}(x)$.

Value of algebra

Algebra serves as the basic language of mathematics. As such, it provides a means of condensing large amounts of data into efficient mathematical statements. Through algebra, we are also able to create a mathematical model of a situation. Further, algebra provides the structure for solving mathematical problems and links numerical and graphical representations of data.

A perpetual debate exists about the value of studying algebra for the average person because it is felt that few people actually use algebra in the workplace. While that is not necessarily true, it is a fact that studying algebra teaches a style of thinking that is important to competent functioning, including the concepts of patterns, functions, and quantitative relationships.

History of variables

Variables are the heart of algebra. Historically, algebra in its earliest stages used ordinary language. In the period from 250-1600 A.D., mathematicians began to use symbols to represent unknown quantities and solve problems for these unknowns. Since 1600 A.D., symbols have been used in all algebraic operations, starting with Francoise Viète, who used letters for mathematical notations.

Soon afterward, René Descarte developed the system of using a, b, c for constants and x, y, z for unknowns.

Today, the particular use of a variable is determined by the mathematical context. The most common uses are as specific unknowns, as generalizers, and as varying quantities. The challenge for students is to learn how values are represented symbolically and to understand the various meanings for letters or shapes in equations, inequalities, formulas, and functions.

Fibonacci sequence

Patterns are an important aspect of mathematics. Italian mathematician Leonardo de Pisa (1175-1245), nicknamed Fibonacci, discovered a unique sequence of numbers with several amazing relationships. The sequence begins with 1, 1, and each following number is the sum of the two preceding numbers. The result is 1, 1, 2, 3, 5, 8, 13, 21, 34, 55, 89, 144, and so on.

Interestingly, the sum of the first 3 numbers is 4, which is one less than the fifth number (5). The sum of the first 4 numbers is 7, one less than the sixth number (8). The relationship holds throughout the sequence.

The Fibonacci sequence describes a variety of phenomena in the world. In music, the keys of a piano have 5 black and 8 white keys in each octave of 13 notes. In nature, the number of spirals on pinecones, pineapples, and in the center of a sunflower is in a Fibonacci sequence, as are the leaves on the stems of many types of plants.

Fibonacci numbers and the golden ratio

Fibonacci ratios are a comparison of two Fibonacci numbers, usually adjacent numbers in the sequence. These ratios, if expressed as decimals, hover around 1.6 to 1.618 and are irrational numbers. Oddly enough, this 1.6 ratio is found in many shapes and objects. The Greeks called it the golden ratio (or golden proportion) and represented it with the letter phi. The Egyptians may have used this ratio in the construction of the pyramids.

Rectangles whose length-to-width ratio is 1.6 are called golden rectangles. Psychologists have discovered that people find golden rectangles more aesthetically pleasing than other rectangles. It is this knowledge that has determined the shape of common objects, such as cereal boxes and picture frames.

The human body has golden proportions, which helps artists to draw figures accurately. For example, the length of an index finger compared with the length from the fingertip to the big knuckle is a ratio of 1.6, as is the length of the arm from the shoulder in relation to the length from the fingertips to the elbow.

Equality and balance scales

Equality is a fundamental concept of algebra, but many students find it difficult to understand. Students may misinterpret the use of the equal sign by thinking it is telling them to perform an operation, as in + or – signs. However, students seem to understand that a balance scale remains balanced if equal amounts are on both sides but becomes unbalanced if items are added or subtracted. Therefore, performing activities with balance scales is often a good hands-on practice for the concept of equality.

Using manipulatives of various shapes on the balance scale can also help with the understanding of different letters in an algebraic equation. If three triangular-shaped objects are equal in weight to two cylinders, the students should be able to make the connection to 3x = 2y. Adding or taking away different shapes also helps with grasping the use of symbols in longer equations.

Representation in algebra

Representation is the display of mathematical relationships graphically, symbolically, pictorially, or verbally.

Graphical representations include bar graphs, line graphs, histograms, line plots, and circle graphs.

Symbolic representations involve the use of symbols and include equations, formulas, and rules.

Pictorial representations include two- and three-dimensional drawings, maps, balance scales, and scale drawings.

Verbal representations are the use of words to express mathematical relationships in speech or writing.

Even though any of these representations can be used in a math problem, there is probably one way that is easier to use and provides more clarity about the situation than the others. Which representation to use should be evaluated for each individual problem. For example, working with numbers in an organized way, such as putting them on a table, often makes patterns more obvious.

Field properties, closure, and denseness

Field properties are the same as those learned in foundational mathematics; however, for algebra, these properties can be expressed using symbols. The basic rules for using symbols are... (1) a, b, and c are real numbers and (2) multiplication is implied when there is no symbol between two variables; that is, ab = a * b. Multiplication can also be indicated by a raised dot (˙).

The rule of closure states that the sum or product of two real numbers is a real number; that is, if a and b are real numbers, then a + b is a real number, and ab is a real number.

Denseness is a rule that says, between any pair of rational numbers, there is at least one rational number. For example, between 4.2 and 4.3, there is the rational number of 4.25. However, the set of natural numbers in not dense because, between two consecutive natural numbers, there may not exist another natural number. For example, between 3 and 4 there exists no other natural number.

Associative, commutative, and distributive

The commutative property shows that the order of the addends, or factors, does not affect the sum or product: a + b = b + a and ab = ba.

The associative property states that the grouping of the addends, or factors, does not affect the sum or product: (a + b) + c = a + (b + c) and (ab)*c = a*(bc).

The distributive property states that multiplying a sum by a number is equal to multiplying each addend by that number: a (b+c) = ab + ac.

Additive identity, multiplicative identity, additive inverse, and multiplicative inverse

The additive identity property states that the sum of any number and zero is that number: a + 0 = a.

The multiplicative identity, or the property of one, says that the product of any number and one is that number: a * 1 = a.

Additive inverse, or the property of opposites, states that the sum of any number and its opposite is zero and is represented by the following statement: a + (-a) = 0.

Multiplicative inverse, or the property of reciprocals, says that the product of any number and its reciprocal is one and is represented by the following statement: a/b * b/a = 1.

Point, line segment, transversal, horizontal, vertical, perpendicular, parallel, collinear, plane, coplanar, and solid

The following terms are commonly used in geometric studies:

- Point – a location found by its coordinates; usually represented on diagrams by a small dot or two crossed lines
- Line segment – the part of a straight line between two points, thus having a fixed length
- Transversal – a line that crosses two or more other lines
- Horizontal – a line or plane that follows the horizon, at a right angle to the vertical
- Vertical – a line or plane that is at a right angle to the horizon
- Perpendicular – a line or plane that is at a right angle to another line or plane
- Parallel – a set of lines or curves that never cross and are the same distance apart at every point along the lines
- Collinear – points that lie in a straight line or share a common straight line
- Plane (or plane figure) – a two-dimensional object, with length and width
- Coplanar – points that lie on the same plane, or share a common plane
- Solid – a three-dimensional object, with a length, width, and thickness

Cartesian coordinate system

The Cartesian coordinate system describes the position of points on a plane or in a space in terms of their distance from lines called axes. The two lines, or axes, are the horizontal x-axis and the vertical y-axis, which are at right angles to each other and thus form a rectangular coordinate system. The point at which the two axes meet is the "origin."

Points along the x-axis and to the right of the origin have a positive value, while those to the left of the origin are negative. Points along the y-axis above the origin are positive, while those below the origin are negative.

The position of a point, labeled (x,y), is described in terms of its distance from the origin. The x-coordinate is the distance of the point from the origin, parallel to the x-axis. The y-coordinate is the distance of the point from the origin, parallel to the y-axis. The x-coordinate is always written first.

Quadrant and dimensions

A quadrant is any of the four regions formed on a plane by the x-axis and the y-axis (not to be confused with the use of the term quadrant for a part of a circle). The 1st quadrant is to the right of the y-axis and above the x-axis. The 2nd quadrant is to the left of the y-axis and above the x-axis. The 3rd quadrant is to the left of the y-axis and below the x-axis. The 4th quadrant is to the right of the y-axis and below the x-axis.

Dimensions are determined by the number of coordinates needed to fix a point in space. If the position of a point on a line or line segment can be described by one coordinate, then the line is one-dimensional. If two coordinates are needed to describe the position of a point in a plane, the plane is two-dimensional. If three coordinates are needed, then the plane is three-dimensional.

Angles

Each type of angle has a distinctive feature:

- Null or zero angle – No rotation (0°)
- Whole turn, or full turn, or round angle, or perigon – A complete turn, or revolution, equal to 360°
- Right angle – A quarter of a full turn, equal to 90°
- Straight or flat angle – half a full turn, equal to 180°
- Acute angle – Any angle smaller than a right angle (< 90°)
- Obtuse angle – Any angle greater than a right angle (> 90°), but smaller than a straight angle (< 180°)
- Reflex angle – Any angle greater than a straight angle (> 180°)
- Positive angle – An angle that is constructed or measured in a counter-clockwise direction
- Negative angle – An angle that is constructed or measure in a clockwise direction

Polygons, vertices, sides, interior and exterior angles, a cyclic, and a diagonal

A polygon is a shape formed from three or more points called vertices (each point is called a vertex) joined by three or more straight lines called sides. The name of most polygons is determined by the number of angles or sides it has.

An interior angle is any of the angles inside a polygon where two sides meet at a vertex. The sum of the interior angles of a polygon is equal to the sum of the interior angles of any other polygon with the same number of sides.

An exterior or external angle is any of the angles formed between a side of a polygon and the extension of the side next to it.
A cyclic is a polygon that can have a circle drawn around it such that each vertex of the polygon lies on the circle's circumference.

A diagonal is a line that joins two vertices of a polygon that are not next to each other.

Polygons

The following list presents several different types of polygons:

- Triangle – 3 sides
- Quadrilateral – 4 sides
- Pentagon – 5 sides
- Hexagon – 6 sides
- Heptagon or septagon – 7 sides
- Octagon – 8 sides
- Nonagon – 9 sides
- Decagon – 10 sides
- Hendecagon – 11 sides
- Dodecagon – 12 sides
- Quindecagon – 15 sides
- Icosagon – 20 sides

N-gon – a polygon that has "n" angles and "n" sides, where n represents any number.

The sum of the interior angles of an n-sided polygon is 180°(n – 2). For example, in a triangle, n is 3, so the sum of the interior angles is 180° (3 – 2) = 180°. In a quadrilateral, n is 4, and the sum of the angles is 180°(4 – 2) = 360°. The sum of the interior angles of a polygon is equal to the sum of the interior angles of any other polygon with the same number of sides.

An equiangular polygon is one in which all the interior angles are equal.
An equilateral polygon is one in which all sides are equal.

Note: An equiangular polygon does not have to be equilateral, and an equilateral polygon does not have to be equiangular.
A convex polygon is one in which all interior angles are less than 180°.

A concave polygon is one in which one or more interior angles are greater than 180°.

A regular polygon is one in which all the sides and interior angles are equal; it is both equilateral and equiangular. Examples of regular polygons are squares, equilateral triangles, regular pentagons, and regular hexagons.

Upper-case letters (A, B, C, etc.) are used to label the vertices of a polygon, while the sides are labeled using lower-case letter (a, b, c, etc.).

Tessellation

Tessellation is the combination of one or more shapes such that, when repeated, the pattern covers a surface plane without leaving any gaps or overlaps. Shapes that fit together in this way are said to tessellate. Another word for tessellation is tiling. For example, a group of squares can tessellate because they fit together completely; however, a group of circles does not tessellate because there are gaps at the curves.

A regular polygon has 3 or more sides and angles, all equal. A regular tessellation includes only one type of congruent (all the same size and shape), regular polygon. Only three regular polygons tessellate in the Euclidean plane: triangles (in a pyramid shape), squares (in a block), and hexagons.

Semi-regular tessellation is a tessellation made up of more than one type of regular polygon. The pattern formed at each vertex where the polygons meet is the same. There are eight semi-regular tessellations. These use a combination of equilateral triangles, squares, hexagons, octagons, and dodecagons.

Triangles

A triangle is a polygon with three sides and three angles. A triangle can be classified according to the length of its sides or magnitude of its angles.

Scalene – The sides are all different lengths, so all three angles are different as well.

Isosceles – Has two equal sides; the angles opposite these sides are also equal. An isosceles triangle has one line of symmetry that divides the triangle into two identical right-angled triangles.

Equilateral –Has three equal sides; each angle measures 60°. An equilateral triangle has three lines of symmetry, each of which divides the triangle into two identical right-angled triangles.
Acute-angled – All three interior angles are less than 90°.

Obtuse-angled – One interior angle is greater than 90°.

Right-angled – One interior angle is equal to 90°; the other two angles are complementary, meaning they sum to 90°.

Congruent, SSS, SAS, AAS, RHS, and similar triangles

Pairs of triangles can have unique features and names. The following pairs are congruent triangles that are exactly the same shape and size.

Side-side-side (SSS) triangles are two triangles in which all three sides of one are equal to all three sides of another, but positioned differently.

Side-angle-side (SAS) triangles are two triangles in which two sides and the included angle of one triangle are the same as the other, but positioned differently.
Angle-angle-side (AAS) triangles are two triangles in which two angles and any side on one triangle are the same as that of the other, but positioned differently.

Right-angle-hypotenuse-side (RHS) triangles are two triangles in which the hypotenuse and one side of a right-angled triangle are the same as the other, but positioned differently.

Similar triangles are the same shape but not necessarily the same size; corresponding angles are equal and corresponding sides are in the same ratio.

Pythagorean theorem

Named after the sixth-century Greek mathematician Pythagoras, this theorem states that, for a right-angled triangle, the square of the hypotenuse (the longest side of a right-angled triangle and always opposite the right (90°) angle) is equal to the sum of the squares of the other two sides. Written in symbols, the Pythagorean theorem has the following formula: $a^2 + b^2 = c^2$, where "c" is the hypotenuse and "a" and "b" are the remaining two sides. The theorem proves that when one side of a triangle is equal to the sum of the squares of the other two sides, the triangle must contain a right angle.

The theorem can be used to find the length of the third side of a right-angled triangle, given the lengths of any two sides. For example, given that the hypotenuse of a right-triangle is 25 and one side is 9, the other side can be found using the formula: $a^2 + b^2 = c^2$, $9 + b^2 = 25$, or $b^2 = 25 - 9$, or $b^2 = 16$, so $b = 4$.

Quadrilaterals

A quadrilateral is a four-sided polygon, and all quadrilaterals tessellate. Each quadrilateral has special properties:

- Square – All sides are equal and all angles are right angles. The opposite sides are parallel, and there are four lines of symmetry. The rotation symmetry is of order 4.
- Rectangle (or oblong) – Opposite sides are equal and parallel, and all interior angles are right angles. There are two lines of symmetry and a rotation symmetry of order 2. The diagonals of a rectangle are of equal length.
- Kite – Two pairs of sides are equal, and one pair of opposite angles are equal. There is only one line of symmetry and no rotation symmetry.
- Parallelogram – Opposite sides are parallel and of equal length, and opposite angles are equal. Most have no lines of symmetry, but do have a rotation symmetry of order 2. The exceptions are rectangles, squares, and rhombuses, which are special types of parallelograms.
- Rhombus – All four sides are equal in length, and opposite angles are equal. There are two lines of symmetry and a rotation symmetry of order 2. A square is a special type of rhombus that has four right angles.
- Trapezoid – One pair of sides is parallel. Most trapezoids have no symmetry, unless the sloping sides, a and b, are the same length. In this case, the trapezoid has one line of symmetry and is called an isosceles trapezoid.
- Arrowhead (or delta) – This concave quadrilateral has two pair of equal adjacent sides. There is one interior angle greater than 180°, and one line of symmetry. There is no rotation symmetry.

Polyhedron

A polyhedron is a solid that has a surface area made of a series of polygons. The polygons are called "faces," and the lines where they meet are called "edges." The corners where three or more faces meet are called "vertices."

A dihedral angle is the angle formed inside a polyhedron where two faces meet.

Euler's theorem, named after 18th-century Swiss mathematician Leonard Euler, is expressed as $V - E + F = 2$, where V is the number of vertices, E is the number of edges and F is the number of faces. For example, a cube has 8 vertices, 12 edges, and 6 faces, so $8 - 12 + 6 = 2$.

The name of a polyhedron is determined by the number of faces it has.

- Tetrahedron – 4 faces
- Pentahedron – 5 faces
- Hexahedron – 6 faces
- Heptahedron – 7 faces
- Octahedron – 8 faces
- Nonahedron – 9 faces
- Decahedron – 10 faces
- Dodecahedron – 12 faces
- Icosahedron – 20 faces

Polyhedra

Convex: Each dihedral angle is less than 180° (for example, a cube).

Concave: At least one dihedral angle is greater than 180°, such that at least one vertex points toward the middle of the solid.

Regular: The faces are identical polygons, and the angles at the vertices are equal. There are five regular polyhedra, called Platonic solids (named after the Greek philosopher, Plato):

Cube – six square faces

Regular Dodecahedron – twelve faces, all of which are regular pentagons

Regular Tetrahedron – four faces, all of which are equilateral triangles

Regular Octahedron – eight faces, all of which are equilateral triangles

Regular Icosahedron – twenty faces, all of which are equilateral triangles

Semi-regular: The faces are more than one type of polygon. For example, an icosidodecahedron is a semi-regular polyhedron with 32 faces, consisting of 20 triangles and 12 pentagons.

Solid

A solid is a three-dimensional object that can be any shape or size. Many solids, such as polyhedra, spheres, cylinders, and cones, have particular properties.

Plan – a two-dimensional drawing of a solid as if viewed directly from above

Elevation – a two-dimensional drawing of a solid as if viewed directly from the front (front elevation) or the side (side elevation); the front is the side nearest the viewer

Diagonal – a line drawn between two vertices that are not on the same edge of the solid

Short diagonals – those that lie across the surface

Long diagonals – those that run through the middle of the solid

Plane section – a flat or plane surface formed by cutting through a solid at any angle

Cross section – a flat or plane surface formed by cutting through a solid at right angles to the axis of rotation symmetry

Frustum – the part below the cross section.

Net – a flat or plane shape composed of polygons that represents the faces of a polyhedron and can be folded to make a polyhedron

Reflection symmetry

Symmetry describes a property of a shape that can be halved and turned such that it fits exactly onto itself. One of two types of symmetry is reflection, also called reflective or line symmetry. This type occurs when a shape can be divided into two parts by a line or plane and each part of the shape is a mirror image of the other. The wings of a butterfly are an example of reflection symmetry.

A line of symmetry, or mirror line, divides a plane into two parts, and each part is a mirror image of the other. A plane can have more than one line of symmetry.

A plane of symmetry divides a solid into two parts, and each part is a mirror image of the other. A solid can have more than one plane of symmetry.

Rotation symmetry

Symmetry describes a property of a shape that can be halved and turned such that it fits exactly onto itself. One of two types of symmetry is rotations, also called rotational symmetry. This type of symmetry occurs when a shape can be turned about a fixed point or line and fit exactly onto itself.

Order of rotation symmetry is the number of times within a revolution (360°) that a shape can be turned to fit exactly onto itself. For example, a four-pointed star has rotation symmetry of order 4 because it can fit onto itself in four different positions.

Center of rotation symmetry is the point around which a plane can be rotated to fit exactly onto itself.

Axis of rotation symmetry is the line around which a solid can be rotated to fit exactly onto itself. For example, a rectangular prism has rotation symmetry of order 4.

Calculating the area of a given shape

The following formulas are used to calculate the area of the given shape:

- Rectangle: area = length * width, a = lw
- Square: area = $(\text{side})^2$, $a = s^2$
- Triangle: area = ½ * (base * perpendicular height), a = ½bh. The perpendicular height is a line from the apex of the triangle that meets the base at a right angle. Any side of the triangle can be the base.
- Parallelogram: area = base * perpendicular height, a = bh. In this case, perpendicular height is a line from a vertex that meets the base at a right angle.

- Trapezoid: area = ½ * (a + b) * h. In this formula, a and b are the lengths of the parallel sides, and h is the perpendicular distance between them.
- Circle: area = $\pi * r^2$ or πr^2, where π (Pi) is approximately 3.14 and r is the radius of the circle. The radius is the distance from the center of the circle to any point on the circumference (edge).

Volume, capacity, and density

Volume is the amount of space that a solid, liquid, or gas occupies. This space is measured by the number of unit cubes that can fit inside it. Common units of measuring volume are based on the units of length, such as cubic centimeters (cm^3) or cubic meters (m^3).

Capacity is the amount that a container can hold. Capacity is often measured in milliliters (ml) or liters (l). Volume and capacity are closely related. A container with a volume of 1 cm^3 holds 1 milliliter of liquid, and a container with a volume of 1000 cm^3 holds 1 liter.

Density is the mass of one unit volume of a material from which an object is made. The shorthand expression is "mass per unit volume." Density is often measured in grams per cubic centimeter (g/cm^3) or kilograms per cubic meter (kg/m^3). The following formula is used to calculate density: Density = mass/volume or D = m/V.

Bimodal and multimodal distribution

One of the three commonly used types of measures of central tendency (average) is mode, which is the value or values that occur most often in a distribution.

Bimodal distribution is one that has two modes. For example, in the distribution of 20, 21, 21, 22, 25, 25, 26, 28, the values of 21 and 25 occur most often, both twice, and are therefore both modes.

Multimodal distribution is one that has three or more modes.

Mode of a frequency distribution is the value with the highest frequency of an item in a group of items. For example, in a group of shoes, a store may have 88 in size 6, 376 in size 7, 255 in size 8, and 142 in size 9. The category with the highest frequency, 376, is size 7, so the mode of this frequency is size 7.

Median and mean of a distribution

Median is the middle value of a distribution that is arranged in size order. The formula used for determining median is ½ (n + 1), where n is the number of values. To find the median of the following distribution, first arrange the distribution in size order: 25, 21, 24, 21, 26, 27, 22, 29, 25 → 21, 21, 22, 24, 25, 25, 26, 27, 29. Then, calculate the median position: median = ½ (9 + 1) = ½ * 10 = 5. The value that is in the 5th position on this distribution list is 25.

Mean, or arithmetic mean, of a distribution is a measure of the general size of the data. The following formula is used to find the mean: sum of values ÷ number of values. For the distribution 1, 6, 8, 4, 7, 10, the sum is 36. There are 6 numbers in the distribution. Therefore, the mean of this distribution is 6 (36 ÷ 6).

Range and quartiles

Range is the difference between the highest and lowest values in a distribution list. For example, in the distribution 3, 1, 6, 4, 7, 12, 9, 5, 8, twelve is the high value and one is the low value; therefore, 12 - 1 = 11, so the range is 11.

The lower, or first quartile (Q_1), is the value that lies one quarter of the way through a distribution arranged in ascending order. The formula for finding the lower quartile position is $(n + 1) \div 4$, where n is the number of values in the distribution.

The upper, or third quartile (Q_3), is the value that lies three-quarters of the way through a distribution arranged in ascending order. The formula for finding the upper quartile position is $3(n + 1) \div 4$.

Standard deviation

Standard deviation from the mean expresses how spread out the values of a distribution are from its mean, while taking into account every value of a distribution. Standard deviation is given in the same units as the original data and is represented by a lower case sigma (σ).

A high standard deviation means that the values are very spread out.

A low standard deviation means that the values are close together.

If every value in a distribution is increased or decreased by the same amount, the mean is increased or decreased by that amount, but the standard deviation stays the same.

If every value in a distribution is multiplied or divided by the same number, the standard deviation and the mean will both be multiplied or divided by that amount.

Pie chart

A pie chart or circle graph is a diagram used to compare parts of a whole. The frequency of a distribution is represented by the area of the sectors within the circle. The diagram has a title to explain what it is showing. Each "slice" or sector of the pie is labeled to tell what it represents or is explained on a key. The size of the slice is determined by the amount of frequency; that is, something that happens 30% of the time is going to get a larger slice than something that happens 20% of the time.

The size of an angle or area can be calculated by the formula: angle = $f * (360° \div \Sigma f)$, where f is the frequency.

The sum of the angles must always be 360°.

Bar charts

A bar chart uses vertical or horizontal bars of equal width to show the frequency of a distribution. For example, a bar chart can show the frequency distribution of car sales according to model.

A compound, or multiple, bar chart uses multiple bars within a category to illustrate more than one set of date. For example, the data on car sales can be separated to show the number of each model sold to men and the number sold to women.

A component bar chart, also known as a composite, sectional, or stacked bar chart, is one that divides each bar into sections to illustrate more than one set of data. That is, the bar can represent total sales, with sections of the bar showing the number sold by model. A component chart could also have bars for each model, but with each bar divided into two sections showing the numbers bought by men and the number by women.

Theoretical and experimental probability

Theoretical probability is a way of calculating the odds of a certain event occurring without actually performing the event. It is based on equally likely outcomes, with no bias or error involved.

The following formula is used to calculate theoretical probability: P (the probability of success for the required or desired outcome) = total successful outcomes ÷ total possible outcomes. For example, given 20 marbles in a bag, 5 red, 8 blue, 4 green, and 3 yellow, the odds of choosing a red one are 5 in 20 or 5 ÷ 20 = 1/4 or 0.25 or 25%.

Experimental probability, or relative frequency, is the number of times an outcome occurs in an experiment or a certain number of events.

The formula, or rule, for calculating experimental probability is: P = total successful outcomes ÷ total events. For example, if a die is thrown 100 times and lands showing the number 5 a total of 10 times, then P = 10 ÷ 100 = 1/10 = 0.2 = 20%. This can be compared to the theoretical probability of 1/6 or 17% (there are 6 sides on a die, each with an equal theoretical probability of rolling face up).

Events

Single event – one that involves only one item, such as tossing a coin

Compound or multiple event – one that involves more than one item, such as a pair of dice

Independent or random event – one that has an outcome that is not affected by any other event; that is, when repeatedly throwing a pair of dice, no throw is affected by any other throw

Dependent or conditional event – one that has an outcome that is affected by another event; for example, once a bag of 20 marbles is reduced by one red marble (originally having 5 red marbles), the odds of getting another red one are changed to 4 out of 19 or 21%.

Mutually exclusive events – two or more events that cannot have a successful outcome at the same time; for example, choosing a spade from a deck of cards is one event and choosing a club is another event. When choosing a card, it cannot be both a club and a spade, so these events are mutually exclusive.

Histogram

A histogram is a special type of bar graph where the data are grouped in intervals (for example 20-29, 30-39, 40-49, etc.). The frequency, or number of times a value occurs in each interval, is indicated by the height of the bar and is called the frequency density. Frequency density can be calculated with the following formula: frequency ÷ class width (the size of the interval). For example, if measuring how much time it takes 20 different people to walk a mile, the frequency would be 20 and the class width would be groups of minutes from the first to finish to the last to finish. Similarly, frequency can be calculated with the formula: class width * frequency density. The total frequency should be the sum of the frequencies in the table.

The intervals do not have to be the same amount but usually are (all data in ranges of 10 or all in ranges of 5, for example). The smaller the intervals, the more detailed the information.

Permutation and combination

Permutation and combination involve the arrangement of items. Use a permutation when order is important and a combination when order has no importance.

For example: It does not matter in what order one picks up pens, pencils, and markers; that's combination. However, it matters in what order numbers are entered into a combination lock; that's permutation. (Maybe it should be renamed a "permutation" lock.)

Two types of permutations and combinations exist within mathematics, those with repetition and those without, as demonstrated in the following examples:

- Permutation with repetition – The same number could repeat in the lock combination, such as 444512.
- Permutation without repetition – Contest results are given by 1st, 2nd, and 3rd place, and two objects cannot be in the same place.
- Combination with repetition – When sorting change according to nickels, dimes, and pennies, order does not matter, but more than one of a particular coin can exist within the quantity of change.
- Combination without repetition – Finding the total number of two-letter combinations that can be made from a three-letter word is an example of a combination with repetition (cat = ca, ct, at, ac, tc, ta).

Stem-and-leaf plot

A stem-and-leaf plot is a method where data is organized visually so that the information is easier to understand. A stem-and-leaf plot is very easy to construct because a simple line separates the stem (the part of the plot listing the tens digit, if displaying two-digit data) from the leaf (the part that shows the ones digit). Thus, the number 45 would appear as 4 | 5. The stem-and-leaf plot for test scores of a group of 11 students might look like the following:

- 9 | 5
- 8 | 1, 3, 8
- 7 | 6, 0, 2, 4, 7
- 6 | 2, 8

A stem-and-leaf plot is similar to a histogram or other frequency plot, but, with a stem-and-leaf plot, all the original data is preserved. In this example, it can be seen at a glance that nearly half the students scored in the 70's, yet all the data has been maintained. These plots can be used for larger numbers, as well. However, they do tend to work best for small sets of data and can become unwieldy with larger sets.

Addition Principle of Counting

The Addition Principle of Counting, or Addition Rule, is used to find the probability of one of any number of outcomes occurring. Expressed symbolically, let E_1 and E_2 be mutually exclusive events (that is, no common outcomes can occur), and let event E describe the situation where either event E_1 or event E_2 will occur. The number of times event E will occur can be expressed as: $n(E) = n(E_1) + n(E_2)$. The addition principle can be generalized for more than two events. In a simple example, there are two types of meat on the cafeteria menu: beef and chicken. Within those two categories, there are 3 beef dishes (3 outcomes) and 4 chicken dishes (4 outcomes). Therefore, $n(E) = 3 + 4 = 7$.

Multiplication Principle of Counting

The Multiplication Principle of Counting, or Multiplication Rule, is used to find the probability of a combination of outcomes occurring, both independent (one event does not affect the other's outcome) or dependent (one event does affect the other) events. For two independent events, the number of possible outcomes for event E, if both E_1 and E_2 must occur, is expressed by: $n(E) = n(E_1) * n(E_2)$. For example: If there are two major highway routes from Houston to St. Louis and three from St. Louis to Cleveland, then there are 2 * 3 = 6 different ways to drive from Houston to Cleveland. For two dependent events, calculate any changes in probability following each outcome, and then multiply the results. For example: Given 20 marbles in a bag, 5 of which are red, the probability of choosing a red one is 5 in 20 on the first draw, but 4 in 19 on the second. Therefore, the calculation becomes $n(E) = 5/20 * 4/19 = 1/19$ or 0.0525.

Data and statistics

- Quantitative data – measurements (such as length, mass, and speed) that provide information about quantities in numbers
- Qualitative data – information (such as colors, scents, tastes, and shapes) that cannot be measured using numbers
- Discrete data – information that can be expressed only by a specific value, such as whole or half numbers; For example, since people can be counted only in whole numbers, a population count would be discrete data.
- Continuous data – information (such as time and temperature) that can be expressed by any value within a given range
- Primary data – information that has been collected directly from a survey, investigation, or experiment, such as a questionnaire or the recording of daily temperatures; Primary data that has not yet been organized or analyzed is called raw data.
- Secondary data – information that has been collected, sorted, and processed by the researcher
- Ordinal data – information that can be placed in numerical order, such as age or weight
- Nominal data – information that cannot be placed in numerical order, such as names or places

Science

Atoms

All matter consists of atoms. Atoms consist of a nucleus and electrons. The nucleus consists of protons and neutrons. The properties of these are measurable; they have mass and an electrical charge. The nucleus is positively charged and consists of protons and neutrons. Electrons are negatively charged and orbit the nucleus. An atom is held together by electromagnetic force between the nucleus and the electrons. The nucleus, which contains protons and neutrons, has considerably more mass than the surrounding electrons. The forces that hold the nucleus of an atom together are usually stronger than the electric forces trying to break it apart. Protons and neutrons are formed from hadrons, which are composed of quarks. Atoms bond together to make molecules. Atoms that have an equal number of protons and electrons are neutral. If the number of protons and electrons is not equal, atoms have positive or negative charges and are known as ions.

Atom, nucleus, electrons, and protons

An atom is one of the most basic units of matter. An atom consists of a central nucleus surrounded by electrons.

The nucleus of an atom consists of protons and neutrons. It is positively charged, dense, and heavier than the surrounding electrons. The plural form of nucleus is nuclei.

Electrons are atomic particles that are negatively charged and orbit the nucleus of an atom.

Along with neutrons, protons make up the nucleus of an atom. The number of protons in the nucleus usually determines the atomic number of an element. Carbon atoms, for example, have six protons. The atomic number of carbon is 6. The number of protons also indicates the charge of an atom.

Atomic number, neutrons, nucleon, and element

The atomic number of an element, also known as the proton number, refers to the number of protons in the nucleus of an atom. It is a unique identifier. It can be represented as "Z." Atoms with a neutral charge have an atomic number that is equal to the number of electrons. The number of protons in the atomic nucleus also determines its electric charge, which in turn determines the number of electrons the atom has in its non-ionized state.

Neutrons are the uncharged atomic particles contained within the nucleus. The number of neutrons in a nucleus can be represented as "N."

Nucleon refers to the collective number of neutrons and protons.

An element is matter with one type of atom. It can be identified by its atomic number. There are 117 elements, 94 of which occur naturally on Earth.

Difference between atoms and molecules

Elements from the periodic table such as hydrogen, carbon, iron, helium, mercury, and oxygen are atoms. Atoms combine to form molecules. For example, two atoms of hydrogen (H) and one atom of oxygen (O) combine to form water (H_2O). Atoms are made up of subatomic particles. Atoms consist of electrons and a nucleus containing at least one proton and one neutron. The one exception to this rule is the hydrogen isotope hydrogen-1, which does not contain a neutron. Protons have a positive charge, while neutrons have no charge. Electrons have a negative charge and orbit the nucleus. The atomic number refers to the number of protons in the nucleus. This number is used to sort elements in the periodic table.

Molecular formation

Electrons in an atom can orbit different levels around the nucleus. They can absorb or release energy, which can change the location of their orbit or even allow them to break free from the atom. The outermost layer is the valence layer, which contains the valence electrons. The valence layer tends to have or share eight electrons. Molecules are formed by a chemical bond between atoms, a bond which occurs at the valence level. Two basic types of bonds are covalent and ionic. A covalent bond is formed when atoms share electrons. An ionic bond is formed when an atom transfers an electron to another atom. A hydrogen bond is a weak bond between a hydrogen atom of one molecule and an electronegative atom (such as nitrogen, oxygen, or fluorine) of another molecule. The Van der Waals force is a weak force between molecules. This type of force is much weaker than actual chemical bonds between atoms.

Atomic model

Atoms are extremely small. A hydrogen atom is about 5×10^{-8} mm in diameter. According to some estimates, five trillion hydrogen atoms could fit on the head of a pin. Atomic radius refers to the average distance between the nucleus and the outermost electron. Models of atoms that include the proton, nucleus, and electrons typically show the electrons very close to the nucleus and revolving around it, similar to how the Earth orbits the sun. However, another model relates the Earth as the nucleus and its atmosphere as electrons, which is the basis of the term "electron cloud." Another description is that electrons swarm around the nucleus. It should be noted that these atomic models are not to scale. A more accurate representation would be a nucleus with a diameter of about 2 cm in a stadium. The electrons would be in the bleachers. This model is similar to the not-to-scale solar system model.

Compounds

Atoms interact by transferring or sharing the electrons furthest from the nucleus. Known as the outer or valence electrons, they are responsible for the chemical properties of an element. Bonds between atoms are created when electrons are paired up by being transferred or shared. If electrons are transferred from one atom to another, the bond is ionic. If electrons are shared, the bond is covalent. Atoms of the same element may bond together to form molecules or crystalline solids. When two or more different types of atoms bind together chemically, a compound is made. The physical properties of compounds reflect the nature of the interactions among their molecules. These interactions are determined by the structure of the molecule, including the atoms they consist of and the distances and angles between them.

Periodic table

The periodic table groups elements with similar chemical properties together. The grouping of elements is based on atomic structure. It shows periodic trends of physical and chemical properties and identifies families of elements with similar properties. It is a common model for organizing and understanding elements. In the periodic table, each element has its own cell that includes varying amounts of information presented in symbol form about the properties of the element. Cells in the table are arranged in rows (periods) and columns (groups or families). At minimum, a cell includes the symbol for the element and its atomic number. The cell for hydrogen, for example, which appears first in the upper left corner, includes an "H" and a "1" above the letter. Elements are ordered by atomic number, left to right, top to bottom.

Matter

Matter refers to substances that have mass and occupy space (or volume). The traditional definition of matter describes it as having three states: solid, liquid, and gas. These different states are caused by differences in the distances and angles between molecules or atoms, which result in differences in the energy that binds them. Solid structures are rigid or nearly rigid and have strong bonds. Molecules or atoms of liquids move around and have weak bonds, although they are not weak enough to readily break. Molecules or atoms of gases move almost independently of each other, are typically far apart, and do not form bonds. The current definition of matter describes it as having four states. The fourth is plasma, which is an ionized gas that has some electrons that are described as free because they are not bound to an atom or molecule.

Conservation of matter and atomic theory

Atomic theory is concerned with the characteristics and properties of atoms that make up matter. It deals with matter on a microscopic level as opposed to a macroscopic level. Atomic theory, for instance, discusses the kinetic motion of atoms in order to explain the properties of macroscopic quantities of matter. John Dalton (1766-1844) is credited with making many contributions to the field of atomic theory that are still considered valid. This includes the notion that all matter consists of atoms and that atoms are indestructible. In other words, atoms can be neither created nor destroyed. This is also the theory behind the conservation of matter, which explains why chemical reactions do not result in any detectable gains or losses in matter. This holds true for chemical reactions and smaller scale processes. When dealing with large amounts of energy, however, atoms can be destroyed by nuclear reactions. This can happen in particle colliders or atom smashers.

Mass, weight, volume, density, and specific gravity

Mass is a measure of the amount of substance in an object.

Weight is a measure of the gravitational pull of Earth on an object or between two bodies.

Volume is a measure of the amount of cubic space occupied. There are many formulas to determine volume. For example, the volume of a cube is the length of one side cubed (a^3) and the volume of a rectangular prism is length times width times height ($l \cdot w \cdot h$). The volume of an irregular shape can be determined by how much water it displaces.

Density is a measure of the amount of mass per unit volume. The formula to find density is mass divided by volume (D=m/V). It is expressed in terms of mass per cubic unit, such as grams per cubic centimeter (g/cm^3).

Specific gravity: This is a measure of the ratio of a substance's density compared to the density of water.

Physical and chemical properties

Both physical changes and chemical reactions are everyday occurrences. The physical properties of a substance refer to attributes such as appearance, color, mass, and volume. Physical changes do not result in different substances. For example, when water becomes ice it has undergone a physical change, but not a chemical change. It has changed its form, but not its composition. It is still H_2O. Chemical properties are concerned with the constituent particles that make up the physicality of a substance. Chemical properties are apparent when chemical changes occur. The chemical properties of a substance are influenced by its electric charge, which is determined in part by the number of protons in the nucleus (the atomic number). The number of electrons is the same as an atom's atomic number. Carbon, for example, has 6 protons and 6 electrons. It is an element's outermost valence electrons that mainly determine its chemical properties. Chemical changes are when a change in a substance results in a different substance. Chemical reactions may release or consume energy.

Elements, compounds, solutions, and mixtures

These are substances that consist of only one type of atom.

These are substances containing two or more elements. Compounds are formed by chemical reactions and frequently have different properties than the original elements. Compounds are decomposed by a chemical reaction rather than separated by a physical one.

These are homogeneous mixtures composed of two or more substances that have become one.

Mixtures contain two or more substances that are combined but have not reacted chemically with each other. Mixtures can be separated using physical methods, while compounds can not.

Some chemical properties of elements include: atomic number, category, group, period, block, weight, electron configuration, electrons per shell, phase, density, sublimation point (the temperature at which elements change from solids to gases without going through a liquid phase), specific heat capacity, oxidation states, electronegativity, ionization energy, atomic radius, and isotopes.

Chemical reactions

Chemical reactions measured in human time can take place quickly or slowly. They can take fractions of a second or billions of years. The rates of chemical reactions are determined by how frequently reacting atoms and molecules interact. Rates are also influenced by the temperature and various properties (such as shape) of the reacting materials. Catalysts accelerate chemical reactions, while inhibitors decrease reaction rates. Some types of reactions release energy in the form of heat and light. Some types of reactions involve the transfer of either electrons or hydrogen ions between reacting ions, molecules, or atoms. In other reactions, chemical bonds are broken down by heat or light to form reactive radicals with electrons that will readily form new bonds. Processes such as the formation of ozone and greenhouse gases in the atmosphere and the burning and processing of fossil fuels are controlled by radical reactions.

Most abundant elements

Aside from dark energy and dark matter, which are thought to account for all but four percent of the universe, the two most abundant elements in the universe are hydrogen (H) and helium (He). After hydrogen and helium, the most abundant elements are oxygen, neon, nitrogen, carbon, silicon, and magnesium. The most abundant isotopes in the solar system are hydrogen-1 and helium-4. Measurements of the masses of elements in the Earth's crust indicate that oxygen (O), silicon (Si), and aluminum (Al) are the most abundant on Earth. Hydrogen in its plasma state is the most abundant chemical element in stars in their main sequences, but is relatively rare on planet Earth.

Past atomic models and theories

There have been many revisions to theories regarding the structure of atoms and their particles. Part of the challenge in developing an understanding of matter is that atoms and their particles are too small to be seen. It is believed that the first conceptualization of the atom was developed by Democritus in 400 B.C. Some of the more notable models are the solid sphere or billiard ball model postulated by John Dalton, the plum pudding or raisin bun model by J.J. Thomson, the planetary or nuclear model by Ernest Rutherford, the Bohr or orbit model by Niels Bohr, and the electron cloud or quantum mechanical model by Louis de Broglie and Erwin Schrodinger. Rutherford directed the alpha scattering experiment that discounted the plum pudding model. The shortcoming of the Bohr model was the belief that electrons orbited in fixed rather than changing ecliptic orbits.

Heat, energy, work, thermal energy, and heat engine

Heat is the transfer of energy from a body or system as a result of thermal contact. Heat consists of random motion and the vibration of atoms, molecules, and ions. The higher the temperature is, the greater the atomic or molecular motion will be.

Energy is the capacity to do work.
Work is the quantity of energy transferred by one system to another due to changes in a system that is the result of external forces, or macroscopic variables. Another way to put this is that work is the amount of energy that must be transferred to overcome a force. Lifting an object in the air is an example of work. The opposing force that must be overcome is gravity. Work is measured in joules (J). The rate at which work is performed is known as power.

Thermal energy is the total kinetic and potential energy present in a system.

Heat engine refers to a machine that converts thermal energy to mechanical energy that can be used to do work.

Thermal contact, entropy, conservation of energy, and perpetual motion

Thermal contact refers to energy transferred to a body by a means other than work. A system in thermal contact with another can exchange energy with it through the process of heat. Thermal contact does not necessarily involve direct physical contact.

Entropy refers to the amount of energy in a system that is no longer available for work. Entropy is also a term used to describe the amount of disorder in a system.

Conservation of energy is a concept that refers to the fact that the total amount of energy in a closed system is constant.

Perpetual motion is the misguided belief that a system can continuously produce more energy than it consumes. Since the law of conservation of energy states that energy cannot be created or destroyed, a true perpetual motion machine is not possible.

Kinetic and potential energy

Kinetic and potential energy are two commonly known types of energy. Kinetic energy refers to the energy of an object in motion. The following formula is used to calculate kinetic energy: $KE = \frac{1}{2} mv^2$, where "KE" stands for kinetic energy, "m" stands for mass, and "v" stands for velocity. Even though an object may appear to be motionless, its atoms are always moving. Since these atoms are colliding and moving, they have kinetic energy. Potential energy refers to a capacity for doing work that is based upon position or configuration. The following formula can be used to calculate potential energy: $PE = mgh$, where "PE" stands for potential energy, "m" stands for mass, "g" stands for gravity, and "h" stands for height.

Laws of thermodynamics

The zeroth laws of thermodynamics states that two objects in thermodynamic equilibrium with a third object are also in equilibrium with each other. Thermodynamic equilibrium basically means that different objects are at the same temperature.

The first law deals with conservation of energy. It states that heat is a form of energy that can not be created or destroyed, only converted.

The second law is that entropy (the amount of energy in a system that is no longer available for work or the amount of disorder in a system) of an isolated system can only increase. The second law also states that heat is not transferred from a lower-temperature system to a higher-temperature one.

The third law of thermodynamics states that as temperature approaches absolute zero, entropy approaches a constant minimum. It also states that a system cannot be cooled to absolute zero.

Energy

Some discussions of energy consider only two types of energy: kinetic energy (the energy of motion) and potential energy (which depends on relative position). There are, however, other types of energy. Electromagnetic waves, for example, are a type of energy contained by a field. Gravitational energy is a form of potential energy. Objects perched any distance from the ground have gravitational energy, or the potential to move. Another type of potential energy is electrical energy, which is the energy it takes to pull apart positive and negative electrical charges. Chemical energy refers to the manner in which atoms form into molecules, and this energy can be released or absorbed when molecules regroup. Solar energy comes in the form of visible light and non-visible light, such as infrared and ultraviolet rays. Sound energy refers to the energy in sound waves.

Energy transformations

Electric to mechanical
Ceiling fan

Chemical to heat
A familiar example of a chemical to heat energy transformation is the internal combustion engine, which transforms the chemical energy (a type of potential energy) of gas and oxygen into heat. This heat is transformed into propulsive energy, which is kinetic. Lighting a match and burning coal are also examples of chemical to heat energy transformations.

Chemical to light
Phosphorescence and luminescence (which allow objects to glow in the dark) occur because energy is absorbed by a substance (charged) and light is re-emitted comparatively slowly. This process is different from the one involved with glow sticks. They glow due to chemiluminescence, in which an excited state is created by a chemical reaction and transferred to another molecule.

Heat to electricity
Examples include thermoelectric, geothermal, and ocean thermal.

Nuclear to heat
Examples include nuclear reactors and power plants.

Mechanical to sound
Playing a violin or almost any instrument

Sound to electric
Microphone

Light to electric
Solar panels

Electric to light
Light bulbs

Heat and temperature

Heat is energy transfer (other than direct work) from one body or system to another due to thermal contact. Everything tends to become less organized and less orderly over time (entropy). In all energy transfers, therefore, the overall result is that the energy is spread out uniformly. This transfer of heat energy from hotter to cooler objects is accomplished by conduction, radiation, or convection. Temperature is considered a measurement of heat or heat energy. More specifically, temperature is the average kinetic energy of an object's particles. When the temperature of an object increases and its atoms move faster, kinetic energy also increases. Temperature is not energy since it changes and is not conserved. Thermometers are used to measure temperature.

Motion and force

A fundamental concept in physics is that objects can change their motion when a force is applied. Newton's laws, the laws of motion, describe how these forces behave and how they can be used to calculate the effects of forces on the motion of objects. Four basic forces are gravity, nuclear weak force, electromagnetic force, and nuclear strong force, with nuclear strong force being the strongest. Linear motion is caused by forces, while rotational motion is caused by torques. The magnitude of the change in motion can be calculated using the relationship F = ma, where "F" stands for force, "m" stands for mass, and "a" stands for acceleration of gravity. Another important concept related to force is that when one object exerts a force on another, a force equal in magnitude and opposite in direction is exerted on the first object.

Gravitational force

Gravitational force is a universal force that causes masses to exert forces on other masses. The strength of the gravitational attractive force between two objects is proportional to their mass and inversely proportional to the square of the distance between them. Gravity is the weakest of the four fundamental forces. Gravity is an attractive force and acts along the imaginary line joining centers of masses. The formula for gravitational force, $F = G[(m_1*m_2)/r^2]$, follows Newton's third law, the law of universal gravitation. Newton's law is widely used to explain and calculate the effects of gravity, but Einstein's theory of general relativity is considered a better model and more accurate. Applying Newton's third law allowed scientists to predict the existence of Neptune. Newton's formula, however, did not work with Mercury, but Einstein's theory of general relativity did.

Newton's laws of motion

Newton's First Law: This is also known as the law of inertia. It states that a body in motion tends to stay in motion and a body at rest tends to stay at rest until another force acts upon it.

Newton's Second Law: This is expressed by the formula F = ma, where "F" is force, "m" is mass, and "a" is acceleration. In other words, force is equal to mass times acceleration. This is applicable when the objects encounter a net external force, but does not tend to be directly applicable to cases where mass varies. The formula is generally not suitable for calculations being made at an atomic level. Quantum mechanics is more suitable for these instances. The formula is also not suitable when objects are approaching the speed of light. Relativity is more suitable for these instances.

Newton's Third Law: This states that for every force there is an equal and opposite force. This also applies to the law of work, the law of energy, and the laws of power.

Simple machines

Simple machines include the incline plane, lever, wheel and axle, and pulley. These simple machines have no internal source of energy. More complex or compound machines can be formed from them. Simple machines provide a force known as a mechanical advantage and make it easier to accomplish a task. The incline plane enables a force less than the object's weight to be used to push an object to a greater height. A lever enables a multiplication of force. The wheel and axle allows for less resistance and is similar to the force of a lever. Single or double pulleys allows for easier direction of force. A wedge is similar to an incline plane in that a smaller force working over a longer distance can produce a larger force. The wedge and screw are forms of the incline plane. The screw is similar to an incline that is wrapped around a shaft.

Friction

Friction is the resistance to motion that occurs where two surfaces touch each other. Generally, the magnitude of the frictional force is affected by the material composition of the surfaces of the objects. Frictional force is independent of the area of contact between two surfaces. While the direction of motion occurs one way, frictional force occurs in the opposite direction. Frictional force is also proportional to the normal force between two surfaces. Two types of friction are static and kinetic. Static friction occurs when there is no relative motion between the surfaces. Kinetic friction occurs when there is relative motion between the surfaces.

Electric charges

The attractive force between the electrons and the nucleus is called the electric force. A positive (+) charge or a negative charge (-) creates a field of sorts in the empty space around it, which is known as an electromagnetic field. The direction of a positive charge is away from it and the direction of a negative charge is towards it. An electron within the force of the field is pulled towards a positive charge because an electron has a negative charge. A particle with a positive charge is pushed away, or repelled. Like charges repel each other and opposite charges attract. Lines of force show the paths of charges. Electric force between two objects is proportional to the inverse square of the distance between the two objects. The electric charge can be negative, zero, or positive. An electric charge is measured with the unit Coulomb (C). It is the amount of charge moved in one second by a steady current of one ampere (1C = 1A * 1s).

Circuits and potential

Electric current is the sustained flow of electrons that are part of an electric charge along a path. This differs from a static electric charge, which is characterized by a discharge or change of charge rather than a continuing flow. The rate of flow of electric charge is expressed using the ampere (amp or A) and can be measured using an ammeter. Movement of electric charge along a path between areas of high electric potential and low electric potential is the definition of a simple circuit. It is a closed conducting path between the high and low points, or the positive and negative charges. An energy supply is required to do the work necessary to move the charge from an area of low electric potential to one of high electric potential. Once at the area of high electric potential, the charge moves or flows back to an area of low electric potential.

Examples of circuits

Current is the measurement of the rate at which charge flows through a circuit point. The formula used to measure current is 1 amp = 1 coulomb/1 second. In other words, a current of 1 ampere means that 1 coulomb of charge passes through a cross section of a wire every second. One example of a circuit is the flow from one terminal of a car battery to the other. The electrolyte solution of water and sulfuric acid provides work in chemical form to start the flow. A frequently used classroom example of circuits involves using a D cell (1.5 V) battery, a small light bulb, and a piece of copper wire to create a circuit to light the bulb. In this example, the light bulb is the load, a device that uses energy. A bell or light could also be used.

Electric charge

Models that can be used to explain the flow of electric current, potential, and circuits include water, gravity, and roller coasters. For example, just as gravity is a force and a mass can have a potential for energy based on its location, so can a charge within an electrical field. Just as a force is required to move an object uphill, a force is also required to move a charge from a low to high potential. Another example is water. Water does not flow when it is level. If it is lifted to a point and then placed on a downward path, it will flow. A roller coaster car requires work to be performed to transport it to a point where it has potential energy (the top of a hill). Once there, gravity provides the force for it to flow (move) downward. If either path is broken, the flow or movement stops or is not completed.

Magnet

A magnet is a piece of metal, such as iron, steel, or magnetite (loadstone) that can affect another substance within its field of force that has like characteristics. Magnets can either attract or repel other substances. Magnets have two poles: north and south. Like poles repel and opposite poles (pairs of north and south) attract. The magnetic field is a set of invisible lines representing the paths of attraction and repulsion. Magnetism can occur naturally, or ferromagnetic materials can be magnetized. Matter that is magnetized can retain its magnetic properties indefinitely and become a permanent magnet. Other matter may lose its magnetic properties, and is considered a temporary magnet. For example, an iron nail can be temporarily magnetized by stroking it repeatedly in the same direction using one pole of another magnet. Once magnetized, it can attract or repel other magnetically inclined materials, such as paper clips. Dropping the nail will cause it to lose its charge.

Magnetic fields

A magnetic field can be formed not only by a magnetic material, but also by electric current flowing through a wire. When a coiled wire is attached to the two ends of a battery, for example, an electromagnet can be formed by inserting a ferromagnetic material such as an iron bar within the coil. When electric current flows through the wire, the bar becomes a magnet. If there is no current, the magnetism is lost. A magnetic domain is when the magnetic fields of atoms are grouped and aligned. These groups form what can be thought of as miniature magnets within a material. This is what happens when an object like an iron nail is temporarily magnetized. Prior to magnetization, the organization of atoms and their various polarities are somewhat random with respect to where the north and south poles are pointing. After magnetization, many of the poles are lined up in one direction, which is what causes the magnetic force exerted by the material.

The motions of subatomic structures (nuclei and electrons) produce a magnetic field. It is the direction of the spin and orbit that indicate the direction of the field. The strength of a magnetic field is known as the magnetic moment. As electrons spin and orbit a nucleus, they produce a magnetic field. Pairs of electrons that spin and orbit in opposite directions cancel each other out, creating a net magnetic field of zero. Materials that have an unpaired electron are magnetic. Those with a weak attractive force are referred to as paramagnetic materials, while ferromagnetic materials have a strong attractive force. A diamagnetic material has electrons that are paired, and therefore does not typically have a magnetic moment. There are, however, some diamagnetic materials that have a weak magnetic field.

Waves

Waves have energy and can transfer energy when they interact with matter. Although waves transfer energy, they do not transport matter. They are a disturbance of matter that transfers energy from one particle to an adjacent particle. There are many types of waves, including sound, seismic, water, light, micro, and radio waves. The two basic categories of waves are mechanical and electromagnetic. Mechanical waves are those that transmit energy through matter. Electromagnetic waves can transmit energy through a vacuum. A transverse wave provides a good illustration of the features of a wave, which include crests, troughs, amplitude, and wavelength. The crest is the maximum upward disturbance of a wave, while the trough is the maximum downward displacement of a wave. Both of these measurements use the wave in its resting position (the position of the wave when there is no disturbance) as the starting point. Amplitude refers to the maximum amount of displacement from the rest position. The wavelength is one complete cycle, which is determined by measuring the distance from a point on the first wave to the corresponding point on the next wave (from crest to crest, for example).

Sound

Sound is a pressure disturbance that moves through a medium in the form of mechanical waves, which transfer energy from one particle to the next. Sound requires a medium to travel through, such as air, water, or other matter since it is the vibrations that transfer energy to adjacent particles, not the actual movement of particles over a great distance. Sound is transferred through the movement of atomic particles, which can be atoms or molecules. Waves of sound energy move outward in all directions from the source. Sound waves consist of compressions (particles are forced together) and rarefactions (particles move farther apart and their density decreases). A wavelength consists of one compression and one rarefaction. Different sounds have different wavelengths. Sound is a form of kinetic energy.

Pitch, loudness, sound intensity, timbre, and oscillation

Pitch is the quality of sound determined by frequency. For example, a musical note can be tuned to a specific frequency. A, for instance, has a frequency of 440 Hz, which is a higher frequency than middle C. Humans can detect frequencies between about 20 Hz to 20,000 Hz.

Loudness is a human's perception of sound intensity.

Sound intensity is measured as the sound power per unit area, and can be expressed in decibels.

Timbre is a human's perception of the type or quality of sound.

Oscillation is a measurement, usually of time, against a basic value, equilibrium, or rest point.

Electromagnetic spectrum

The electromagnetic spectrum is defined by frequency (f) and wavelength (λ). Frequency is typically measured in hertz and wavelength is usually measured in meters. Frequency is inversely proportional to wavelength, a relationship expressed by the formula $f = v/\lambda$, where "f" is frequency, "v" is phase speed or phase velocity, and "λ" is wavelength. Frequency refers to the number of occurrences of an event in a given time period. Frequency multiplied by wavelength always equals the speed of light, which is $3.0 * 10^9$. Electromagnetic waves occur when a charged object is accelerated or decelerated. Electromagnetic waves include radio waves (which have the longest wavelength), microwaves, infrared radiation (radiant heat), visible light, ultraviolet radiation, x-rays, and gamma rays. The energy of electromagnetic waves is carried in packets that have a magnitude that is inversely proportional to the wavelength. Radio waves have a range of wavelengths, from about 10^{-1} to 10^{-5} meters, while their frequencies range from 10^5 to about 10^{-1}.

Visible light

Light is the portion of the electromagnetic spectrum that is visible because of its ability to stimulate the retina. It is absorbed and emitted by electrons, atoms, and molecules that move from one energy level to another. Visible light interacts with matter through molecular electron excitation (which occurs in the human retina) and through plasma oscillations (which occur in metals). Visible light is between ultraviolet and infrared light on the spectrum. Wavelengths of visible light range from 380 nanometers (nm) to 760 nm. Different wavelengths correspond to different colors. The color red has the longest wavelength, while the wavelength of violet is on the short end of the spectrum. The human brain interprets or perceives visible light, which is emitted from the sun and other stars, as color. For example, when the entire wavelength reaches the retina, the brain perceives the color white. When no part of the wavelength reaches the retina, the brain perceives the color black.

Doppler effect

The Doppler effect refers to the effect the relative motion of the source of the wave and the location of the observer has on waves. The Doppler effect is easily observable in sound waves. What a person hears when a train approaches or a car honking its horn passes by are examples of the Doppler effect. The pitch of the sound is different not because the emitted frequency has changed, but because the received frequency has changed. The frequency is higher (as is the pitch) as the train approaches, the same as emitted just as it passes, and lower as the train moves away. This is because the wavelength changes. The Doppler effect can occur when an observer is stationary, and can also occur when two trains approach and pass each other. Electromagnetic waves are also affected in this manner. The motion of the medium can also affect the wave. For waves that do not travel in a medium, such as light waves, it is the difference in velocity that determines the outcome.

Kinetic theory of gases

The kinetic theory of gases assumes that gas molecules are small compared to the distances between them and that they are in constant random motion. The attractive and repulsive forces between gas molecules are negligible. Their kinetic energy does not change with time as long as the temperature remains the same. The higher the temperature is, the greater the motion will be. As the temperature of a gas increases, so does the kinetic energy of the molecules. In other words, gas will occupy a greater volume as the temperature is increased and a lesser volume as the temperature is decreased. In addition, the same amount of gas will occupy a greater volume as the temperature increases, but pressure remains constant. At any given temperature, gas molecules have the same average kinetic energy. The ideal gas law is derived from the kinetic theory of gases.

Inorganic compounds

The main trait of inorganic compounds is that they lack carbon. Inorganic compounds include mineral salts, metals and alloys, non-metallic compounds such as phosphorus, and metal complexes. A metal complex has a central atom (or ion) bonded to surrounding ligands (molecules or anions). The ligands sacrifice the donor atoms (in the form of at least one pair of electrons) to the central atom. Many inorganic compounds are ionic, meaning they form ionic bonds rather than share electrons. They may have high melting points because of this. They may also be colorful, but this is not an absolute identifier of an inorganic compound. Salts, which are inorganic compounds, are an example of inorganic bonding of cations and anions. Some examples of salts are magnesium chloride ($MgCl_2$) and sodium oxide (Na_2O). Oxides, carbonates, sulfates, and halides are classes of inorganic compounds. They are typically poor conductors, are very water soluble, and crystallize easily. Minerals and silicates are also inorganic compounds.

Organic compounds

Two of the main characteristics of organic compounds are that they include carbon and are formed by covalent bonds. Carbon can form long chains, double and triple bonds, and rings. While inorganic compounds tend to have high melting points, organic compounds tend to melt at temperatures below 300° C. They also tend to boil, sublimate, and decompose below this temperature. Unlike inorganic compounds, they are not very water soluble. Organic molecules are organized into functional groups based on their specific atoms, which helps determine how they will react chemically. A few groups are alkanes, nitro, alkenes, sulphides, amines, and carbolic acids. The hydroxyl group (-OH) consists of alcohols. These molecules are polar, which increases their solubility. By some estimates, there are more than 16 million organic compounds.

Reading chemical equations

Chemical equations describe chemical reactions. The reactants are on the left side before the arrow and the products are on the right side after the arrow. The arrow indicates the reaction or change. The coefficient, or stoichiometric coefficient, is the number before the element, and indicates the ratio of reactants to products in terms of moles. The equation for the formation of water from hydrogen and oxygen, for example, is $2H_2$ (g) + O_2 (g) $\rightarrow$ $2H_2O$ (l). The 2 preceding hydrogen and water is the coefficient, which means there are 2 moles of hydrogen and 2 of water. There is 1 mole of oxygen, which does not have to be indicated with the number 1. In parentheses, g stands for gas, l stands for liquid, s stands for solid, and aq stands for aqueous solution (a substance dissolved in water). Charges are shown in superscript for individual ions, but not for ionic compounds. Polyatomic ions are separated by parentheses so the ion will not be confused with the number of ions.

Balancing equations

An unbalanced equation is one that does not follow the law of conservation of mass, which states that matter can only be changed, not created. If an equation is unbalanced, the numbers of atoms indicated by the stoichiometric coefficients on each side of the arrow will not be equal. Start by writing the formulas for each species in the reaction. Count the atoms on each side and determine if the number is equal. Coefficients must be whole numbers. Fractional amounts, such as half a molecule, are not possible. Equations can be balanced by multiplying the coefficients by a constant that will produce the smallest possible whole number coefficient. $H_2 + O_2 \rightarrow H_2O$ is an example of an unbalanced equation. The balanced equation is $2H_2 + O_2 \rightarrow 2H_2O$, which indicates that it takes two moles of hydrogen and one of oxygen to produce two moles of water.

Water

The important properties of water (H_2O) are high polarity, hydrogen bonding, cohesiveness, adhesiveness, high specific heat, high latent heat, and high heat of vaporization. It is essential to life as we know it, as water is one of the main if not the main constituent of many living things. Water is a liquid at room temperature. The high specific heat of water means it resists the breaking of its hydrogen bonds and resists heat and motion, which is why it has a relatively high boiling point and high vaporization point. It also resists temperature change. In its solid state, water floats. Most substances are heavier in their solid forms. Water is cohesive, which means it is attracted to itself. It is also adhesive, which means it readily attracts other molecules. If water tends to adhere to another substance, the substance is said to be hydrophilic. Water makes a good solvent. Substances, particularly those with polar ions and molecules, readily dissolve in water.

Hydrogen bonds

Hydrogen bonds are weaker than covalent and ionic bonds, and refer to the type of attraction in an electronegative atom such as oxygen, fluorine, or nitrogen. Hydrogen bonds can form within a single molecule or between molecules. A water molecule is polar, meaning it is partially positively charged on one end (the hydrogen end) and partially negatively charged on the other (the oxygen end). This is because the hydrogen atoms are arranged around the oxygen atom in a close tetrahedron. Hydrogen is oxidized (its number of electrons is reduced) when it bonds with oxygen to form water. Hydrogen bonds tend not only to be weak, but also short-lived. They also tend to be numerous. Hydrogen bonds give water many of its important properties, including its high specific heat and high heat of vaporization, its solvent qualities, its adhesiveness and cohesiveness, its hydrophobic qualities, and its ability to float in its solid form. Hydrogen bonds are also an important component of proteins, nucleic acids, and DNA.

Solutions

A solution is a homogeneous mixture. A mixture is two or more different substances that are mixed together, but not combined chemically. Homogeneous mixtures are those that are uniform in their composition. Solutions consist of a solute (the substance that is dissolved) and a solvent (the substance that does the dissolving). An example is sugar water. The solvent is the water and the solute is the sugar. The intermolecular attraction between the solvent and the solute is called solvation. Hydration refers to solutions in which water is the solvent. Solutions are formed when the forces of the molecules of the solute and the solvent are as strong as the individual molecular forces of the solute and the solvent. An example is that salt (NaCl) dissolves in water to create a solution. The Na^+ and the Cl^- ions in salt interact with the molecules of water and vice versa to overcome the individual molecular forces of the solute and the solvent.

Mixtures, suspensions, colloids, emulsions, and foams

A mixture is a combination of two or more substances that are not bonded. Suspensions are mixtures of heterogeneous materials. Particles are usually larger than those found in true solutions. Dirt mixed vigorously with water is an example of a suspension. The dirt is temporarily suspended in water, but the two separate once the mixing is ceased. A mixture of large (1 nm to 500 nm) particles is called a colloidal suspension. The particles are termed dispersants and the dispersing medium is similar to the solvent in a solution. Sol refers to a liquid or a solid that also has solids dispersed through it, such as milk or gelatin. An aerosol spray is a colloid suspension of gas and the solid or liquid being dispersed. An emulsion refers to a liquid or a solid that has a liquid dispersed through it. A foam is a liquid that has gas dispersed through it.

Acids

When they are dissolved in aqueous solutions, some properties of acids are that they conduct electricity, change blue litmus paper to red, have a sour taste, react with bases to neutralize them, and react with active metals to free hydrogen. A weak acid is one that does not donate all of its protons or disassociate completely. Strong acids include hydrochloric, hydroiodic, hydrobromic, perchloric, nitric, and sulfuric. They ionize completely. Superacids are those that are stronger than 100 percent sulfuric acid. They include fluoroantimonic, magic, and perchloric acids. Acids can be used in pickling, a process used to remove rust and corrosion from metals. They are also used as catalysts in the processing of minerals and the production of salts and fertilizers. Phosphoric acid (H_3PO_4) is added to sodas and other acids are added to foods as preservatives or to add taste.

Bases

When they are dissolved in aqueous solutions, some properties of bases are that they conduct electricity, change red litmus paper to blue, feel slippery, and react with acids to neutralize their properties. A weak base is one that does not completely ionize in an aqueous solution, and usually has a low pH. Strong bases can free protons in very weak acids. Examples of strong bases are hydroxide compounds such as potassium, barium, and lithium hydroxides. Most are in the first and second groups of the periodic table. A superbase is extremely strong compared to sodium hydroxide and cannot be kept in an aqueous solution. Superbases are organized into organic, organometallic, and inorganic classes. Bases are used as insoluble catalysts in heterogeneous reactions and as catalysts in hydrogenation.

Salts

Some properties of salts are that they are formed from acid base reactions, are ionic compounds consisting of metallic and nonmetallic ions, dissociate in water, and are comprised of tightly bonded ions. Some common salts are sodium chloride ($NaCl$), sodium bisulfate, potassium dichromate ($K_2Cr_2O_7$), and calcium chloride ($CaCl_2$). Calcium chloride is used as a drying agent, and may be used to absorb moisture when freezing mixtures. Potassium nitrate (KNO_3) is used to make fertilizer and in the manufacture of explosives. Sodium nitrate ($NaNO_3$) is also used in the making of fertilizer. Baking soda (sodium bicarbonate) is a salt, as are Epsom salts [magnesium sulfate ($MgSO_4$)]. Salt and water can react to form a base and an acid. This is called a hydrolysis reaction.

pH

The potential of hydrogen (pH) is a measurement of the concentration of hydrogen ions in a substance in terms of the number of moles of H^+ per liter of solution. All substances fall between 0 and 14 on the pH scale. A lower pH indicates a higher H^+ concentration, while a higher pH indicates a lower H^+ concentration. Pure water has a neutral pH, which is 7. Anything with a pH lower than water (0 to 6) is considered acidic. Anything with a pH higher than water (8 to 14) is a base. Drain cleaner, soap, baking soda, ammonia, egg whites, and sea water are common bases. Urine, stomach acid, citric acid, vinegar, hydrochloric acid, and battery acid are acids. A pH indicator is a substance that acts as a detector of hydrogen or hydronium ions. It is halochromic, meaning it changes color to indicate that hydrogen or hydronium ions have been detected.

Earth's life-sustaining system

Life on earth is dependent on:

- All three states of water – gas (water vapor), liquid, and solid (ice)
- A variety of forms of carbon, the basis of life (carbon-based units)
- In the atmosphere, carbon dioxide in the forms of methane and black carbon soot produce the greenhouse effect that provides a habitable atmosphere.
- The earth's atmosphere and electromagnetic field, which shield the surface from harmful radiation and allow useful radiation to go through

- The earth's relationship to the sun and the moon, which creates the four seasons and the cycles of plant and animal life
- The combination of water, carbon, and nutrients, which provides sustenance for life and regulates the climate system in a habitable temperature range with non-toxic air.

Earth system science

The complex and interconnected dynamics of the continents, atmosphere, oceans, ice, and life forms are the subject of earth system science. These interconnected dynamics require an interdisciplinary approach that includes chemistry, physics, biology, mathematics, and applied sciences in order to study the Earth as an integrated system and determine (while considering human impact and interaction) the past, present, and future states of the earth. Scientific inquiry in this field includes exploration of:

- Extreme weather events as they pertain to a changing climate
- Earthquakes and volcanic eruptions as they pertain to tectonic shifts
- Losses in biodiversity in relation to the changes in the earth's ecosystems
- Causes and effects in the environment
- The sun's solar variability in relation to the earth's climate
- The atmosphere's increasing concentrations of carbon dioxide and aerosols
- Trends in the earth's systems in terms of changes and their consequences

Earth science disciplines

Modern science is approaching the study of the earth in an integrated fashion that sees the earth as an interconnected system that is impacted by humankind and, therefore, must include social dimensions. Traditionally, though, the following were the earth science disciplines:

- Geology is the study of the origin and structure of the earth and of the changes it has undergone and is in the process of undergoing. Geologists work from the crust inward.
- Meteorology is the study of the atmosphere, including atmospheric pressure, temperature, clouds, winds, precipitation, etc. It is also concerned with describing and explaining weather.
- Oceanography is the study of the oceans, which includes studying their extent and depth, the physics and chemistry of ocean waters, and the exploitation of their resources.
- Ecology is the study of living organisms in relation to their environment and to other living things. It is the study of the interrelations between the different components of the ecosystem.

Geological eras

Geologists divide the history of the earth into units of time called eons, which are divided into eras, then into periods, then into epochs and finally into ages. Dates are approximate of course, and there may be variations of a few million years. (Million years ago is abbreviated as Ma.) Some of the most commonly known periods are:

- Hadean Period – About 4.5 to 3.8 billion years ago
- Archaean Period – 3.8 to 2.5 billion years ago
- Proterozoic Period – 2.5 billion to 542 Ma
- Cambrian Period – 542 to 488 Ma
- Ordovician Period – 488 to 443 Ma
- Silurian Period – 443 to 416 Ma

- Devonian Period – 416 to 359 Ma
- Carboniferous Period – 359 to 290 Ma
- Permian Period – 290 to 248 Ma
- Triassic Period – 251 to 200 Ma
- Jurassic Period – 200 to 150 Ma
- Cretaceous Period – 150 to 65 Ma
- Paleogene Period – 65 to 28 Ma
- Neogene Period – 28 to 2 Ma
- Quaternary Period – about 2 Ma to the present

Development of life on earth

The evolution of life on earth is believed to have occurred as follows:

- Igneous rocks formed. (Hadean)
- The continents formed. (Archaean Eon)
- One-celled creatures such as hydras, jellyfish, and sponges appeared about 600 Ma.
- Flatworms, roundworms, and segmented worms appeared about 550 Ma.
- Moss, arthropods, octopus, and eels appeared. (Cambrian Period)
- Mushrooms, fungi, and other primitive plants appeared; sea animals began to use calcium to build bones and shells. (Ordovician Period)
- Fish with jaws appeared. (Silurian Period)
- Fish developed lungs and legs (frogs) and went on land; ferns appeared. (Devonian period)
- Reptiles developed the ability to lay eggs on land and pine trees appeared. (Carboniferous Period)
- Dinosaurs dominated the land during the Triassic and Jurassic Periods.
- Flying insects, birds, and the first flowering plants appeared; dinosaurs died out. (Cretaceous Period)
- Mammals evolved and dominated; grasses became widespread. (50 Ma)
- Hominids appeared more than 2 Ma.

Planets

In order of their distance from the sun (closest to furthest away), the planets are: Mercury, Venus, Earth, Mars, Jupiter, Saturn, Uranus, Neptune, and Pluto (there is debate about whether Pluto should be classified as a planet). All the planets revolve around the sun, which is an average-sized star in the spiral Milky Way galaxy. They revolve in the same direction in nearly circular orbits. If the planets were viewed by looking down from the sun, they would rotate in a counter-clockwise direction. Pluto's orbit is so highly inclined at 18 degrees that at times its ellipse is nearer to the sun than to its neighbor, Neptune. All the planets are in or near the same plane, called the ecliptic, and the axis of rotation is nearly perpendicular to the ecliptic. The exceptions are Uranus and Pluto, which are tipped on their sides.

Terrestrial and Jovian Planets

The Terrestrial Planets are: Mercury, Venus, Earth, and Mars. These are the four planets closest to the sun. They are called terrestrial because they all have a compact, rocky surface similar to the Earth's. Venus, Earth, and Mars have significant atmospheres, but Mercury has almost no atmosphere.

The Jovian Planets are: Jupiter (the largest planet), Saturn, Uranus, and Neptune. They are called Jovian (Jupiter-like) because of their huge sizes in relation to that of the Earth, and because they all have a gaseous nature like Jupiter. Although gas giants, some or all of the Jovian Planets may have small, solid cores.

Pluto does not have the characteristics necessary to fit into either the Terrestrial or the Jovian group.

The sun represents 99.85% of all the matter in our solar system. Combined, the planets make up only 0.135% of the mass of the solar system, with Jupiter having twice the mass of all the other planets combined. The remaining 0.015% of the mass comes from comets, planetary satellites, asteroids, meteoroids, and interplanetary medium.

Hydrosphere

The hydrosphere is anything on earth that is related to water, whether it is in the air, on land, or in a plant or animal system. A water molecule consists of only two atoms of hydrogen and one of oxygen, yet it is what makes life possible. Unlike the other planets, earth is able to sustain life because its temperature allows water to be in its liquid state most of the time. Water vapor and ice are of no use to living organisms.

The hydrologic cycle is the journey water takes as it assumes different forms. Liquid surface water evaporates to form the gaseous state of a cloud, and then becomes liquid again in the form of rain. This process takes about 10 days if water becomes a cloud. Water at the bottom of the ocean or in a glacier is not likely to change form, even over periods of thousands of years.

Aquifers

An aquifer is an underground water reservoir formed from groundwater that has infiltrated from the surface by passing through the soil and permeable rock layers (the zone of aeration) to a zone of saturation where the rocks are impermeable.

There are two types of aquifers. In one, the water is under pressure (confined) as the supply builds up between layers of impermeable rocks and has to move back towards the surface, resulting in a spring or artesian well. The second type of aquifer is called "unconfined" because it has room to expand and contract, and the water has to be pumped out. The highest level of the aquifer is called the water table. If water is pumped out of the aquifer such that the water table dips in a specific area, that area is called a cone of depression.

Freshwater biomes, estuaries, intertidal zones, and subtidal zones

Freshwater biomes are areas of relatively slow-moving water, such as rivers, lakes, and ponds. Since the water is not moving so quickly as to move life forms along, insects and fish have time to grow, and plants have time to attach themselves to the soil.

Estuaries are coastline regions where the fresh water from rivers mixes with the salt water of the ocean. This mix is attractive to numerous types of marine life (and birds). It is especially suitable for laying eggs because the water is quite still and its brackishness hides newborn fish.

The intertidal zone is the space on the coastline that is under water during high tide and dry during low tide. It is usually rocky, and contains abundant amounts of algae, small marine life, and many birds looking for food.

The subtidal zone, which may have large sandy plains, is always under water near the coast. Coral reefs and most of the world's fish are here because the waves create abundant life-sustaining oxygen in the water.

Euphotic , bathyal, and abyssal zone

Beyond the subtidal zone, the ocean floor drops away to the deep ocean biome, which has three layers:

- The euphotic zone is the surface area of deep ocean water where there is a lot of sunshine and oxygen and therefore many small photosynthetic organisms. However, there are few nutrients because they fall to the bottom.
- The bathyal zone is the area further down that has dim light and no little organisms. It does, however, have some fish that go to feed on the organisms on the surface.
- The abyssal zone is the bottom of the ocean where it is pitch black. There are no producers and little oxygen. This zone is very cold and has high pressure. There are predator fish and living organisms that feed on whatever falls from the surface.

Biosphere

Biosphere is the term used by physical geographers to describe the living world of trees, bugs, and animals. It refers to any place where life exists on earth, and is the intersection of the hydrosphere, the atmosphere, the land, and the energy that comes from space. The biosphere includes the upper areas of the atmosphere where birds and insects can travel, areas deep inside caves, and hydrothermal vents at the bottom of the ocean. Factors that affect the biosphere include:

- The distance and tilt between the earth and the sun – This produces temperatures that are conducive to life and causes the seasons.
- Climate, daily weather, and erosion – These change the land and the organisms on and in it.
- Earthquakes, tornadoes, volcanoes, tsunamis, and other natural phenomena – These all change the land.
- Chemical erosion – This changes the composition of rocks and organic materials, as well as how bacteria and single-celled organisms break down organic and inorganic materials.

Ecological system and biome

An ecological system, or ecosystem, is the community of all the living organisms in a specific area interacting with non-living factors such as temperature, sunlight, atmospheric pressure, weather patterns, wind, types of nutrients, etc. An ecosystem's development depends on the energy that passes in and out of it. The boundaries of an ecosystem depend on the use of the term, whether it refers to an ecosystem under a rock or in a valley, pond, or ocean.

A biome is a general ecosystem type defined by the plants and animals that live there and the local climate patterns. Examples include tropical rainforests or savannas, deserts, grasslands, deciduous forests, tundra, woodlands, and ice caps. There can be more than one type of biome within a larger climate zone. The transition area between two biomes is an ecotone, which may have characteristics of both biomes.

Erosion

Erosion is the process that breaks down matter, whether it is a rock that is broken into pebbles or mountains that are rained on until they become hills. Erosion always happens in a downhill direction. The erosion of land by weather or breaking waves is called denudation. Mass wasting is the movement of masses of dirt and rock from one place to another. This can occur in two ways: mechanical (such as breaking a rock with a hammer) or chemical (such as pouring acid on a rock to dissolve it). If the material changes color, it indicates that a break down was chemical in nature. Whatever is broken down must go somewhere, so erosion eventually builds something up. For example, an eroded mountain ends up in a river that carries the sediment towards the ocean, where it builds up and creates a wetland or delta at the mouth of the river.

Climates

Climate is the atmospheric condition in a certain location near the surface of the earth. Scientists have determined the following different types of climates:

- Polar (ice caps)
- Polar (tundra)
- Subtropical (dry summer)
- Subtropical (dry winter)
- Subtropical (humid)
- Subtropical (marine west coast)
- Subtropical (Mediterranean)
- Subtropical (wet)
- Tropical (monsoon)
- Tropical (savannah/grasslands)
- Tropical (wet)

Several factors make up and affect climates. These include:

- Temperature
- Atmospheric pressure
- The number of clouds and the amount of dust or smog
- Humidity
- Winds

The moistest and warmest of all the climates is that of the tropical rainforest. It has daily convection thunderstorms caused by the surface daytime heat and the high humidity, which combine to form thunderclouds.

Layers of the earth

The earth has several distinct layers, each with its own properties:

- Crust is the outermost layer of the earth that is comprised of the continents and the ocean basins. It has a variable thickness (35-70 km in the continents and 5-10 km in the ocean basins) and is composed mostly of alumino-silicates.
- Mantle is about 2900 km thick, and is made up mostly of ferro-magnesium silicates. It is divided into an upper and lower mantle. Most of the internal heat of the earth is located in the mantle. Large convective cells circulate heat, and may cause plate tectonic movement.

- Core is separated into the liquid outer core and the solid inner core. The outer core is 2300 km thick (composed mostly of nickel-iron alloy), and the inner core (almost entirely iron) is 12 km thick. The earth's magnetic field is thought to be controlled by the liquid outer core.

Earth's atmosphere

The earth's atmosphere is 79% nitrogen, 20% oxygen, and 1% other gases. The oxygen was originally produced almost entirely by algae-type plants. The atmosphere has four layers:

- Troposphere – This is the layer closest to the earth where all weather takes place. It is the region that contains rising and falling packets of air. Air pressure at sea level is 0.1 atmospheres, but the top of the troposphere is about 10% of that amount.
- In the stratosphere, air flow is mainly horizontal. The upper portion has a thin layer of concentrated ozone (a reactive form of oxygen) that is largely responsible for absorbing the sun's ultraviolet rays.
- Mesosphere is the coldest layer. Temperatures drop to -100°C at the top.
- Thermosphere is divided into the lower ionosphere and the higher exosphere. This layer is very thin and has many ionized atoms with a net electrical charge. The aurora and Van Allen Belts are here. This layer also absorbs the most energetic photons from the sun and reflects radio waves, enabling long distance radio communication.

Paleontology

Paleontology is the study of prehistoric plant and animal life through the analysis of fossil remains. These fossils reveal the ecologies of the past and the path of evolution for both extinct and living organisms. A historical science, paleontology seeks information about the identity, origin, environment, and evolution of past organisms and what they can reveal about the past of the earth as a whole. Paleontology explains causes as opposed to conducting experiments to observe effects. It is related to the fields of biology, geology, and archaeology, and is divided into several sub-disciplines concerned with the types of fossils studied, the process of fossilization, and the ecology and climate of the past. Paleontologists also help identify the composition of the earth's rock layers by the fossils that are found, thus identifying potential sites for oil, mineral, and water extraction.

Rock record

The Law of Superposition logically assumes that the bottom layer of a series of sedimentary layers is the oldest, unless it has been overturned or older rock has been pushed over it.

In addition, since igneous intrusions can cut through or flow above other rocks, these other rocks are older. For example, molten rock (lava) flows out over already present, older rocks.

Another guideline for the rock record is that rock layers are older than the folds and faults in them because the rocks must exist before they can be folded or faulted.

If a rock contains atomic nuclei, reference tables of the half lives of commonly used radio isotopes can be used to match the decay rate of known substances to the nuclei in a rock, and thereby determine its age.

Ages of rocks can also be determined from contact metamorphism, the re-crystallization of pre-existing rocks due to changes in physical and chemical conditions, such as heat, pressure, and chemically active fluids that might be present in lava or polluted waters.

Matching rocks and geologic events

Geologists physically follow rock layers from one location to another by a process called "walking the outcrop." Geologists walk along the outcropping to see where it goes and what the differences and similarities of the neighboring locations they cross are.

Similar rock types or patterns of rock layers that are similar in terms of thickness, color, composition, and fossil remains tell geologists that two locations have a similar geologic history.

Fossils are found all over the earth, but are from a relatively small time period in earth's history. Therefore, fossil evidence helps date a rock layer, regardless of where it occurs.

Volcanic ash is a good time indicator since ash is deposited quickly over a widespread area. Matching the date of an eruption to the ash allows for a precise identification of time. Similarly, the meteor impact at the intersection of the Cretaceous and Tertiary Periods left a time marker. Wherever the meteor's iridium content is found, geologists are able to date rock layers.

Fossil and rock record

Reference tables are used to match specimens and time periods. For example, the fossil record has been divided into time units of the earth's history. Rocks can therefore be dated by the fossils found with them. There are also reference tables for dating plate motions and mountain building events in geologic history.

Since humans have been around for a relatively short period of time, fossilized human remains help to affix a date to a location.

Some areas have missing geologic layers because of erosion or other factors, but reference tables specific to a region will list what is complete or missing.

The theory of uniformitarianism assumes that geologic processes have been the same throughout history. Therefore, the way erosion or volcanic eruptions happen today is the same as the way these events happened millions of years ago because there is no reason for them to have changed. Therefore, knowledge about current events can be applied to the past to make judgments about events in the rock record.

Fossils can show how animal and plant life have changed or remained the same over time. For example, fossils have provided evidence of the existence of dinosaurs even though they no longer roam the earth, and have also been used to prove that certain insects have been around forever.

Fossils have been used to identify four basic eras: Proterozoic, the age of primitive life; Paleozoic, the age of fishes; Mesozoic, the age of dinosaurs; and Cenozoic, the age of mammals.

Most ancient forms of life have disappeared, and there are reference tables that list when this occurred. Fossil records also show the evolution of certain life forms, such as the horse from the eohippus. However, the majority of changes do not involve evolution from simple to complex forms, but rather an increase in the variety of forms.

Mountains

A mountain is a portion of the earth that has been raised above its surroundings by volcanic action or tectonic plate movement. Mountains are made up of igneous, metamorphic, and sedimentary rocks, and most lie along active plate boundaries. There are two major mountain systems. The Circum-Pacific encircles the entire Pacific Ocean, from New Guinea up across Japan and the Aleutians and down to southern South America. The Alpine-Himalaya stretches from northern Africa across the Alps and to the Himalayas and Indonesia.

Orogeny is the term for the process of natural mountain formation. Therefore, physical mountains are orogens.

Folded mountains are created through the folding of rock layers when two crustal plates come together. The Alps and Himalayas are folded mountains. The latter was formed by the collision of India with Asia.
Fault-block mountains are created from the tension forces of plate movements. These produce faults that vertically displace one section to form a mountain.

Dome mountains are created from magma pushing up through the earth's crust.

Volcanoes

Volcanoes are classified according to their activity level. An active volcano is in the process of erupting or building to an eruption; a dormant volcano has erupted before and may erupt again someday, but is not currently active; and an extinct volcano has died out volcanically and will not erupt ever again. Active volcanoes endanger plant and animal life, but lava and ash add enriching minerals to the soil.There are three types of volcanic mountains:

- Shield volcanoes are the largest volcanic mountains because of a repeated, viscous lava flow from small eruptions over a long period of time that cause the mountain to grow.
- Cinder cone volcanoes, or linear volcanoes, are small in size, but have massive explosions through linear shafts that spread cinders and ash around the vent. This results in a cone-shaped hill.
- Composite volcanoes get their name from the mix of lava and ash layers that build the mountain.

Major subdivisions

The three major subdivisions of rock are:

- Igneous (magmatites) – This type is formed from the cooling of liquid magma. In the process, minerals crystallize and amalgamate. If solidification occurs deep in the earth (plutonic rock), the cooling process is slow. This allows for the formation of large crystals, giving rock a coarse-grained texture (granite). Quickly cooled magma has a glassy texture (obsidian).
- Metamorphic – Under conditions of high temperature and pressure within the earth's crust, rock material melts and changes structure, transitioning or metamorphosing into a new type of rock with different minerals. If the minerals appear in bands, the rock is foliated. Examples include marble (unfoliated) and slate (foliated).
- Sedimentary – This is the most common type of rock on earth. It is formed by sedimentation, compaction, and then cementation of many small particles of mineral,

animal, or plant material. There are three types of sedimentary rocks: clastic, clay, and sand that came from disintegrated rocks; chemical (rock salt and gypsum), formed by evaporation of aqueous solutions; and biogenic (coal), formed from animal or plant remnants.

Glaciers

Glaciers start high in the mountains, where snow and ice accumulate inside a cirque (a small semicircular depression). The snow becomes firmly packed into masses of coarse-grained ice that are slowly pulled down a slope by gravity. Glaciers grow with large amounts of snowfall and retreat (diminish) if warm weather melts more ice than can be replaced. Glaciers once covered large areas of both the northern and southern hemispheres with mile-thick ice that carved out valleys, fjords, and other land formations. They also moved plants, animals, and rocks from one area to another. There were two types of glaciers: valley, which produced U-shaped erosion and sharp-peaked mountains; and continental, which moved over and rounded mountain tops and ridges. These glaciers existed during the ice ages, the last of which occurred from 2.5 million years ago to 12,000 years ago.

Planet definition

On August 24, 2006, the International Astronomical Union redefined the criteria a body must meet to be classified as a planet, stating that the following conditions must be met:

- "A planet orbits around a star and is neither a star nor a moon."
- "Its shape is spherical due to its gravity."
- "It has 'cleared' the space of its orbit."

A dwarf planet such as Pluto does not meet the third condition. Small solar system bodies such as asteroids and comets meet only the first condition.

The solar system developed about 4.6 billion years ago out of an enormous cloud of dust and gas circling around the sun. Four rocky planets orbit relatively close to the sun. Their inside orbit is separated from the outside orbit of the four, larger gaseous planets by an asteroid belt. Pluto, some comets, and several small objects circle in the Kuiper belt outside Neptune's orbit. The Oort cloud, composed of icy space objects, encloses the planetary system like a shell.

Moon

Earth's moon is the closest celestial body to earth. Its proximity has allowed it to be studied since the invention of the telescope. As a result, its landforms have been named after astronomers, philosophers, and other scholars. Its surface has many craters created by asteroids since it has no protective atmosphere. These dark lowlands looked like seas to early astronomers, but there is virtually no water on the moon except possibly in its polar regions. These impact craters and depressions actually contain solidified lava flows. The bright highlands were thought to be continents, and were named terrae. The rocks of the moon have been pounded by asteroids so often that there is a layer of rubble and dust called the regolith. Also because there is no protective atmosphere, temperatures on the moon vary widely, from 265°F to -255°F.

Sun

A star begins as a cloud of hydrogen and some heavier elements drawn together by their own mass. This matter then begins to rotate. The core heats up to several million degrees Fahrenheit, which causes the hydrogen atoms to lose their shells and their nuclei to fuse. This releases enormous amounts of energy. The star then becomes stable, a stage called the main sequence. This is the stage our sun is in, and it will remain in this stage until its supply of hydrogen fuel runs out. Stars are not always alone like our sun, and may exist in pairs or groups. The hottest stars shine blue-white; medium-hot stars like our sun glow yellow; and cooler stars appear orange. The earth's sun is an average star in terms of mass, light production, and size. All stars, including our sun, have a core where fusion happens; a photosphere (surface) that produces sunspots (cool, dark areas); a red chromosphere that emits solar (bright) flares and shooting gases; and a corona, the transparent area only seen during an eclipse.

Comets, asteroids, and meteoroids

Comets are celestial bodies composed of dust, rock, frozen gases, and ice. Invisible until they near the sun, the heat causes them to emit volatile components in jets of gas and dust. The coma is the comet's fog-like envelope that glows as it reflects sunlight and releases radiation. Solar winds blow a comet away from the sun and give it a tail of dust or electrically charged molecules. Each orbit of a comet causes it to lose matter until it breaks up or vaporizes into the sun.

Asteroids are irregularly-shaped boulders, usually less than 60 miles in diameter, that orbit the sun. Most are made of graphite; about 25% are silicates, or iron and nickel. Collisions or gravitational forces can cause them to fly off and possibly hit a planet.

Meteoroids are fragments of asteroids of various sizes. If they come through earth's atmosphere, they are called meteors or shooting stars. If they land on earth, they are called meteorites, and create craters on impact (the Barringer Crater in Arizona).

Subfields of biology

There are a number of subfields of biology:

- Zoology is the study of animals
- Botany is the study of plants
- Biophysics is the application of the laws of physics to the processes of organisms and the application of the facts about living things to human processes and inventions
- Biochemistry is the study of the chemistry of living organisms, including diseases and the pharmaceutical drugs used to cure them
- Cytology is the study of cells
- Histology is the study of the tissues of plants and animals
- Organology is the study of tissues organized into organs
- Physiology is the study of the way organisms function, including metabolism, the exchange of matter and energy in nutrition, the senses, reproduction and development, and the work of the nervous system and brain
- Genetics is the study of heredity as it relates to the transmission of genes
- Ethology is the study of animal behavior
- Ecology is the study of the relationship of living organisms to their environments

Kingdoms of life forms

All living creatures can be classified into one of five kingdoms:

- The Moneran Kingdom contains the simplest known organisms (prokaryotes). Members have just one chromosome, reproduce asexually, may have flagella, and are very simple in form. Members are either bacteria or blue-green algae.
- The Protist Kingdom contains the simplest eukaryotes. They have a true nucleus surrounded by a membrane that separates it from the cytoplasm. Most are one-celled and have no complex tissues like plants. Members include protozoa, algae, and slime molds.
- The Fungi Kingdom members have no chlorophyll, so they don't make their own food like plants. They reproduce using spores. Fungi are made up of filaments called hyphae that, in larger fungi, can interlace to form a tissue called mycelium. Fungi include mushrooms and microscopic organisms that may be parasitic.
- The Plant Kingdom consists of all multi-celled organisms that have chlorophyll and make their own food. Plants have differentiated tissues and reproduce either sexually or asexually.
- The Animal Kingdom consists of all multi-celled organisms that have no chlorophyll and have to feed on existing organic material. Animals have the most complex tissues and can move about.

Invertebrates

Invertebrates are animals with no internal skeletons. They can be divided into three groups:

- Marine Invertebrates live in oceans and seas. Marine invertebrates include sponges, corals, jellyfish, snails, clams, octopuses, squids, and crustaceans, none of which live on the surface.
- Freshwater Invertebrates live in lakes and rivers. Freshwater invertebrates include worms on the bottom, microscopic crustaceans, and terrestrial insect larvae that live in the water column, but only where there is no strong current. Some live on the surface of the water.
- Terrestrial Invertebrates live on dry ground. Terrestrial invertebrates include insects, mollusks (snails, slugs), arachnids, and myriapods (centipedes and millipedes). Terrestrial invertebrates breathe through a series of tubes that penetrate into the body (trachea) and deliver oxygen into tissues.

Underground terrestrial invertebrates are generally light-colored with atrophied eyes and no cuticle to protect them from desiccation. They include worms that live underground and in caves and rock crevices. This group also includes insects such as ants that create colonies underground.

Vertebrate groups

The vertebrates, animals with an internal skeleton, are divided into four groups:

- Fish – This group is the most primitive, but is also the group from which all other groups evolved. Fish live in water, breathe with gills, are cold-blooded, have fins and scales, and are typically oviparous. Fish typically have either cartilaginous skeletons (such as rays and sharks) or bony skeletons.
- Amphibians – The skin of animals in this group is delicate and permeable, so they need water to keep it moist. Amphibians are oviparous. The young start out in water with gills, but the adults use lungs.
- Reptiles and birds – The skin of animals in this group has very hard, horn-like scales. Birds have exchanged scales for feathers. Reptiles and birds are oviparous, although birds care for

their eggs and reptiles do not. Members have a cloaca, an excretory and reproductive cavity that opens to the outside. Reptiles are cold-blooded, but birds are warm-blooded.
- Mammals – These are the most highly evolved vertebrates. Mammals have bodies covered with fur; are warm-blooded; are viviparous, meaning they give birth to live young which are fed with milk from female mammary glands; and are tetrapods (four-legged). Most live on the ground (except whales and dolphins) and a few fly (bats).

Hunters and prey animals

The interaction between predators and their prey is important to controlling the balance of an ecosystem.

Hunters are carnivorous animals at the top of the ecological pyramid that eat other animals. Hunters tend to be territorial, leaving signs to warn others to stay out or risk a fight. Hunters are equipped to capture with claws, curved beaks, spurs, fangs, etc. They try to use a minimum amount of energy for each capture, so they prey upon the more vulnerable (the old, ill, or very young) when given a choice. Predators never kill more than they can eat. Some hunters have great speed, some stalk, and some hunt in groups.

Prey animals are those that are captured by predators for food. They are usually herbivores further down the ecological pyramid. Prey animals have special characteristics to help them flee from predators. They may hide in nests or caves, become totally immobile to escape detection, have protective coloration or camouflage, have warning coloration to indicate being poisonous, or have shells or quills for protection.

Life processes

Living things share many processes that are necessary to survival, but the ways these processes and interactions occur is highly diverse. Processes include those related to:
- Nutrition is the process of obtaining, ingesting, and digesting foods; excreting unused or excess substances; and extracting energy from the foods to maintain structure.
- Transport (circulation) is the process of circulating essential materials such as nutrients, cells, hormones, and gases (oxygen and hydrogen) to the places they are needed by moving them through veins, arteries, and capillaries. Needed materials do not travel alone, but are "piggybacked" on transporting molecules.
- Respiration is the process of breathing, which is exchanging gases between the interior and exterior using gills, trachea (insects), or lungs.
- Regulation is the process of coordinating life activities through the nervous and endocrine systems.
- Reproduction and growth is the process of producing more of one's own kind and growing from birth to adulthood. The more highly evolved an animal is, the longer its growth time is.
- Locomotion (in animals) is the process of moving from place to place in the environment by using legs, flight, or body motions.

Organisms that interfere with cell activity

Viruses, bacteria, fungi, and other parasites may infect plants and animals and interfere with normal life functions, create imbalances, or disrupt the operations of cells.

- Viruses enter the body by inhalation (airborne) or through contact with contaminated food, water, or infected tissues. They affect the body by taking over the cell's protein synthesis mechanism to make more viruses. They kill the host cell and impact tissue and organ operations. Examples of viruses include measles, rabies, pneumonia, and AIDS.
- Bacteria enter the body through breaks in the skin or contaminated food or water, or by inhalation. They reproduce rapidly and produce toxins that kill healthy host tissues. Examples include diphtheria, bubonic plague, tuberculosis, and syphilis.
- Fungi feed on healthy tissues of the body by sending rootlike tendrils into the tissues to digest them extracellularly. Examples include athlete's foot and ringworm.
- Parasites enter the body through the skin, via insect bites, or through contaminated food or water. Examples include tapeworms, malaria, or typhus.

Autotrophs, producers, herbivores, carnivores, omnivores, and decomposers

Energy flows in one direction: from the sun, through photosynthetic organisms such as green plants (producers) and algae (autotrophs), and then to herbivores, carnivores, and decomposers.

Autotrophs are organisms capable of producing their own food. The organic molecules they produce are food for all other organisms (heterotrophs).

Producers are green plants that manufacture food by photosynthesis.

Herbivores are animals that eat only plants (deer, rabbits, etc.). Since they are the first animals to receive the energy captured by producers, herbivores are called primary consumers.

Carnivores, or secondary consumers, are animals that eat the bodies of other animals for food. Predators (wolves, lions, etc.) kill other animals, while scavengers consume animals that are already dead from predation or natural causes (buzzards). Omnivores are animals that eat both plants and other animals (humans). Decomposers include saprophytic fungi and bacteria that break down the complex structures of the bodies of living things into simpler forms that can be used by other living things. This recycling process releases energy from organic molecules.

Abiotic and biotic factors

Abiotic factors are the physical and chemical factors in the environment that are nonliving, but upon which the growth and survival of living organisms depends. These factors can determine the types of plants and animals that will establish themselves and thrive in a particular area. Abiotic factors include:

- Light intensity available for photosynthesis
- Temperature range
- Available moisture
- Type of rock substratum
- Type of minerals
- Type of atmospheric gases
- Relative acidity (pH) of the system

Biotic factors are the living components of the environment that affect, directly or indirectly, the ecology of an area, possibly limiting the type and number of resident species. The relationships of predator/prey, producer/consumer, and parasite/host can define a community. Biotic factors include:

- Population levels of each species
- The food requirements of each species
- The interactions between species
- The wastes produced

Hydrocarbons and carbohydrates

Carbon is an element found in all living things. Two types of carbon molecules that are essential to life are hydrocarbons and carbohydrates.

Hydrocarbons, composed only of hydrogen and carbon, are the simplest organic molecules. The simplest of these is methane, which has one carbon atom and four hydrogen atoms. Methane is produced by the decomposition of animal or vegetable matter, and is part of petroleum and natural gas.

Carbohydrates are compounds made of hydrogen, carbon, and oxygen. There are three types of these macromolecules (large molecules):

Sugars are soluble in water and, although they have less energy than fats, provide energy more quickly.

Starches, insoluble in water, are long chains of glucose that act as reserve substances. Potatoes and cereals are valuable foods because they are rich in starch. Animals retain glucose in their cells as glucogen, a special type of starch.

Cellulose, composed of glucose chains, makes up the cells and tissues of plants. It is one of the most common organic materials.

Lipids, proteins, and nucleic acids

Besides hydrocarbons and carbohydrates, there are three other types of carbon molecules that are essential to life: lipids, proteins, and nucleic acids.

Lipids are compounds that are insoluble or only partially soluble in water. There are three main types: fats, which act as an energy reserve for organisms; phospholipids, which are one of the essential components of cell membranes; and steroids such as cholesterol and estrogen, which are very important to metabolism.

Proteins are complex substances that make up almost half the dry weight of animal bodies. These molecules contain hydrogen, carbon, oxygen, and other elements, chiefly nitrogen and sulfur. Proteins make up muscle fibers and, as enzymes, act as catalysts.

Nucleic acids are large molecules (polymers) composed of a large number of simpler molecules (nucleotides). Each one has a sugar containing five carbons (pentose), a phosphorous compound (phosphate group), and a nitrogen compound (nitrogenated base). Nucleic acids facilitate perpetuation of the species because they carry genetic information as DNA and RNA.

How plants manufacture food

Plants are the only organisms capable of transforming inorganic material from the environment into organic matter by using water and solar energy. This transformation is made possible by chloroplasts, flat structures inside plant cells. Chloroplasts, located primarily in the leaves, contain chlorophyll (the pigment capable of absorbing light and storing it in chemical compounds), DNA, ribosomes, and numerous enzymes. Chloroplasts are surrounded by a membrane. The leaves of plants are the main producers of oxygen, which helps purify the air.

The chlorophyll in chloroplasts is responsible for the light, or luminous, phase of photosynthesis. The energy it absorbs breaks down water absorbed through the roots into hydrogen and oxygen to form ATP molecules that store energy. In the dark phase, when the plant has no light, the energy molecules are used to attach carbon dioxide to water and form glucose, a sugar.

Role of a cell

The cell is the basic organizational unit of all living things. Each piece within a cell has a function that helps organisms grow and survive. There are many different types of cells, but cells are unique to each type of organism. The one thing that all cells have in common is a membrane, which is comparable to a semi-permeable plastic bag. The membrane is composed of phospholipids. There are also some transport holes, which are proteins that help certain molecules and ions move in and out of the cell. The cell is filled with a fluid called cytoplasm or cytosol.

Within the cell are a variety of organelles, groups of complex molecules that help a cell survive, each with its own unique membrane that has a different chemical makeup from the cell membrane. The larger the cell, the more organelles it will need to live.

Eukaryotic cells

Eukaryotic cells have a nucleus, a big dark spot floating somewhere in the center that acts like the brain of the cell by controlling eating, movement, and reproduction. A nuclear envelope surrounds the nucleus and its contents, but allows RNA and proteins to pass through. Chromatin, made up of DNA, RNA, and nuclear proteins, is present in the nucleus. The nucleus also contains a nucleolus made of RNA and protein.

Mitochondria are very small organelles that take in nutrients, break them down, and create energy for the cell through a process called cellular respiration. There might be thousands of mitochondria depending on the cell's purpose. A muscle cell needs more energy for movement than a cell that transmits nerve impulses, for example. Mitochondria have two membranes: a cover and the inner cristae that folds over many times to increase the surface work area. The fluid inside the mitochondria, the matrix, is filled with water and enzymes that take food molecules and combine them with oxygen so they can be digested.

Chloroplasts

Chloroplasts, which make plants green, are the food producers of a plant cell. They differ from an animal cell's mitochondria, which break down sugars and nutrients. Photosynthesis occurs when the energy from the sun hits a chloroplast and the chlorophyll uses that energy to combine carbon dioxide and water to make sugars and oxygen. The nutrition and oxygen obtained from plants makes them the basis of all life on earth. A chloroplast has two membranes to contain and protect the inner parts. The stroma is an area inside the chloroplast where reactions occur and starches are created. A thylakoid has chlorophyll molecules on its surface, and a stack of thylakoids is called a granum. The stacks of sacs are connected by stromal lamellae, which act like the skeleton of the chloroplast, keeping all the sacs a safe distance from each other and maximizing the efficiency of the organelle.

Passive and active transport

Passive transport within a cell does not require energy and work. For example, when there is a large concentration difference between the outside and the inside of a cell, the pressure of the greater concentration, not energy, will move molecules across the lipid bilayer into the cell. Another example of passive transport is osmosis, which is the movement of water across a membrane. Too much water in a cell can cause it to burst, so the cell moves ions in and out to help equalize the amount of water.

Active transport is when a cell uses energy to move individual molecules across the cell membrane to maintain a proper balance. Proteins embedded in the lipid bilayer do most of the transport work. There are hundreds of different types of proteins because they are specific. For instance, a protein that moves glucose will not move calcium. The activity of these proteins can be stopped by inhibitors or poisons, which can destroy or plug up a protein.

Mitotic cell replication

Mitosis is the duplication of a cell and all its parts, including the DNA, into two identical daughter cells. There are five phases in the life cycle of a cell:

- Prophase is the process of duplicating everything in preparation for division.
- Metaphase – The cell's different pieces align themselves for the split. The DNA lines up along a central axis and the centrioles send out specialized tubules that connect to the centromere. The centromere has two strands of a chromosome (condensed DNA) attached to it.
- Anaphase – Half of the chromosomes go one way and half go another.
- Telophase – When the chromosomes get to the side of the cell, the cell membrane closes in and splits the cell into two pieces. This results in two separate cells, each with half of the original DNA.
- Interphase is the normal state of the cell, or the resting stage between divisions. During this stage, the cell duplicates nucleic acids in preparation for the next division.

Microbes

Microbes are the smallest, simplest, and most abundant organisms on earth. Their numbers are incalculable, and a microscope is required to see them. There is a huge variety of microbes, including bacteria, fungi, some algae, and protozoa. Microbes can be harmful or helpful. Microbes can be heterotrophic (eat other things) or autotrophic (make food for themselves). They can be solitary or colonial, sexual or asexual. Examples include mold, a multi-cellular type of fungus, and yeasts, which are single-celled (but may live in colonies).

A mushroom is a fungus that lives as a group of strands underground called hyphae that decompose leaves or bark on the ground. When it reproduces, it develops a mushroom whose cap contains spores. Mold is a type of zygote fungi that reproduces with a stalk, but releases zygospores.

Good bacteria can be those that help plants absorb the nitrogen needed for growth or help grazing animals break down the cellulose in plants. Some bad bacteria are killed by the penicillin developed from a fungus.

Roots, stems, and leaves

Roots are structures designed to pull water and minerals from soil or water. In large plants such as trees, the roots usually go deep into the ground to not only reach the water, but also to support and stabilize the tree. There are some plant species that have roots above ground, and there are also plants called epiphytes that live in trees with their roots clinging to the branches. Some roots, like carrots and turnips, serve as food. Roots are classified as primary and lateral (like a trunk and branches). The apical meristem is the tip of a root or shoot that helps the plant increase in length. Root hairs are fuzzy root extensions that help with the absorption of water and nutrients.

The majority of the plant above ground is made up of the stems (trunk and branches) and leaves. Stems transport food and water and act as support structures. Leaves are the site for photosynthesis, and are connected to the rest of the plant by a vascular system.

Gymnosperms, cycads, and conifers

Gymnosperms are plants with vascular systems and seeds but no flowers (flowers are an evolutionary advancement). The function of the seed is to ensure offspring can be produced by the plant by providing a protective coating that lets the plant survive for long periods until it germinates. It also stores food for the new plant to use until it can make its own. Seeds can be spread over a wide area.

Cycads are sturdy plants with big, waxy fronds that make them look like ferns or palms. They can survive in harsh conditions if there is warm weather. For reproduction, they have big cones located in the center of the plant. The female plant grows a fruit in the middle of the stem.

Conifers are trees that thrive in northern latitudes and have cones. Examples of conifers are pine, cedar, redwood, and spruce. Conifers are evergreens because they have needles that take full advantage of the sun year round. They are also very tall and strong because of the chemical substance xylem in their systems.

Angiosperms

Angiosperms are plants that have flowers. This is advantageous because the plant's seeds and pollen can be spread not only by gravity and wind, but also by insects and animals. Flowers are able to attract organisms that can help pollinate the plant and distribute seeds. Some flowering plants also produce fruit. When an animal eats the fruit, the plant seeds within will be spread far and wide in the animal's excrement.

There are two kinds of angiosperm seeds: monocotyledons (monocots) and dicotyledons (dicots). A cotyledon is the seed leaf or food package for the developing plant. Monocots are the simple flowering plants such as grasses, corn, palm trees, and lilies. They always have three petals on their flowers, and their leaves are long strands (like a palm frond). A dicot has seeds with two cotyledons, or two seed leaves of food. Most everyday flowers are dicots with four or five petals and extremely complex leaves with veins. Examples include roses, sunflowers, cacti, and cherry trees.

Arthropods

Arthropods have a number of unique characteristics:

- They have an exoskeleton (outside instead of inside).
- They molt. As the arthropod grows, it must shed its old shell and grow a new one.
- They have several legs, which are jointed.
- Their advanced nervous systems allow for hunting, moving around, finding a mate, and learning new behaviors for adaptation.
- They develop through metamorphosis. As arthropods develop, they change body shape.

There are two types of metamorphosis:

- Complete – The entire body shape changes. An example is butterflies, which change from worm-like larvae to insects with wings.
- Gradual – The arthropod starts off small with no wings, and then molts and grows wings. Grasshoppers are an example.

Arthropods include spiders, crustaceans, and the enormous insect species (26 orders) called uniramians. Ranging from fleas to mosquitoes, beetles, dragonflies, aphids, bees, flies, and many more, uniramians have exoskeletons made of chitin, compound eyes, complex digestive systems, and usually six legs. This group is extremely diverse. Some can fly, some have toxins or antennae, and some can make wax, silk, or honey.

Reptiles

One group of vertebrates is the reptile. This group includes:

- Crocodilia is a group of reptiles that can grow quite large, and includes alligators and crocodiles. Normally found near the water in warmer climates, Crocodilia might be more closely related to birds than other reptiles.
- Squamata is the order of reptiles that includes snakes and lizards. Snakes are special because they have no legs and no ears. They feel vibrations, smell with their tongues, have specialized scales, and can unhinge their jaws to swallow prey that is larger than they are. Like snakes, lizards have scales, but they differ in that they have legs, can dig, can climb trees, and can grab things.
- Chelonia is the order of reptiles that includes turtles and tortoises. It is a special group because its members have shells. Different varieties live in forests, water, and deserts, or anywhere the climate is warm enough. They also live a long time, even hundreds of years. Turtles are typically found near water and tortoises on land, even dry areas.

Reproduction in mammals

When classified according to how they reproduce, there are three types of mammals:

- Monotremes are rare mammals that lay eggs. These were the first mammals, and are more closely related to reptiles than other mammals. Examples include the duck-billed platypus and the spiny anteater.

- Marsupials are special mammals. They give birth to live young, but the babies mature in pouches, where they are carried and can feed on milk. Many are found in Australia. The isolation of this island continent prevented placental mammals from taking hold. Examples of marsupials include kangaroos, possums, and koalas.
- Placental mammals give birth from the females' placenta to live young. The young may be able to walk immediately, or they may need to be carried. They are still dependent on parental care for at least a short time. Placental mammals are the dominant form of mammals. Members of this group include cetaceans such as whales and dolphins, which are mammals that evolved but returned to the ocean.

Respiratory system

The respiratory system exchanges gases with the environment. Amphibians exchange gases through their moist skin and fish use gills, but mammals, birds, and reptiles have lungs. The human respiratory system is made up of the nose, mouth, pharynx, trachea, and two lungs. The purpose of the respiratory system is to bring oxygen into the body and expel carbon dioxide.

The respiratory system can inhale viruses, bacteria, and dangerous chemicals, so it is vulnerable to toxins and diseases such as pneumonia, which causes the lungs to fill with fluid until they cannot take in enough oxygen to support the body. Emphysema, often caused by smoking tobacco, destroys the tissues in the lungs, which cannot be regenerated.

The respiratory system interacts with the digestive system in that the mouth and pharynx are used to swallow food and drink, as well as to breathe. It interacts with the circulatory system in that it provides fresh oxygen through blood vessels that pass through the lungs. This oxygen is then carried by the circulatory system throughout the body.

Skeletal system

The human body has an endoskeleton, meaning it is inside the body. It is made up of bones instead of the hard plate of exoskeletons or fluids in tubes, which comprise the hydrostatic system of the starfish. The purpose of the skeleton is to support the body, provide a framework to which the muscles and organs can connect, and protect the inner organs. The skull protects the all-important brain and the ribs protect the internal organs from impact. The skeletal system interacts with the muscular system to help the body move, and softer cartilage works with the calcified bone to allow smooth movement of the body. The skeletal system also interacts with the circulatory system in that the marrow inside the bones helps produce both white and red blood cells.

Nervous system

The nervous system is divided into two parts: the central nervous system (brain and spinal cord) and the peripheral nervous system (a network of billions of neurons of different types throughout the entire body). The neurons are connected end to end, and transmit electrical impulses to each other. Efferent neurons send impulses from the central system to the limbs and organs. Afferent neurons receive sensory information and transmit it back to the central system.

The nervous system is concerned with senses and action. In other words, it senses something and then acts upon it. An example is a predator sensing prey and attacking it. The nervous system also automatically senses activity inside the body and reacts to stimuli. For example, the first bite of a meal sets the whole digestive system into motion.

The nervous system interacts with every other system in the body because all the tissues and organs need instruction, even when individuals are not aware of any activity occurring. For instance, the endocrine system is constantly working to produce hormones or adrenalin as needed.

Producers, consumers, and decomposers

The food chain, or food web, is a series of events that happens when one organism consumes another to survive. Every organism is involved in dozens of connections with others, so what happens to one affects the environment of the others. In the food chain, there are three main categories:

- Producers – Plants and vegetables are at the beginning of the food chain because they take energy from the sun and make food for themselves through photosynthesis. They are food sources for other organisms.
- Consumers – There are three levels of consumers: the organisms that eat plants (primary consumers, or herbivores); the organisms that eat the primary consumers (secondary consumers, or carnivores); and, in some ecosystems, the organisms that eat both plants and animals (tertiary consumers, or omnivores).
- Decomposers – These are the organisms that eat dead things or waste matter and return the nutrients to the soil, thus returning essential molecules to the producers and completing the cycle.

System of classification

The main characteristic by which living organisms are classified is the degree to which they are related, not the degree to which they resemble each other. The science of classification is called taxonomy, a difficult science since the division lines between groups is not always clear. Some animals have characteristics of two separate groups.

The basic system of taxonomy involves placing an organism into a major kingdom (Moneran, Protist, Fungi, Plants, and Animals), and then dividing those kingdoms into phyla, then classes, then orders, then families, and finally genuses. For example, the family cat is in the kingdom of animals, the phylum of chordates, the class of mammals, the order of carnivores, the family of felidae, and the genus of felis. All species of living beings can be identified with Latin scientific names that are assigned by the worldwide binomial system. The genus name comes first, and is followed by the name of the species. The family cat is *felis domesticus.*

Although not part of taxonomy, behavior is also considered in identifying living beings. For example, birds are identified according to their songs or means of flight.

Genetics, genes, and chromosomes

Genetics is the science devoted to the study of how characteristics are transmitted from one generation to another. In the 1800s, Gregor Mendel discovered the three laws of heredity that explain how genetics works.

Genes are the hereditary units of material that are transmitted from one generation to the next. They are capable of undergoing mutations, can be recombined with other genes, and can determine the nature of an organism, including its color, shape, and size. Genotype is the genetic makeup of an individual based on one or more characteristics, while phenotype is the external manifestation of the genotype. For example, genotype can determine hair color, and phenotype is the actual color of the hair.

Chromosomes are the structures inside the nucleus of a cell made up primarily of deoxyribonucleic acid (DNA) and proteins. The chromosomes carry the genes. The numbers vary according to the species, but they are always the same for each species. For example, the human has 46 chromosomes, and the water lily has 112.

Interactions among humans, natural hazards, and the environment

In science class, students will learn that the human population on earth can be affected by various factors from both their natural environments and from the technologies they use in their daily lives. These factors can be positive or negative, so students need to learn how to prepare for, respond to, and evaluate the consequences of environmental occurrences over a long period of time.

Natural disasters are a negative experience, but so are human-made disasters such as pollution and deforestation. Students need to understand that science is involved in the interactions between the human population, natural hazards, and the environment. They should know that the aim of science is to make these interactions balanced and positive. Science is a discipline that can help find ways to increase safety during and remediate after natural disasters, advance technology and transportation in an environmentally safe manner, prevent and cure diseases, and remediate the environmental damage that has already been done.

Personal and social perspectives

Learning must be relevant, so when students study science in the context of personal and social perspectives, they see the practical application of the textbook knowledge. They are given an understanding of the issues around them that can be solved by science and the means to act on those issues.

Science should be taught within the social context of history so that students can see where society has been and how far it has come thanks to scientific advancements related to tools, medicine, transportation, and communication. Students should also understand how these advances developed in response to resources, needs, and values.

Students need to review the process of scientific inquiry through the centuries to get a sense of the benefits of intellectual curiosity, the inter-relatedness of science, and the development of civilization. Students should question the role science has played in the development of various cultures by considering how computers, refrigeration, vaccines, microscopes, fertilizers, etc. have improved the lives of people.

Personal health

Among the personal and social perspectives of science are the issues of personal and public health care. In this area, students learn such things as:

- The importance of regular exercise to the maintenance and improvement of health
- The need for risk assessment and educated decisions to prevent injuries and illnesses because of the potential for accidents and the existence of hazards.
- The risk of illness and the social and psychological factors associated with the use of tobacco products

- The dangers of abusing alcohol and other drug substances, including addiction and damage to body functions
- The energy and nutrition values of various foods, their role in growth and development, and the requirements of the body according to variable factors
- The complexities of human sexuality and the dangers of sexually transmitted diseases
- The relationship between environmental and human health, and the need to monitor soil, water, and air standards

Risk and benefit analysis

Risk analysis considers the type of hazard and estimates the number of people who might be exposed and the number likely to suffer consequences. The results are used to determine options for reducing or eliminating risks. For example, the Center for Disease Control must analyze the risk of a certain new virus strain causing a pandemic, how many people and what age groups need to be vaccinated first, and what precautions can be taken to guard against the spread of the disease. Risk and benefit analysis involves having students consider the dangers of natural (major storms), chemical (pollution), biological (pollen and bacteria), social (occupational safety and transportation), and personal (smoking, dieting, and drugs) hazards. Students then use a systematic approach to think critically about these hazards, apply probability estimates to the risks, and compare them to estimated and perceived personal and social benefits.

Science and technology

The interactions of science and technology with society include:

- Scientific knowledge and the procedures used by scientists influence the way many people think about themselves, others, and the environment.
- Technology influences society through its products and processes. It influences quality of life and the ways people act and interact. Technological changes are often accompanied by social, political, and economic changes. Science and technology contribute enormously to economic growth and productivity. The introduction of the cell phone into society is a perfect example of technology influencing society, quality of life, human interaction, and the economy.
- Societal challenges often inspire questions for scientific research, and social priorities often influence research priorities through the availability of research funding.
- Science and technology have been advanced through the contributions of many different people in a variety of cultures during different time periods in history. Scientists and engineers work in colleges, businesses and industries, research institutes, and government agencies, touching many lives in a variety of settings.

Inquiry-based science

If learning in the science classroom is inquiry based, children should see themselves as being involved in the process of learning. They should feel free to express curiosity and skepticism, change ideas and procedures, take risks, and exchange information with their classmates. Inquiry-based learning in science begins with observations of details, sequences, events, changes, similarities and differences, etc. Observations are followed by investigations based on scientific standards and safety that are designed by students. Designs should allow for verification, extension, or dismissal of ideas. Investigations should involve choosing tools, handling materials, measuring, observing, and recording data. The results of an investigation can take the form of a journal, report, drawing, graph, or chart. The summary of the observations and investigation should include explanations, solutions, and connections to other ideas, as well as further questions, an assessment of the quality of the work, a description of any problems encountered, and a description of the strengths and weaknesses of the investigation. Finally, students should reflect together about the lessons learned from the investigation.

Components of scientific experimentation

A hypothesis is a tentative supposition about a phenomenon (or a fact or set of facts) made in order to examine and test its logical or empirical consequences through investigation or methodological experimentation.
A theory is a scientifically proven, general principle offered to explain phenomena. A theory is derived from a hypothesis and verified by experimentation and research.

A scientific law is a generally accepted conclusion about a body of observations to which no exceptions have been found. Scientific laws explain things, but do not describe them.

A control is a normal, unchanged situation used for comparison against experimental data.

Constants are factors in an experiment that remain the same.

Independent variables are factors, traits, or conditions that are changed in an experiment. A good experiment has only one independent variable so that the scientist can track one thing at a time. The independent variable changes from experiment to experiment.

Dependent variables are changes that result from variations in the independent variable.

Scientific processes

Science is not just the steps of experimentation. While the process of posing a question, forming a hypothesis, testing the hypothesis, recording data, and drawing a conclusion is at the heart of scientific inquiry, there are other processes that are important as well. Once the scientist has completed the testing of a hypothesis and possibly come up with a theory, the scientist should then go through the process of getting feedback from colleagues, publishing an article about the work in a peer-reviewed journal, or otherwise reporting the results to the scientific community, replicating the experiment for verification of results (by the original scientist or others), and developing new questions. Science is not just a means of satisfying curiosity, but is also a process for developing technology, addressing social issues, building knowledge, and solving everyday problems.

Drawing a conclusion

Conclusions are based on data analysis and background research. The scientist has to take a hard look at the results of an experiment and check the accuracy of the data to draw preliminary conclusions. These should be compared to the background research to find out if the preliminary conclusion can be supported by previous research experiments. If the results do not support the hypothesis, or if they are contrary to what the background research predicted, then further research is needed. The focus should be on finding a reason for the different results. Finally, the scientist provides a discussion of findings that includes a summary of the results of the experiment, a statement as to whether the hypothesis was proven or disproven, a statement of the relationship between the independent and dependent variable, a summary and evaluation of the procedures of the experiment (including comments about successes and effectiveness), and suggestions for changes/modifications in procedures for further studies.

Mathematics Practice Test

Number Sense and Operations

1. In the base-5 number system, what is the sum of 303 and 2222?
   a. 2030
   b. 2525
   c. 3030
   d. 3530

2. Kim's current monthly rent is $800. She is moving to another apartment complex, where the monthly rent will be $1,100. What is the percent increase in her monthly rent amount?
   a. 25.5%
   b. 27%
   c. 35%
   d. 37.5%

3. Which of the following statements is true?
   a. The set of whole numbers is a subset of the set of natural numbers.
   b. The set of integers is a subset of the set of natural numbers.
   c. The set of integers is a subset of the set of rational numbers.
   d. The set of rational numbers is a subset of the set of integers.

4. Which of the following represents 55 in the base-2 system?
   a. 110
   b. 1101
   c. 101,111
   d. 110,111

5. Marlon pays $45 for a jacket that has been marked down 25%. What was the original cost of the jacket?
   a. $80
   b. $75
   c. $65
   d. $60

6. Which of the following statements is true?
   a. A number is divisible by 6 if the number is divisible by both 2 and 3.
   b. A number is divisible by 4 if the sum of all digits is divisible by 8.
   c. A number is divisible by 3 if the last digit is divisible by 3.
   d. A number is divisible by 7 if the sum of the last two digits is divisible by 7.

7. Which of the following is an irrational number?

a. $4.\overline{2}$

b. $\sqrt{2}$

c. $\frac{4}{5}$

d. $\frac{21}{5}$

8. Robert buys a car for $24,210. The price of the car has been marked down by 10%. What was the original price of the car?

a. $25,900

b. $26,300

c. $26,900

d. $27,300

9. Carlos spends $\frac{1}{8}$ of his monthly salary on utility bills. If his utility bills total $320, what is his monthly salary?

a. $2,440

b. $2,520

c. $2,560

d. $2,600

10. Which of the following is closed under the operation of division?

a. whole numbers

b. integers

c. nonzero rational numbers

d. irrational numbers

11. Which of the following accurately describes the set of integers?

a. the set of counting numbers

b. the set of counting numbers, plus zero

c. the set of numbers that may be written as the ratio of $\frac{a}{b}$, where $b \neq 0$

d. the set of counting numbers, zero, and the negations of the counting numbers

12. Which of the following correctly compares the sets of rational and irrational numbers?

a. The set of rational numbers is a subset of the set of irrational numbers.

b. The set of irrational numbers is a subset of the set of rational numbers.

c. The sets of irrational and rational numbers are disjoint.

d. The sets of irrational and rational numbers are equal.

13. Which of the following illustrates the multiplicative inverse property?

a. The product of a and 1 is a.

b. The product of $\frac{1}{a}$ and a is 1.

c. The variable a, raised to the negative 1 power, is equal to the ratio of 1 to a.

d. The product of a and $-a$ is $-a^2$.

14. For any natural numbers, a, b, and c, assume $a|b$ and $a|c$. Which of the following statements is *not* necessarily true?
a. $b|c$
b. $a|(b-c)$
c. $a|bc$
d. $a|(b+c)$

15. Which of the following equations may be used to convert $0.\bar{4}$ to a fraction?
a. $10x - x = 4.\bar{4} - 0.\bar{4}$
b. $100x - x = 4.\bar{4} - 0.\bar{4}$
c. $10x - x = 44.\bar{4} - 4.\bar{4}$
d. $100x - 10x = 4.\bar{4} - 0.\bar{4}$

16. Jason decides to donate 1% of his annual salary to a local charity. If his annual salary is $45,000, how much will he donate?
a. $4.50
b. $45
c. $450
d. $4,500

17. Kendra uses the pie chart below to represent the allocation of her annual income. Her annual income is $40,000.

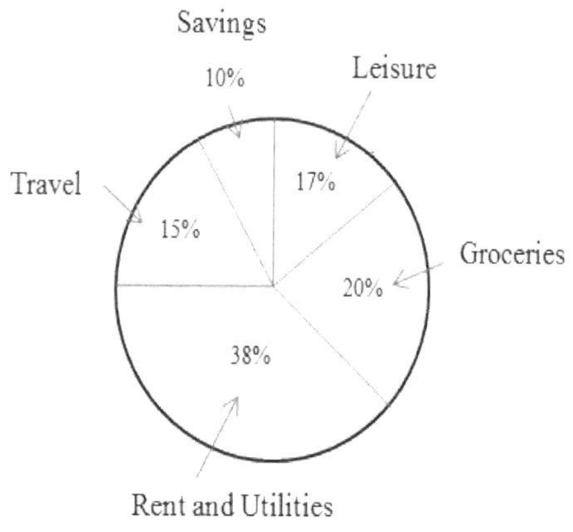

Which of the following statements is true?
a. The amount of money she spends on travel and savings is more than $11,000.
b. The amount of money she spends on rent and utilities is approximately $15,000.
c. The amount of money she spends on groceries and savings is more than $13,000.
d. The amount of money she spends on leisure is less than $5,000.

18. Which of the following correctly represents the expanded form of 0.867?
a. $8 \cdot \frac{1}{10^0} + 6 \cdot \frac{1}{10^1} + 7 \cdot \frac{1}{10^2}$
b. $8 \cdot \frac{1}{10^2} + 6 \cdot \frac{1}{10^3} + 7 \cdot \frac{1}{10^4}$
c. $8 \cdot \frac{1}{10^3} + 6 \cdot \frac{1}{10^2} + 7 \cdot \frac{1}{10^1}$
d. $8 \cdot \frac{1}{10^1} + 6 \cdot \frac{1}{10^2} + 7 \cdot \frac{1}{10^3}$

19. Which expression is represented by the diagram below?

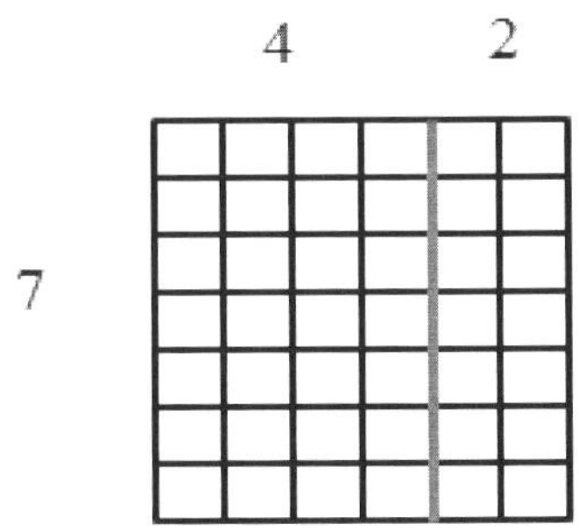

a. $7 + (4 + 2)$
b. $7 \cdot (4 \cdot 2)$
c. $7 + (4 \cdot 2)$
d. $7 \cdot (4 + 2)$

20. $b|a$ if
a. $a = b \cdot q$
b. $a = b + q$
c. $b = a \cdot q$
d. $b = a + q$

21. Which of the following sets is *not* closed under subtraction?
a. integers
b. real numbers
c. natural numbers
d. rational numbers

22. A dress is marked down 45%. The cost, after taxes, is $39.95. If the tax rate is 8.75%, what was the original price of the dress?
a. $45.74
b. $58.61
c. $66.79
d. $72.31

23. Amy saves $450 every 3 months. How much does she save after 3 years?
a. $4,800
b. $5,200
c. $5,400
d. $5,800

24. The table below shows the average amount of rainfall Houston receives during the summer and autumn months.

Month	Amount of Rainfall (in inches)
June	5.35
July	3.18
August	3.83
September	4.33
October	4.5
November	4.19

What percentage of rainfall received during this timeframe, is received during the month of October?

a. 13.5%
b. 15.1%
c. 16.9%
d. 17.7%

25. Which of the following represents 30,490?

a. 3.049×10^{-4}
b. 3.049×10^{3}
c. 30.490×10^{3}
d. 3.049×10^{4}

Algebra and Functions

26. Which of the following formulas may be used to represent the sequence 1, 2, 4, 8, 16, ...?

a. $y = 2x$
b. $y = x + 2$
c. $y = 2^{x-1}$
d. $y = x^2$

27. Which of the following formulas may be used to represent the sequence 8, 13, 18, 23, 28, ...?

a. $a_n = 5n + 3$
b. $a_n = n + 5$
c. $a_n = n + 8$
d. $a_n = 5n + 8$

28. Which of the following graphs does *not* represent a function?

a.

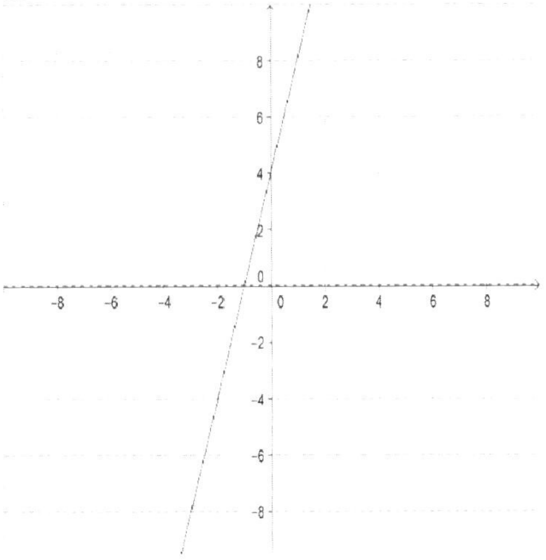

b.

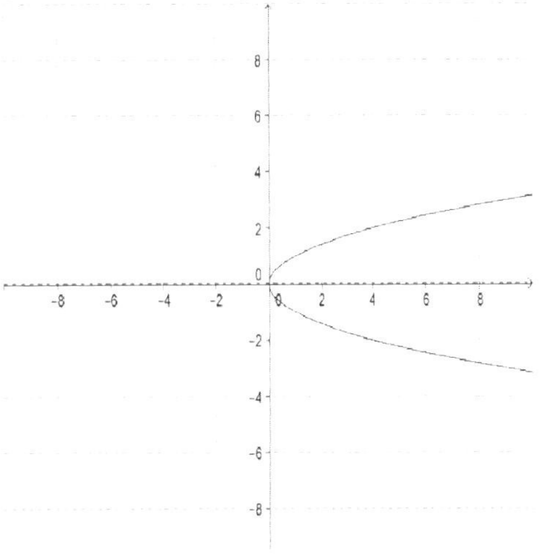

c.

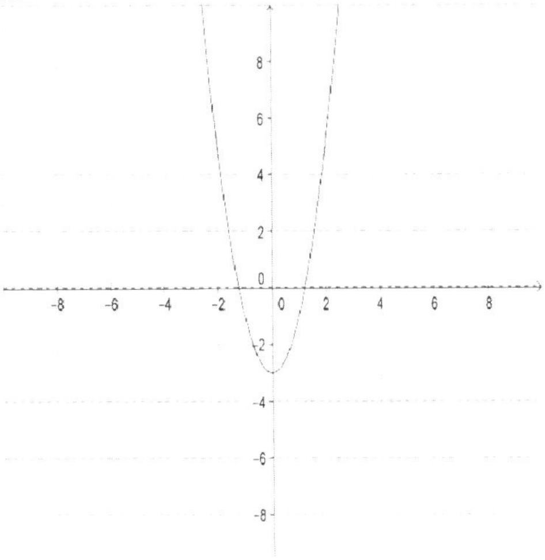

d.

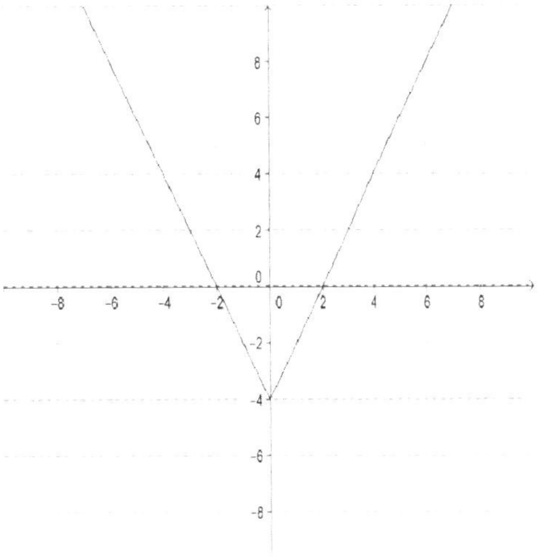

29. Which of the following represents a proportional relationship?

a.

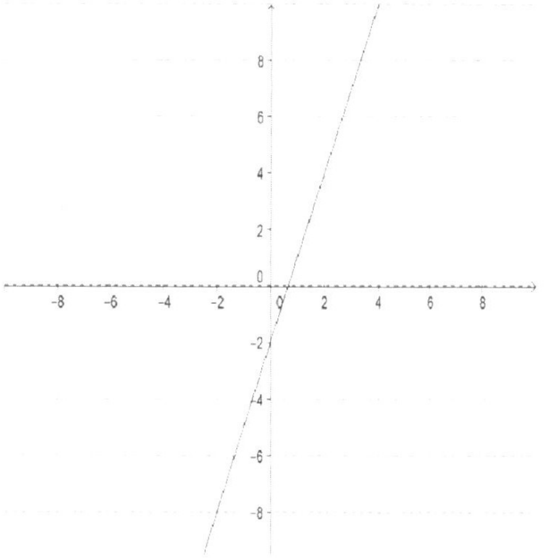

b.

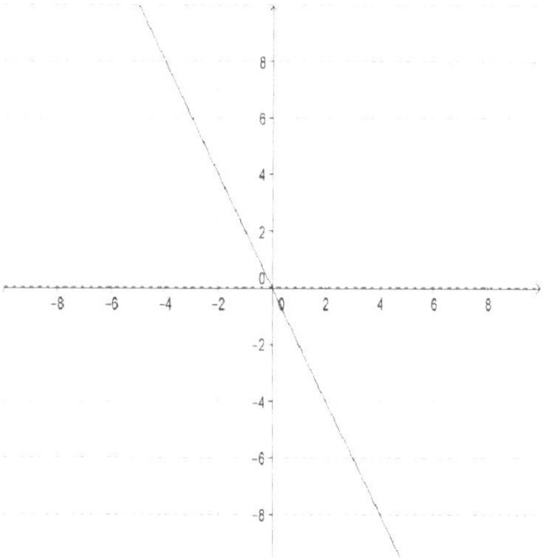

c.

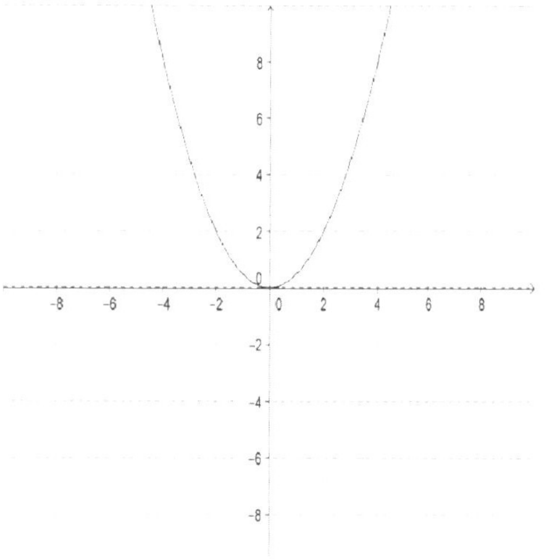

d.

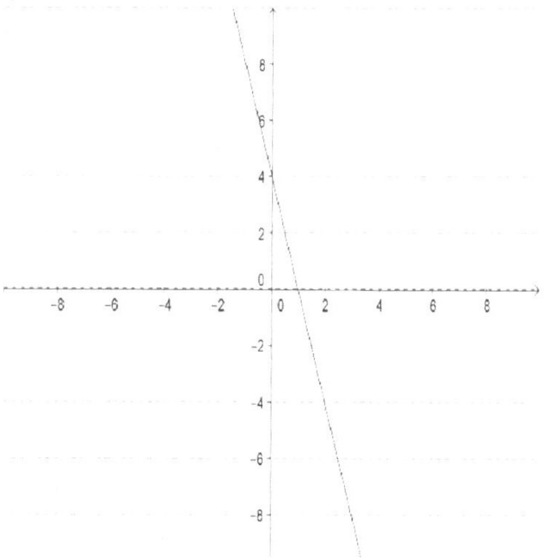

30. Which of the following represents the graph of $y = (x - 4)^2 + 3$?

a.

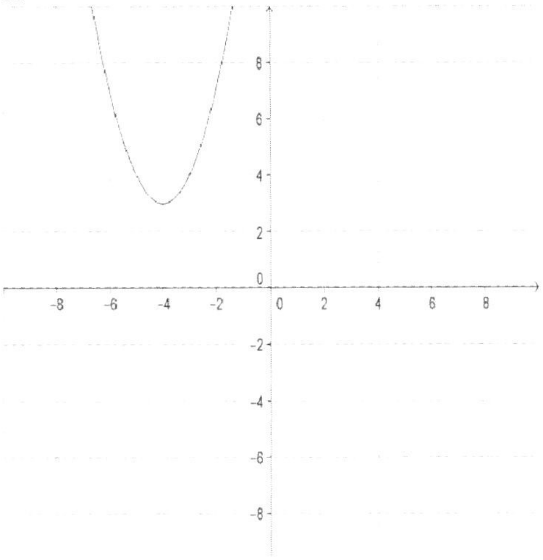

b.

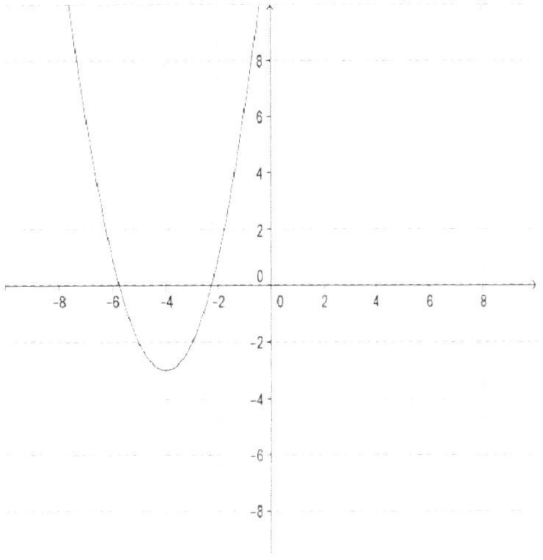

c.

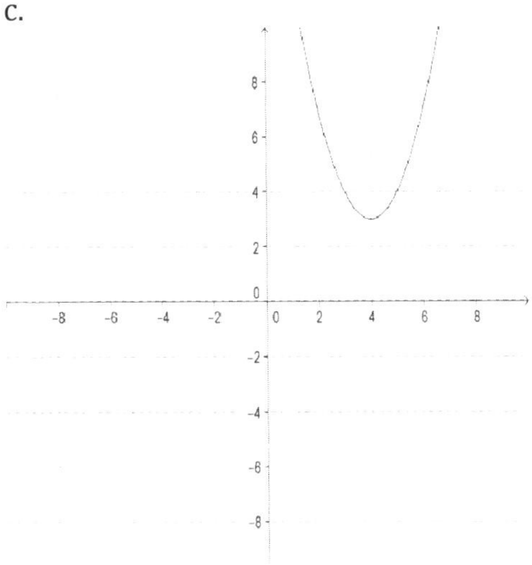

d.

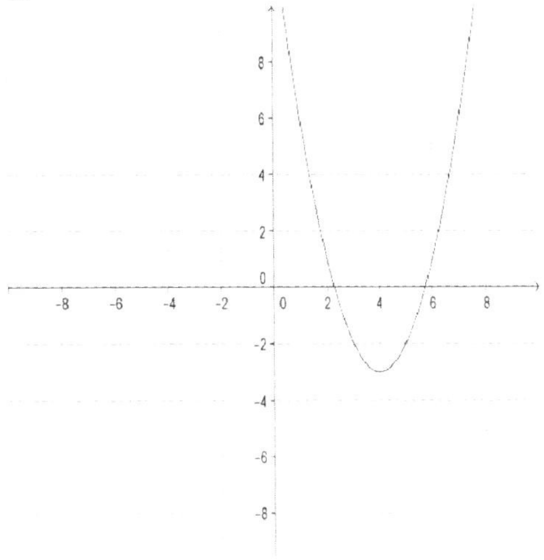

31. The expression $2x^2 - 4x - 30$ is equal to the product of $(x - 5)$ and which other factor?

a. $(2x - 10)$
b. $(2x + 25)$
c. $(2x + 7)$
d. $(2x + 6)$

32. What is the constant of proportionality represented by the table below?

x	y
2	−8
5	−20
7	−28
10	−40
11	−44

a. −12
b. −8
c. −6
d. −4

33. Which of the following represents an inverse proportional relationship?
a. $y = 3x$
b. $y = \frac{1}{3}x$
c. $y = \frac{3}{x}$
d. $y = 3x^2$

34. Which of the following expressions is equivalent to $-3x(x-2)^2$?
a. $-3x^3 + 6x^2 - 12x$
b. $-3x^3 - 12x^2 + 12x$
c. $-3x^2 + 6x$
d. $-3x^3 + 12x^2 - 12x$

35. Which of the following graphs represents the solution to $y \geq 3x - 6$?

a.

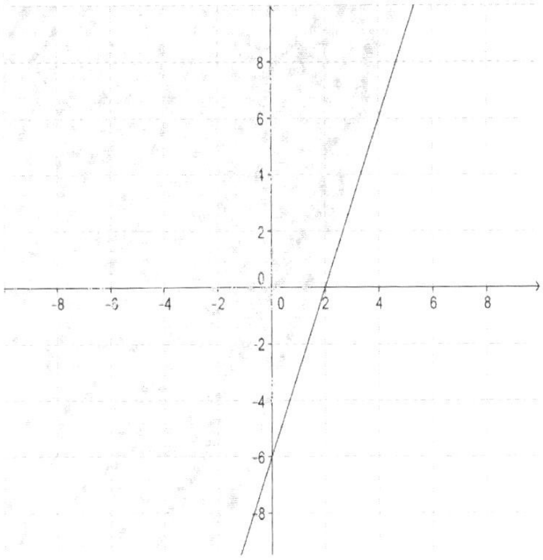

b.

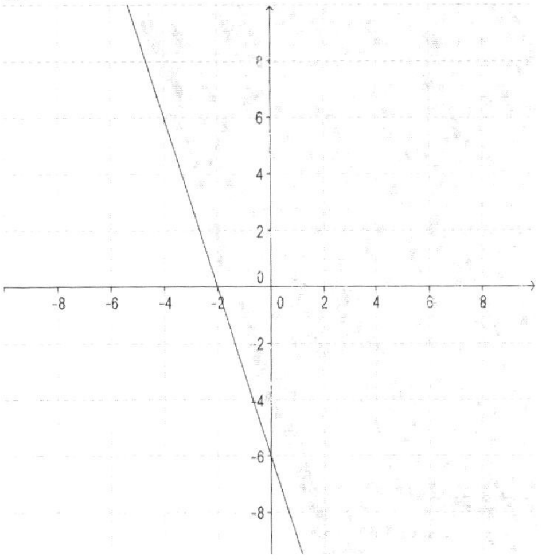

c.

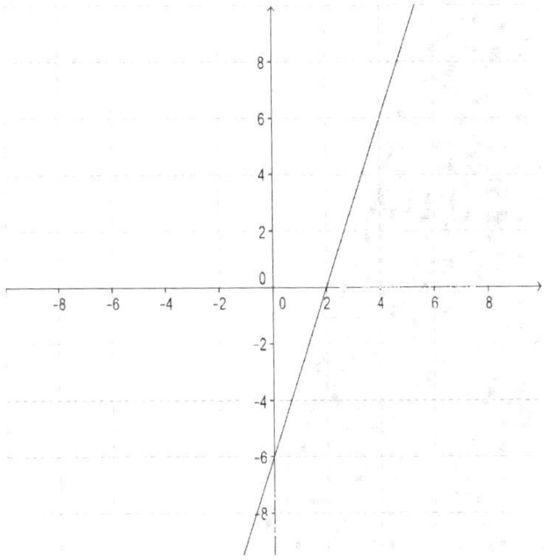

d.

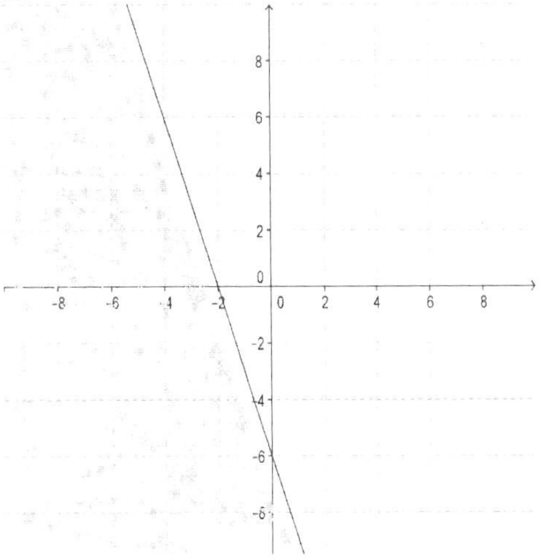

36. If $f(x) = \frac{x^3-2x+1}{3x}$, what is $f(2)$?

a. $\frac{1}{3}$

b. $\frac{1}{2}$

c. $\frac{5}{6}$

d. $\frac{5}{2}$

37. The variables x and y are in a linear relationship. The table below shows a few sample values. Which of the following graphs correctly represents the linear equation relating x and y?

x	y
−2	−11
−1	−8
0	−5
1	−2
2	1

a.

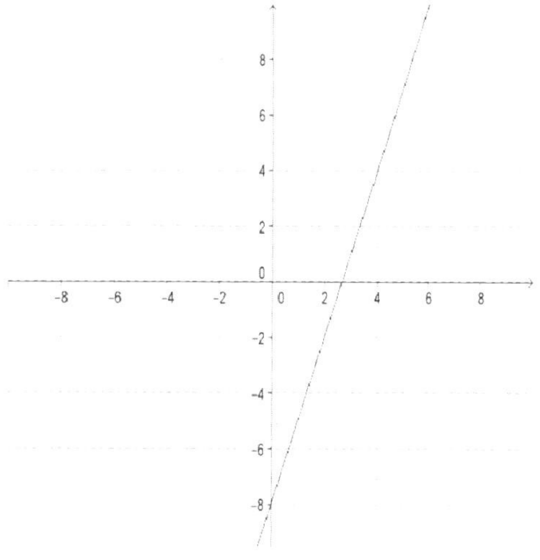

b.

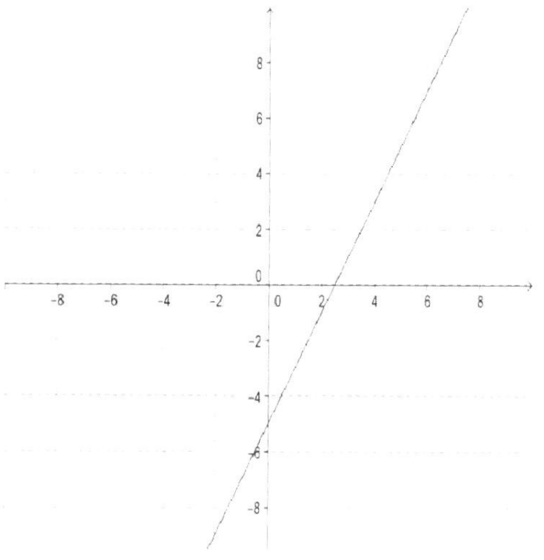

c.

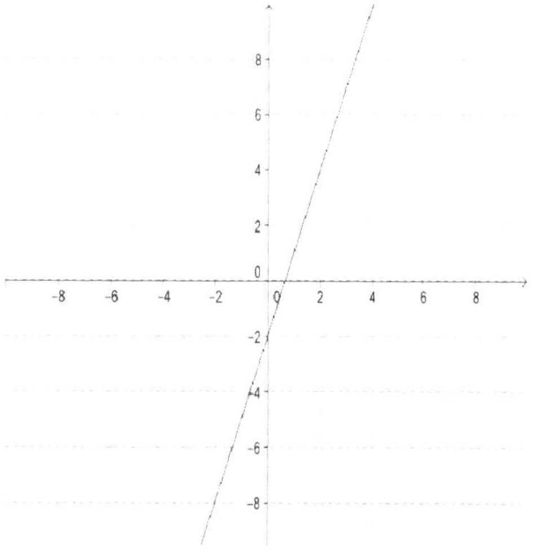

d.

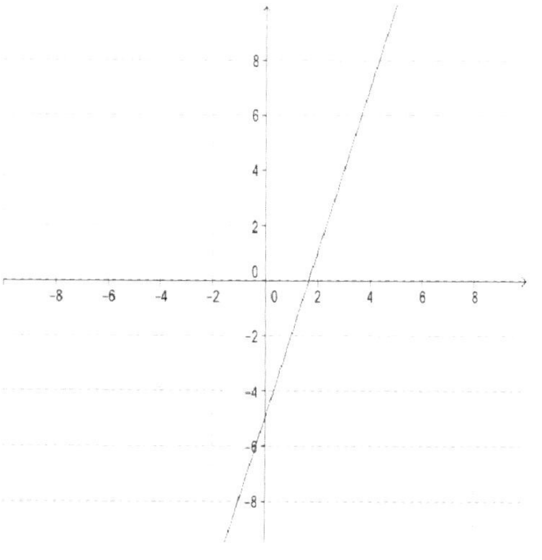

38. Which of the following is the graph of the equation $y = -4x - 6$?

a.

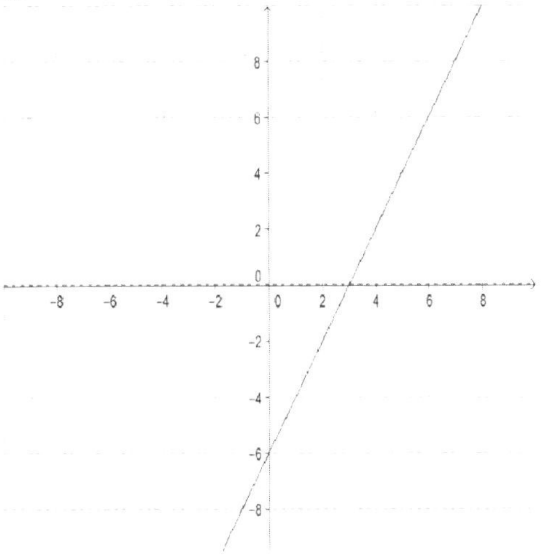

b.

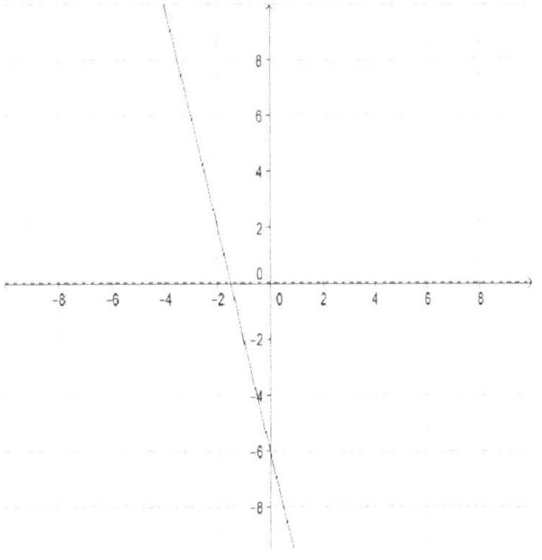

c.

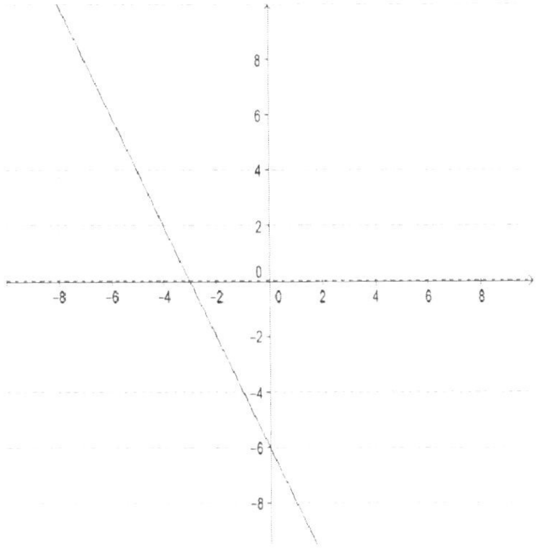

d.

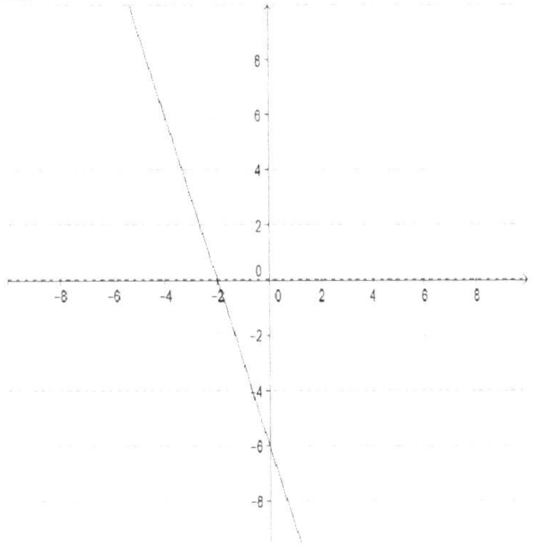

39. Given the graph below, what is the average rate of change from $f(2)$ to $f(5)$?

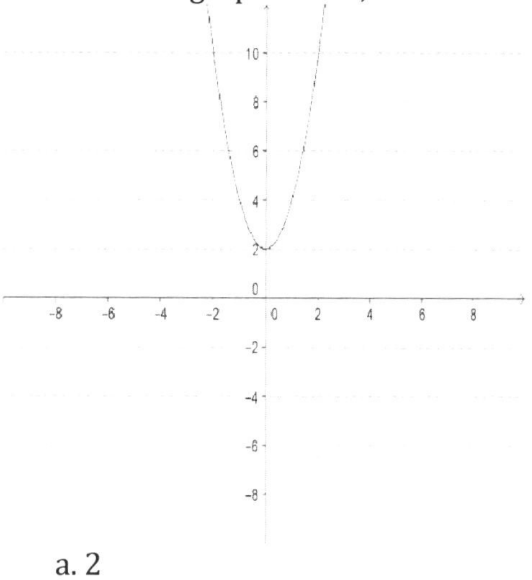

a. 2
b. 14
c. 21
d. 42

40. Elijah pays a $30 park entrance fee, plus $4 for every ticket purchased. Which of the following equations represents the cost?

a. $y = 30x + 4$
b. $y = 34x$
c. $y = 4x + 30$
d. $y = 34x + 30$

41. What is the solution to the system of linear equations graphed below?

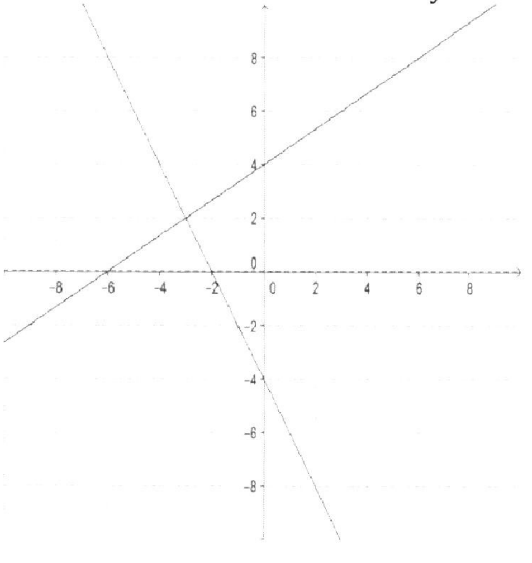

a. (2, −3)
b. (−3, −2)
c. (−2, 3)
d. (−3, 2)

42. What is the solution to the system of linear equations below?

$$4x - 2y = -38$$
$$2x + 3y = 17$$

a. $(-5, 9)$
b. $(-2, 11)$
c. $(-3, 7)$
d. $(-4, 11)$

43. Which of the following graphs represents the solution to the system of inequalities below?

$$2x - 3y \geq -11$$
$$-2x + 4y \geq 14$$

a.

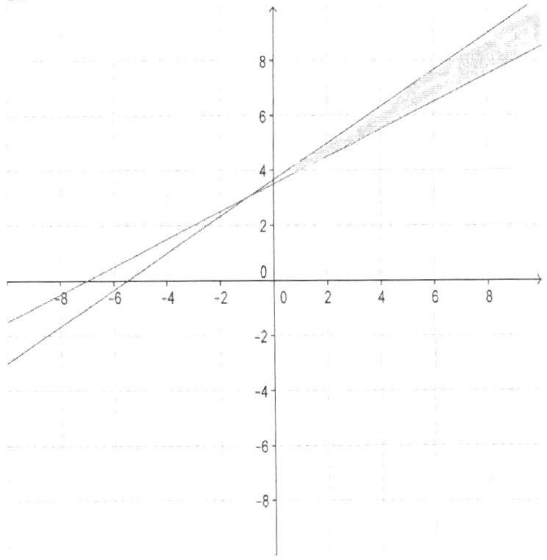

b.

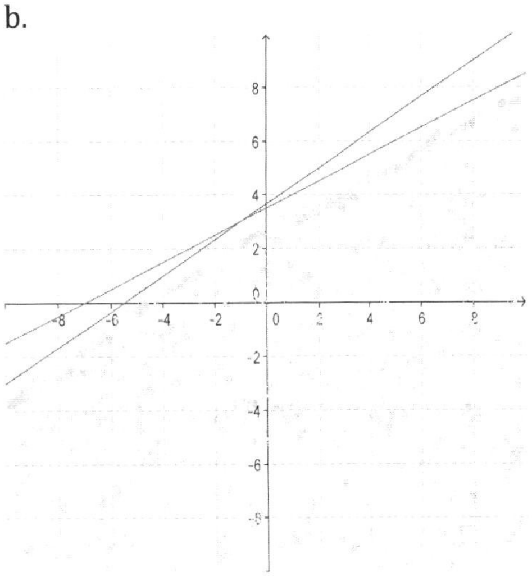

c.

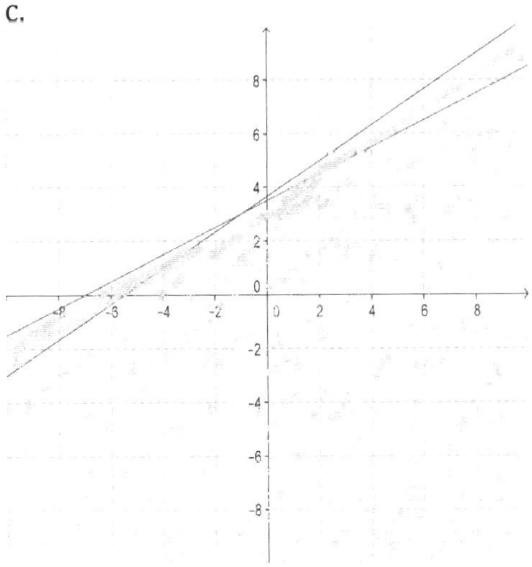

d.

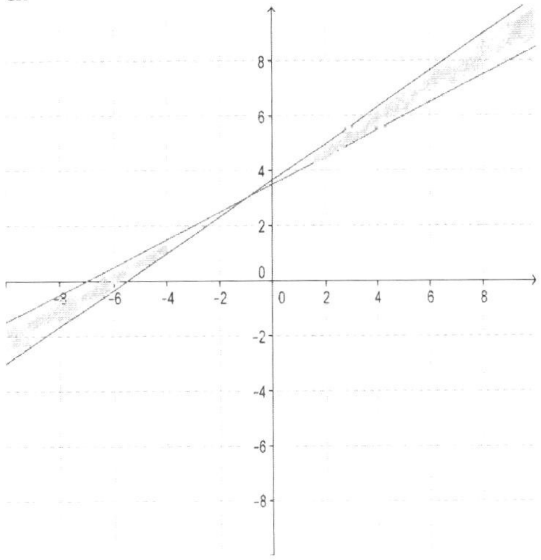

44. Robert drops a ball from his balcony. The height of the ball is modeled by the function $f(x) = -2x^2 + x + 11$, where $f(x)$ represents the height of the ball and x represents the number of seconds. Which of the following best represents the number of seconds that will pass before the ball reaches the ground?

a. 1.4
b. 1.9
c. 2.1
d. 2.6

45. Which type of function is represented by the table of values below?

x	y
−2	0.25
−1	0.5
0	1
1	2
2	4

a. linear
b. quadratic
c. cubic
d. exponential

46. What linear equation includes the data in the table below?

x	y
−3	1
1	−11
3	−17
5	−23
9	−35

a. $y = -3x - 11$
b. $y = -6x - 8$
c. $y = -3x - 8$
d. $y = -12x - 11$

47. Which of the following equations represents a line perpendicular to the one graphed below and passing through the point (3, 2)?

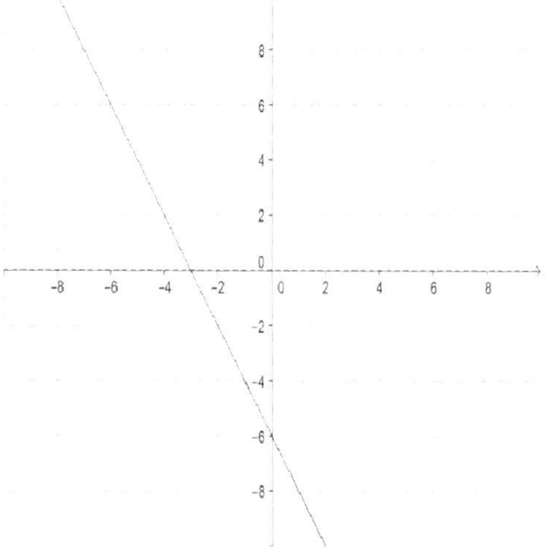

a. $y = \frac{1}{2}x + 2$
b. $y = \frac{1}{2}x + \frac{1}{2}$
c. $y = \frac{3}{2}x + \frac{1}{2}$
d. $y = 2x + 2$

48. Which of the following equations represents a line parallel to the one graphed below and passing through the point (−1, 4)?

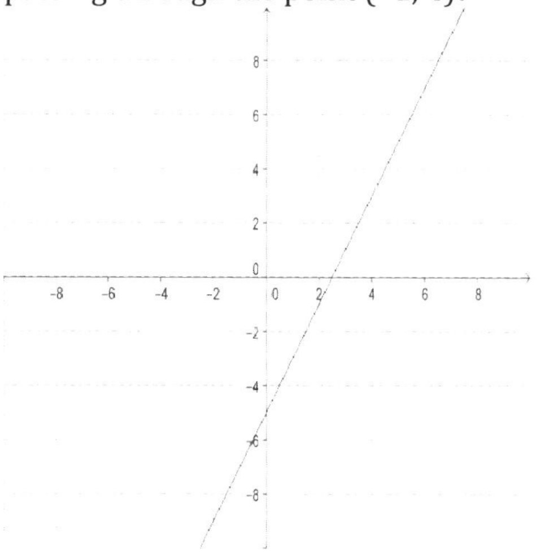

a. $y = 2x - 2$
b. $y = 3x + 6$
c. $y = 3x - 4$
d. $y = 2x + 6$

49. Hannah's monthly gym membership cost is represented by the graph shown below. Which of the following statements is correct?

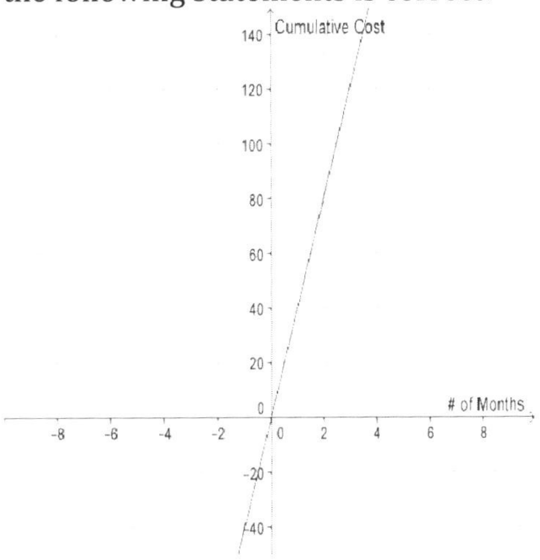

a. The cost is linear, but not proportional.
b. The cost is linear and proportional.
c. The cost is proportional, but not linear.
d. The cost represents an inverse proportional relationship.

50. Amanda saves \$0.02 during Month 1. During each subsequent month, she plans to save twice as much as she did the previous month. Which of the following equations represents the amount she will save during the *n*th month?

a. $a_n = 0.02 \cdot 2^{n-1}$
b. $a_n = 0.02 + 2^n$
c. $a_n = 0.02 \cdot 2^n$
d. $a_n = 2n - 1.98$

51. Kevin saves \$3 during Month 1. During each subsequent month, he plans to save 4 more dollars than he saved during the previous month. Which of the following equations represents the amount he will save during the *n*th month?

a. $a_n = 3n - 1$
b. $a_n = 3n + 4$
c. $a_n = 4n + 3$
d. $a_n = 4n - 1$

52. What is $\lim_{n\to\infty} \frac{n^2+1}{n}$?

a. 0
b. 1
c. 2
d. There is no limit.

53. What is $\lim_{n\to\infty} \frac{5n+2}{n}$?

a. 0
b. 2
c. 5
d. There is no limit.

54. The initial term of a sequence is 3. Each term in the sequence is $\frac{2}{3}$ the amount of the previous term. What is the sum of the terms, as n approaches infinity?

a. 6
b. 9
c. 12
d. 15

55. Mandy can buy 4 containers of yogurt and 3 boxes of crackers for $9.55. She can buy 2 containers of yogurt and 2 boxes of crackers for $5.90. How much does one box of crackers cost?

a. $1.75
b. $2.00
c. $2.25
d. $2.50

56. What is the derivative of $f(x) = 9x^2$?

a. 3x
b. 9x
c. 18x
d. $18x^2$

57. Which of the following functions converges?

a. $f(x) = \frac{x^2}{x}$
b. $f(x) = 2x$
c. $f(x) = \frac{4x}{x} + 1000$
d. $f(x) = \frac{3x^2+100}{x}$

58 McKenzie shades $\frac{1}{5}$ of a piece of paper. Then, she shades an additional area $\frac{1}{5}$ the size of what she just shaded. Next, she shades another area $\frac{1}{5}$ as large as the previous one. As she continues the process to infinity, what is the limit of the shaded fraction of the paper?

a. $\frac{1}{5}$
b. $\frac{1}{4}$
c. $\frac{1}{3}$
d. $\frac{1}{2}$

59. Which of the following functions has a limit of 0?

a. $f(x) = 2x$
b. $f(x) = \frac{4}{x}$
c. $f(x) = \frac{x}{8}$
d. $f(x) = \frac{3x+1}{x}$

60. What is the derivative of $g(x) = x^{ab}$?
   a. $ab \cdot x^{ab}$
   b. $ab \cdot x^{ab-1}$
   c. $a \cdot x^{ab}$
   d. $b \cdot x^{ab-1}$

61. Which of the following graphs represents an inverse proportional relationship?

a.

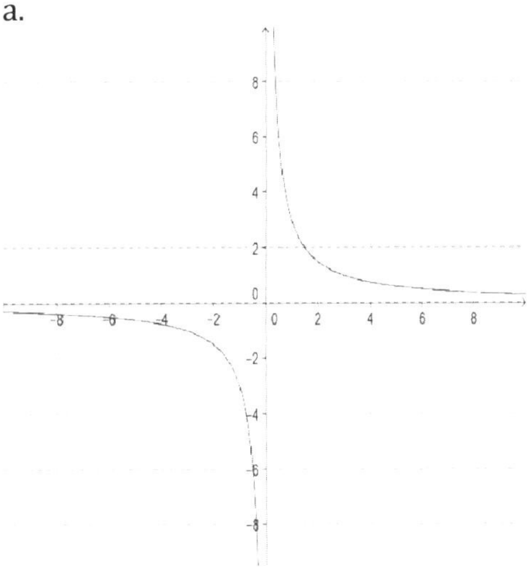

b.

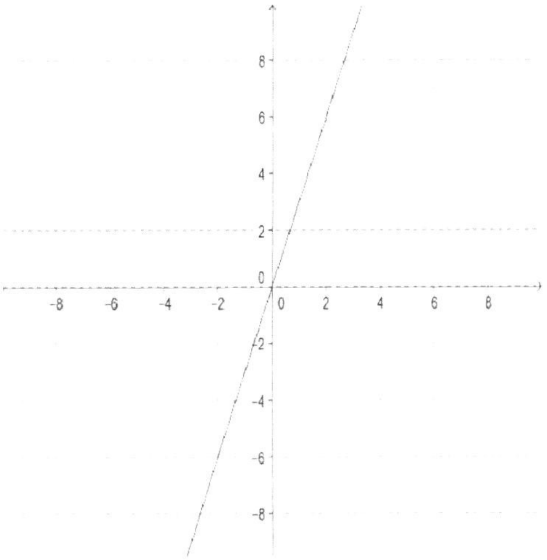

c.

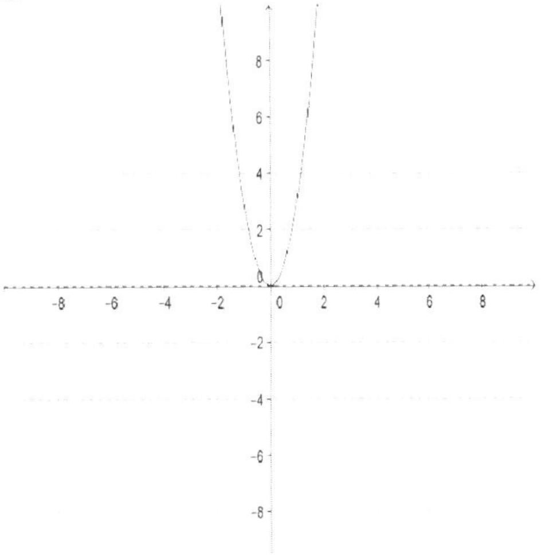

d.

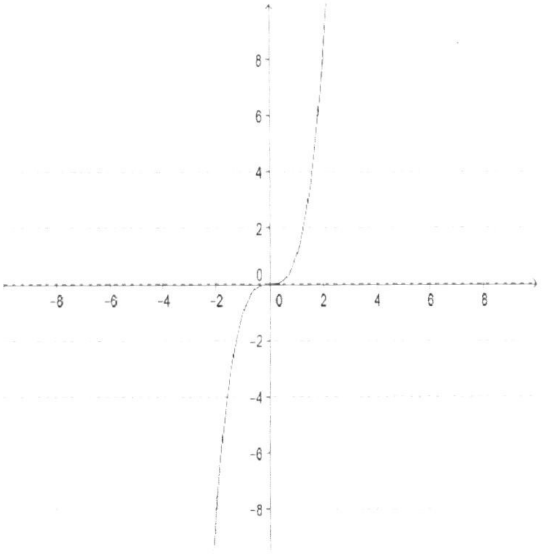

62. What is the sum of the first 50 even, positive integers?
   a. 1,250
   b. 2,025
   c. 2,550
   d. 3,250

63. The graph of the parent function $y = x^2$ is shifted 5 units to the left and 4 units down. Which of the following equations represents the transformed function?

a. $y = (x - 5)^2 - 4$
b. $y = (x + 5)^2 - 4$
c. $y = (x - 5)^2 + 4$
d. $y = (x + 5)^2 + 4$

64. Which of the following represents a function?

a. $\{(2, 9), (3, 4), (6, 8), (-1, 5), (3, -1)\}$
b. $\{(8, 7), (7, 9), (2, 1), (4, 3), (3, 6)\}$
c. $\{(-4, 6), (2, 1), (-4, -2), (3, 8), (9, 2)\}$
d. $\{(2, 6), (6, 5), (5, 9), (2, 0), (-3, 1)\}$

65. A car is accelerated. Which of the following accurately describes the appearance of the position-time graph?

a. It is a line with a positive slope.
b. It is a line with a negative slope.
c. It is a curve with an increasing slope.
d. It is a curve with a decreasing slope.

66. Tom needs to buy ink cartridges and printer paper. Each ink cartridge costs $30. Each ream of paper costs $5. He has $100 to spend. Which of the following inequalities may be used to find the combinations of ink cartridges and printer paper that he may purchase?

a. $30c + 5p \leq 100$
b. $30c + 5p < 100$
c. $30c + 5p > 100$
d. $30c + 5p \geq 100$

67. Hannah spends at least $16 on 4 packages of coffee. Which of the following inequalities represents the possible costs?

a. $16 \geq 4p$
b. $16 < 4p$
c. $16 > 4p$
d. $16 \leq 4p$

68. $f(x) = \frac{x+1}{2x}$. What is the equation of the horizontal asymptote?

a. $y = \frac{1}{4}$
b. $y = \frac{1}{2}$
c. $y = 0$
d. $y = 2$

69. $g(x) = \frac{x}{x+3}$. What is the equation of the horizontal asymptote?

a. y = 0
b. y = 0.5
c. y = 1
d. y = 3

70. What is $\lim_{x \to -\infty} \frac{4x^2}{x+2}$?

a. −4000
b. −400
c. 0
d. There is no limit.

71. What is $\lim_{x \to -2}(3x^3 - 6x^2 + 4)$?

a. −44
b. −42
c. 4
d. 52

72. Jackson can decorate a cake in 3 hours. Eli can decorate the same cake in 2 hours. If they work together, how long will it take them to decorate the cake?

a. 0.8 hours
b. 1.2 hours
c. 1.5 hours
d. 1.8 hours

73. Robert needs to buy milk and bread. Each gallon of milk costs \$3. Each loaf of bread costs \$2. He intends to spend at least \$20. Which of the following graphs represents the possible combinations of gallons of milk and loaves of bread that he may purchase?

a.

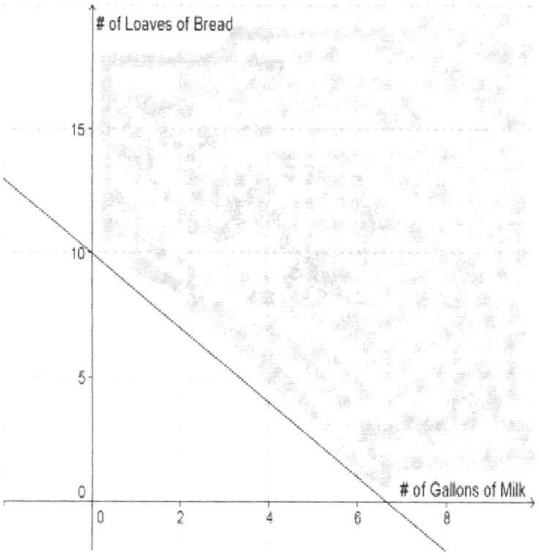

b.

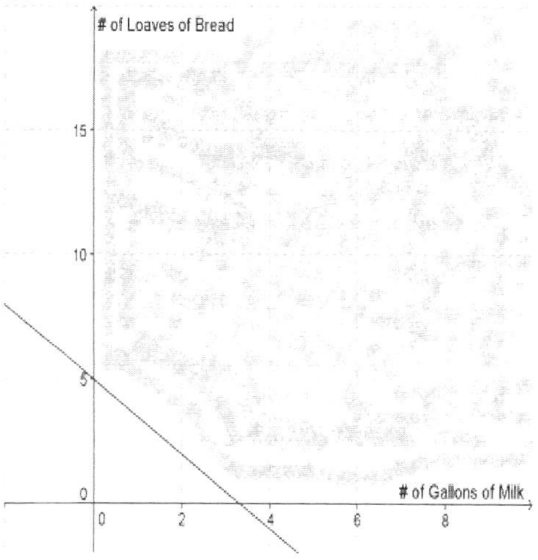

c.

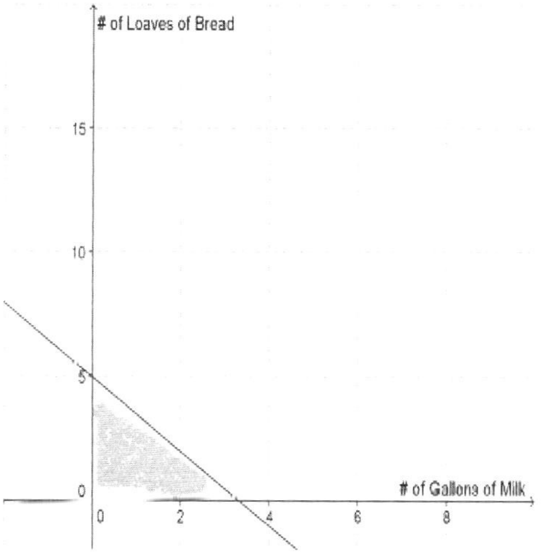

d.

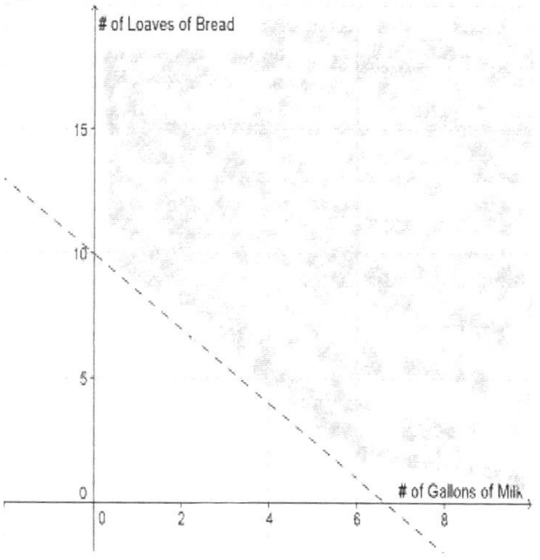

74. Kayla has a $75 budget to purchase gifts for her colleagues. She wants to buy coffee mugs and note pads. She may purchase a maximum of 30 items. Each coffee mug costs $6 and each note pad costs $3. Which of the following graphs correctly shows the possible combinations of coffee mugs and note pads that she may buy?

a.

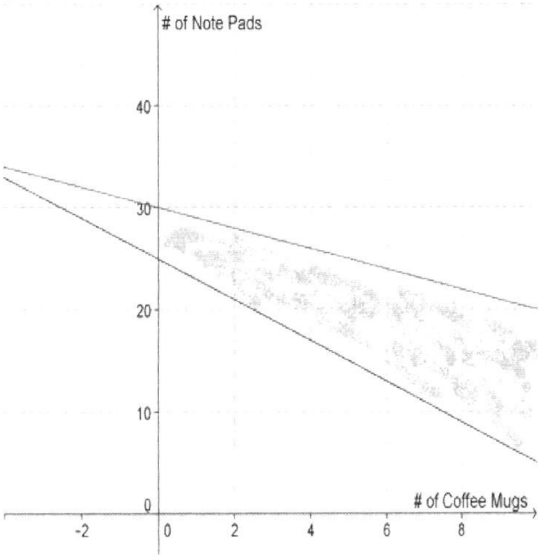

b.

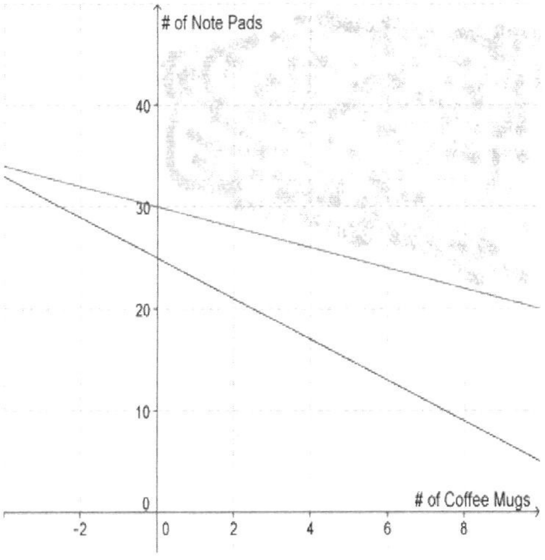

c.

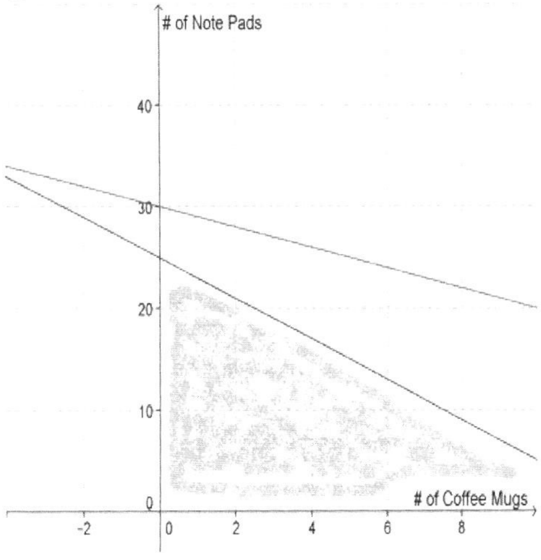

d.

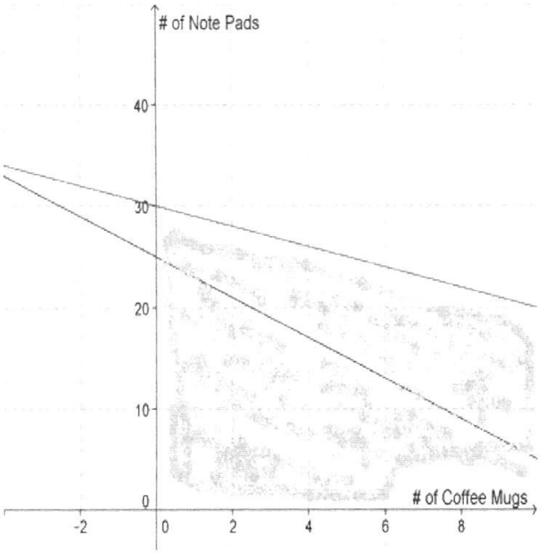

75. Which of the following tables contains points in an exponential function?

a.

x	y
−2	−24
1	12
3	36
5	60
8	96

b.

x	y
−2	12
0	0
2	12
4	48
6	108

c.

x	y
−1	−1
1	1
3	27
5	125
6	216

d.

x	y
−1	0.5
0	1
3	8
5	32
6	64

Measurement and Geometry

76. A city is at an elevation of 6,700 feet. Which of the following best represents the elevation in miles?

a. 0.77 miles
b. 1.27 miles
c. 1.56 miles
d. 1.89 miles

77. A can has a radius of 1.5 inches and a height of 3 inches. Which of the following best represents the volume of the can?

a. 17.2 in^3
b. 19.4 in^3
c. 21.2 in^3
d. 23.4 in^3

78. A ball has a diameter of 7 inches. Which of the following best represents the volume?

a. 165.7 in^3
b. 179.6 in^3
c. 184.5 in^3
d. 192.3 in^3

79. A gift box has a length of 14 inches, a height of 8 inches, and a width of 6 inches. How many square inches of wrapping paper are needed to wrap the box?

a. 56
b. 244
c. 488
d. 672

80. Aidan has a plastic container in the shape of a square pyramid. He wants to fill the container with chocolate candies. If the base has a side length of 6 inches and the height of the container is 9 inches, how many cubic inches of space may be filled with candies?

a. 98
b. 102
c. 108
d. 112

81. Eric has a beach ball with a radius of 9 inches. He is planning to wrap the ball with wrapping paper. Which of the following is the best estimate for the number of square feet of wrapping paper he will need?

a. 4.08
b. 5.12
c. 7.07
d. 8.14

82. Each base of a triangular prism has a base length of 9 cm and a height of 12 cm. The height of the prism is 15 cm. What is the volume of the prism?

a. 652 cm^3
b. 720 cm^3
c. 792 cm^3
d. 810 cm^3

83. The two prisms shown below are similar. What is the measurement of x?

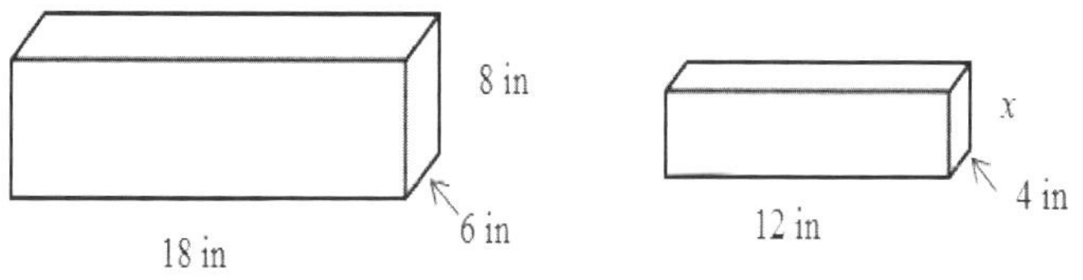

a. $4\frac{3}{4}$ in
b. $5\frac{1}{3}$ in
c. $5\frac{2}{3}$ in
d. $5\frac{3}{4}$ in

84. Given that the two horizontal lines in the diagram below are parallel, which pair of angles is congruent?

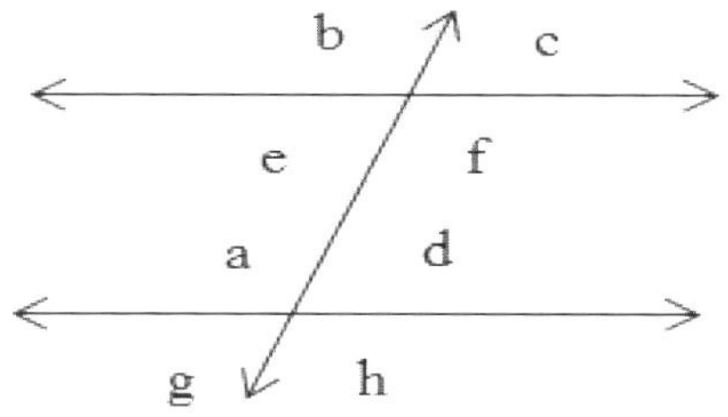

a. e and b
b. d and h
c. g and c
d. d and f

85. Given the diagram below, which of the following theorems may be used to verify that lines a and b are parallel?

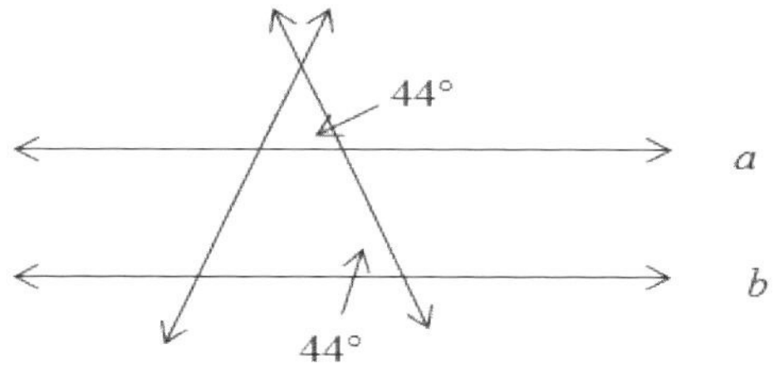

a. Alternate Interior Angles Converse Theorem
b. Alternate Exterior Angles Converse Theorem
c. Consecutive Interior Angles Converse Theorem
d. Corresponding Angles Converse Theorem

86. Given the diagram below, what is the measure of the inscribed angle?

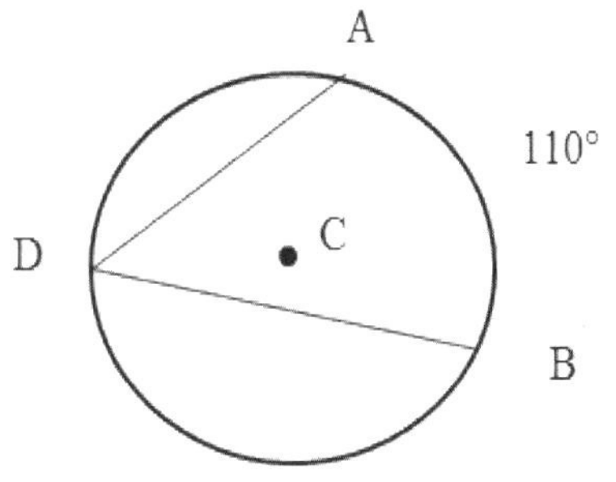

a. 37°
b. 45°
c. 55°
d. 57°

87. A tree with a height of 15 feet casts a shadow that is 5 feet in length. A man standing at the base of the shadow formed by the tree is 6 feet tall. How long is the shadow cast by the man?

a. 1.5 feet
b. 2 feet
c. 2.5 feet
d. 3 feet

88. Which of the following best represents the measurement of *x*, shown in the triangle below?

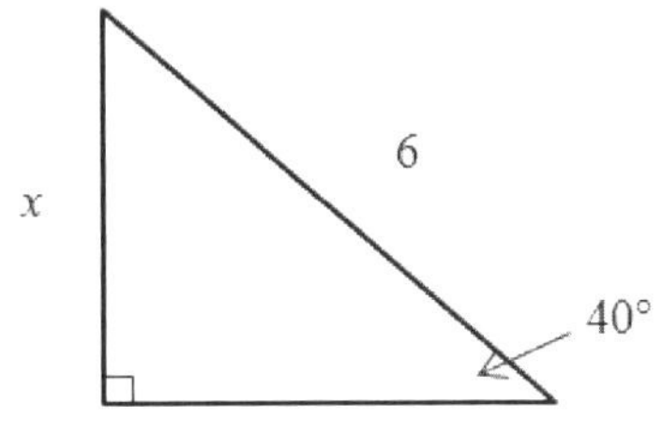

a. 2.6
b. 3.1
c. 3.9
d. 4.4

89. What is the area of the shaded region in the figure shown below?

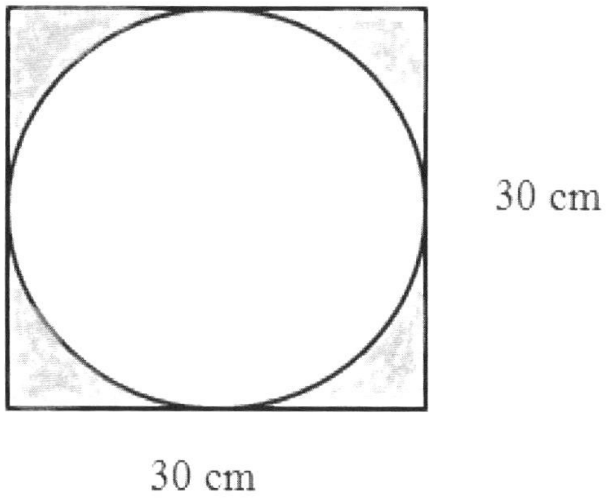

a. 177 cm^2
b. 181 cm^2
c. 187 cm^2
d. 193 cm^2

90. Which of the following postulates proves the congruence of the triangles below?

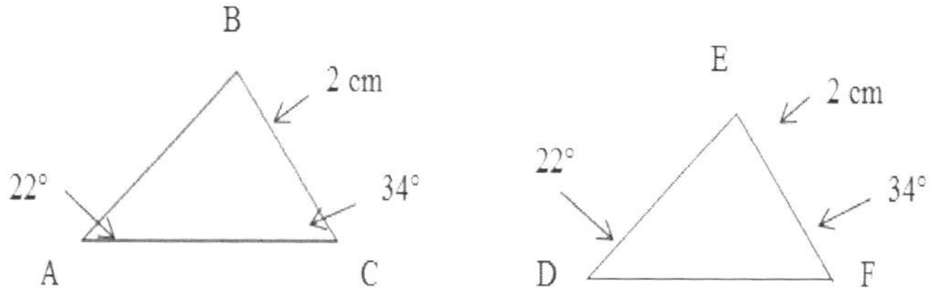

a. ASA
b. AAS
c. SAS
d. SSS

91. A man standing on a flat, level surface casts a shadow that is 6.2 ft in length. The man is 5.8 ft tall. Which of the following best represents the distance from the top of his head to the end of the shadow?

a. 7 ft
b. 7.5 ft
c. 8 ft
d. 8.5 ft

92. A cylindrical carrot stick is sliced with a knife. Which of the following shapes is *not* a possible cross-section?

a. circle
b. rectangle
c. ellipse
d. triangle

93. What is the value of x, shown in the diagram below?

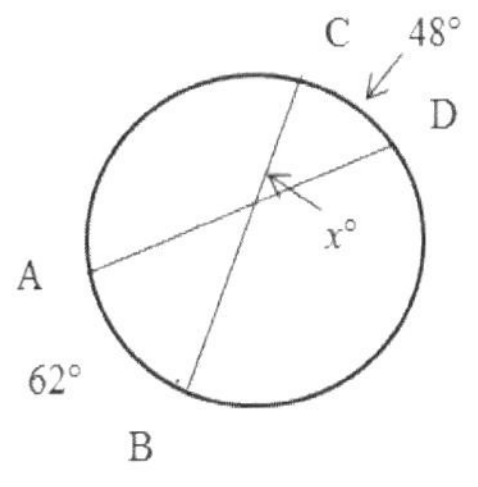

a. 16
b. 24
c. 48
d. 55

94. What is the value of x, shown in the diagram below?

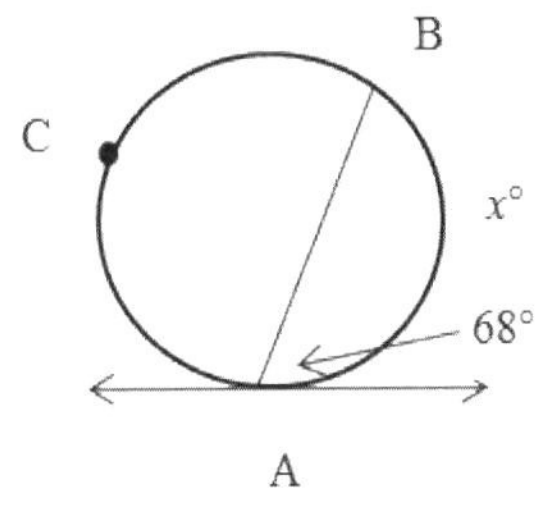

a. 68°
b. 76°
c. 128°
d. 136°

95. Which of the following represents the net of a triangular prism?

a.

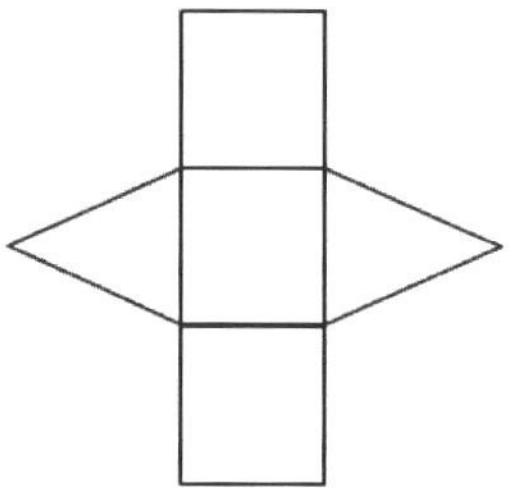

b.

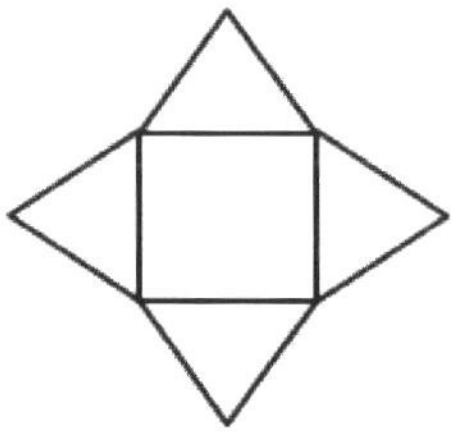

c.

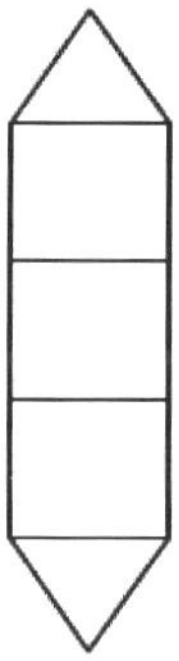

d.

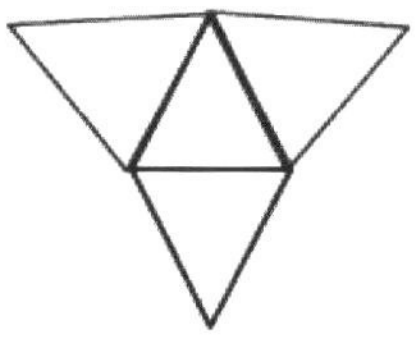

96. A convex three-dimensional figure has 9 edges and 6 vertices. How many faces does it have?

a. 4
b. 5
c. 6
d. 8

97. Given that the two horizontal lines in the diagram below are parallel, which of the following statements is correct?

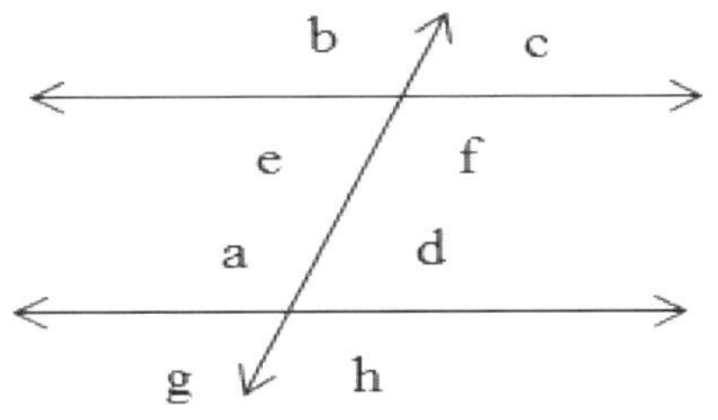

a. Angles b and g are complementary.
b. Angles d and c are supplementary.
c. Angles a and e are supplementary.
d. Angles e and h are congruent.

98. Which of the following postulates may be used to prove the similarity of ΔABC and ΔADE?

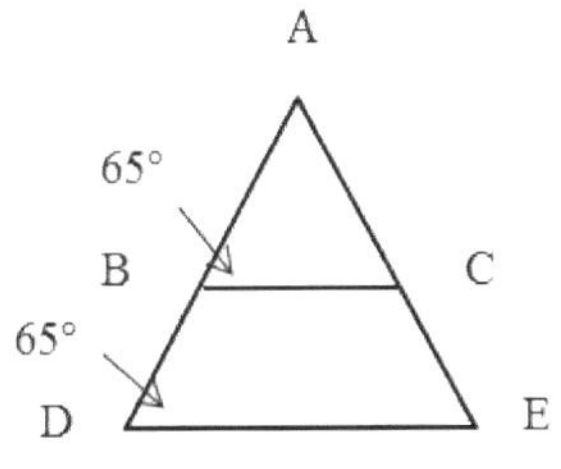

a. ASA
b. AA
c. SAS
d. SSS

99. Which of the following transformations has been applied to ΔABC?

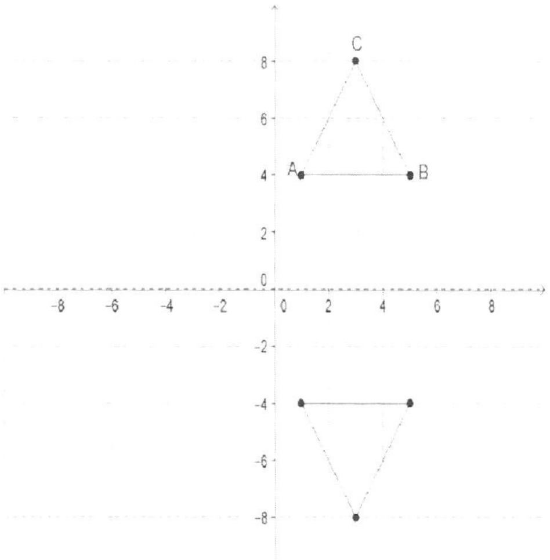

a. translation
b. rotation of 90 degrees
c. reflection
d. dilation

100. Which of the following steps were applied to ΔABC?

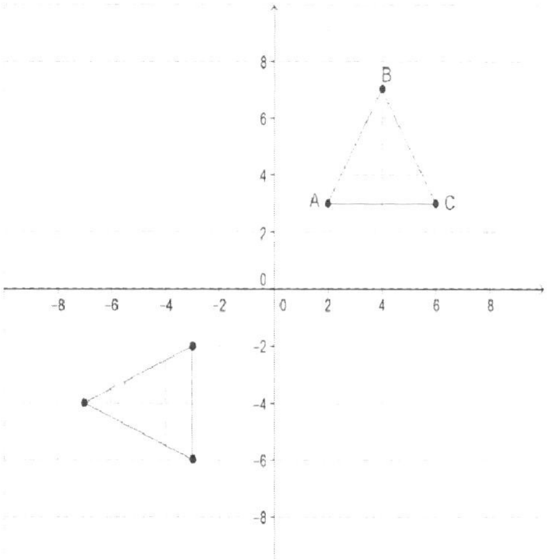

a. reflection across the x-axis and rotation of 90 degrees
b. reflection across the x-axis and rotation of 180 degrees
c. reflection across the x-axis and rotation of 270 degrees
d. reflection across the y-axis and rotation of 180 degrees

101. What is the midpoint of the line segment below?

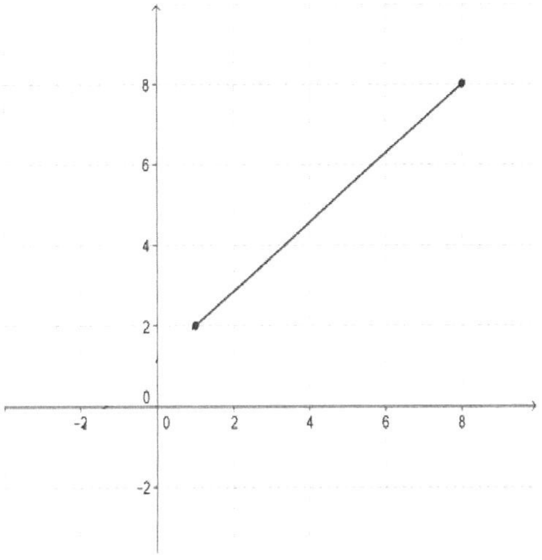

a. (3.5, 4)
b. (4, 4)
c. (4.5, 5)
d. (5, 5)

102. What is the distance on a coordinate plane from (−8, 6) to (4, 3)?

a. $\sqrt{139}$
b. $\sqrt{147}$
c. $\sqrt{153}$
d. $\sqrt{161}$

103. What is the perimeter of the trapezoid graphed below?

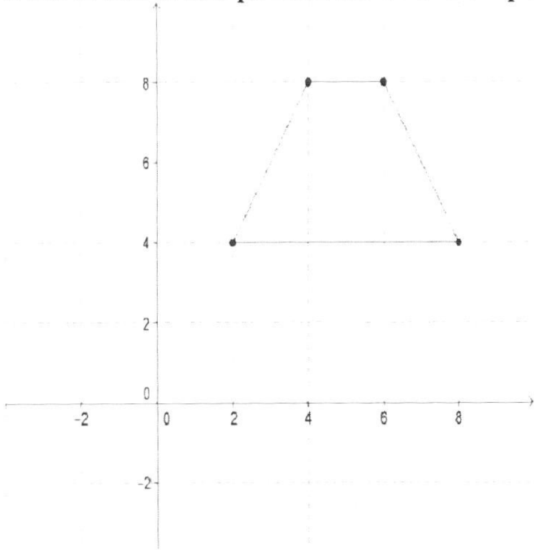

a. $4 + \sqrt{10}$
b. $8 + 4\sqrt{5}$
c. $4 + 2\sqrt{5}$
d. $8 + 2\sqrt{22}$

104. What is the area of the figure graphed below?

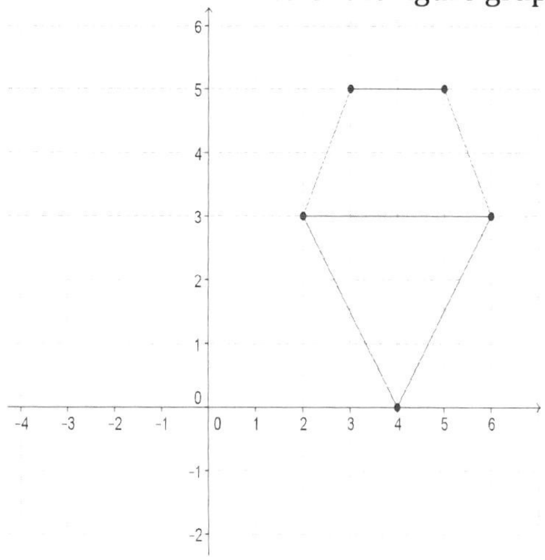

a. 11 $units^2$
b. 11.5 $units^2$
c. 12 $units^2$
d. 12.5 $units^2$

105. What scale factor was applied to the larger triangle to obtain the smaller triangle below?

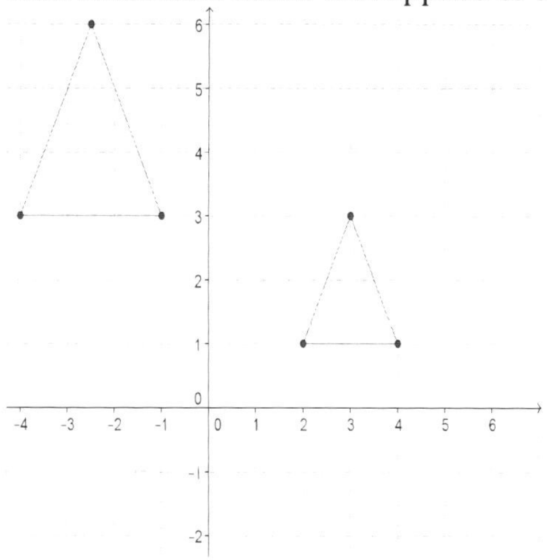

a. $\frac{1}{4}$
b. $\frac{1}{3}$
c. $\frac{1}{2}$
d. $\frac{2}{3}$

106. Which of the following pairs of equations represents the lines of symmetry in the figure below?

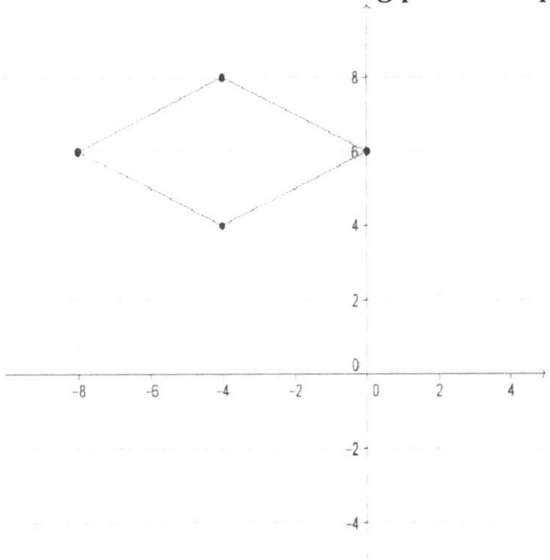

a. $x = -4, y = 6$
b. $x = 4, y = 6$
c. $y = -4, x = 6$
d. $y = 4, x = -6$

107. Which of the following pairs of shapes may tessellate a plane?
a. regular pentagons and squares
b. regular pentagons and equilateral triangles
c. equilateral triangles and regular hexagons
d. regular octagons and equilateral triangles

108. Andrea must administer $\frac{1}{12}$ of a medicine bottle to a patient. If the bottle contains $3\frac{4}{10}$ fluid ounces of medicine, how much medicine should be administered?
a. $\frac{17}{60}$ fluid ounces
b. $\frac{15}{62}$ fluid ounces
c. $\frac{3}{19}$ fluid ounces
d. $\frac{17}{67}$ fluid ounces

109. What is the slope of the leg marked x in the triangle graphed below?

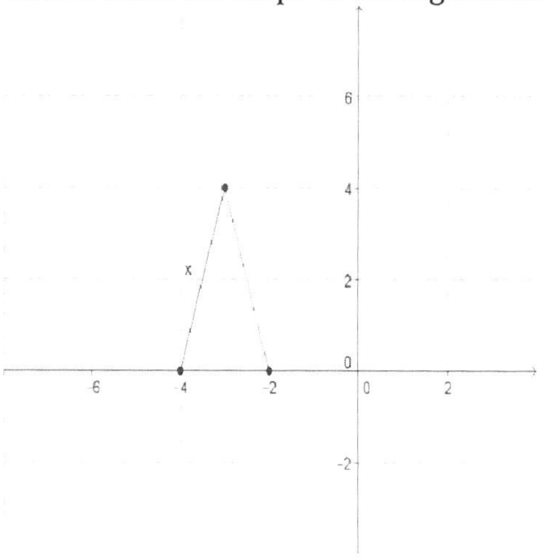

a. 2
b. 3.5
c. 4
d. 4.5

110. Ann must walk from Point A to Point B and then to Point C. Finally, she will walk back to Point A. If each unit represents 5 miles, which of the following best represents the total distance she will have walked?

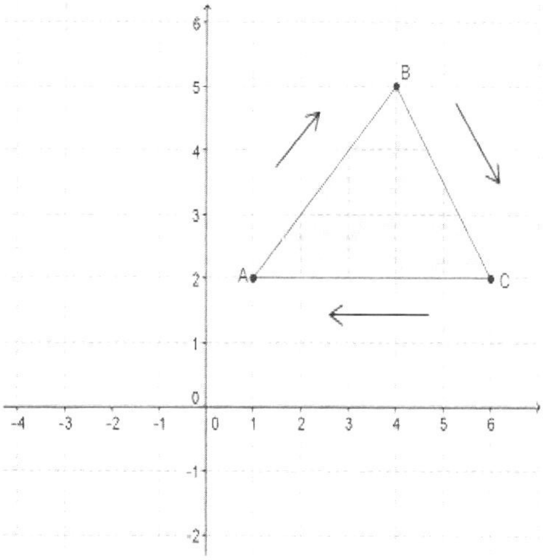

a. 42 miles
b. 48 miles
c. 56 miles
d. 64 miles

111. Which of the following measurements is the best approximation of 2,012 square inches?
a. 11.85 ft^2
b. 12.28 ft^2
c. 13.97 ft^2
d. 15.29 ft^2

112. What is the length of the hypotenuse in the triangle shown below?

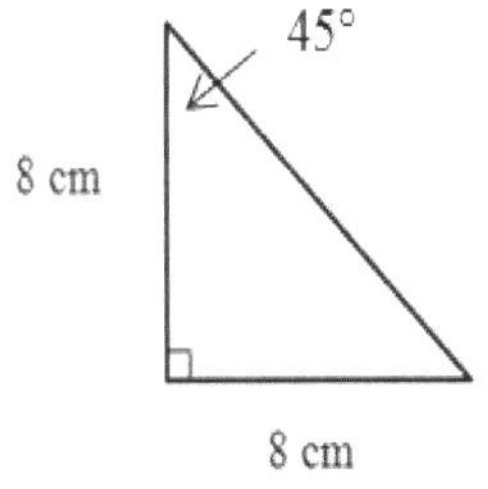

a. 4 cm
b. $8\sqrt{3}$ cm
c. 16 cm
d. $8\sqrt{2}$ cm

Statistics, Probability, and Discrete Mathematics

113. For which of the following data sets would the mean be an appropriate measure of center to use?
a. 7, 15, 20, 24, 27, 28, 31, 36, 41, 50
b. 6, 7, 8, 8, 9, 9, 10, 20, 34, 50
c. 5, 18, 30, 42, 43, 44, 46, 48, 49, 50
d. 8, 10, 12, 13, 14, 16, 20, 22, 24, 2200

114. A student scores 82 on a final exam. The class average is 87, with a standard deviation of 2 points. How many standard deviations below the class average is the student's score?
a. 1.5
b. 2
c. 2.5
d. 3

115. A student scores 61 on a test. The class average is 81, with a standard deviation of 10 points. What percentage of the class scored below this student?
a. 1.26%
b. 1.43%
c. 1.96%
d. 2.28%

116. A student scores 96 on a test. The class average is 84, with a standard deviation of 4 points. What percentage of the class scored below this student?
a. 78.89%
b. 82.77%
c. 92.67%
d. 99.87%

117. A student scores 68 on a final exam. Another student scores 84 on the exam. The class average is 80, with a standard deviation of 8 points. What percentage of the class scored within the range of these two students' scores?

a. 44.32%
b. 48.54%
c. 58.39%
d. 62.47%

118. Class A, with a total of 28 students, had a final exam average of 85 and a standard deviation of 4.5 points. Class B, with a total of 30 students, had a final exam average of 88, with a standard deviation of 4 points. Which of the following statements is true?

a. There is no significant difference between the classes, as evidenced by a p-value greater than 0.05.
b. There is no significant difference between the classes, as evidenced by a p-value less than 0.05.
c. There is a significant difference between the classes, as evidenced by a p-value greater than 0.05.
d. There is a significant difference between the classes, as evidenced by a p-value less than 0.05.

119. A beverage manufacturer claims to include 20 ounces in each bottle. A random sample of 30 bottles shows a mean of 19.8 ounces, with a standard deviation of 0.2 ounces. Which of the following statements is correct?

a. The manufacturer's claim is likely true, as evidenced by a p-value less than 0.01.
b. The manufacturer's claim is likely true, as evidenced by a p-value greater than 0.01.
c. The manufacturer's claim is likely false, as evidenced by a p-value less than 0.01.
d. The manufacturer's claim is likely false, as evidenced by a p-value greater than 0.01.

120. An oatmeal manufacturer claims to include 18 ounces in each container, with a standard deviation of 0.3 ounces. A random sample of 25 containers shows a mean of 17.9 ounces. Which of the following statements is true?

a. The manufacturer's claim is likely true, as evidenced by a p-value less than 0.05.
b. The manufacturer's claim is likely true, as evidenced by a p-value greater than 0.05.
c. The manufacturer's claim is likely false, as evidenced by a p-value less than 0.05.
d. The manufacturer's claim is likely false, as evidenced by a p-value greater than 0.05.

121. A professor claims that the average on his final exam is 82. A random sample of 30 students shows an exam mean of 83 and a standard deviation of 2 points. Which of the following statements is true?

a. The professor's claim is likely true, as evidenced by a p-value less than 0.05.
b. The professor's claim is likely false, as evidenced by a p-value less than 0.05.
c. The professor's claim is likely true, as evidenced by a p-value greater than 0.05.
d. The professor's claim is likely false, as evidenced by a p-value greater than 0.05.

122. Which of the following describes a sampling technique that will likely increase the sampling error?

a. choosing every 5th person from a list
b. grouping a sample according to gender and then choosing every 10th person from a list
c. using an intact group
d. assigning numbers to a sample and then using a random number generator to choose numbers

123. What is the area under the normal curve between ±2 standard deviations?

a. approximately 68%
b. approximately 90%
c. approximately 95%
d. approximately 99%

124. Which of the following best represents the standard deviation of the data below?
3, 4, 4, 5, 6, 12, 12, 15

a. 2.9
b. 3.4
c. 4.1
d. 4.6

125. Given the boxplots below, which of the following statements is correct?

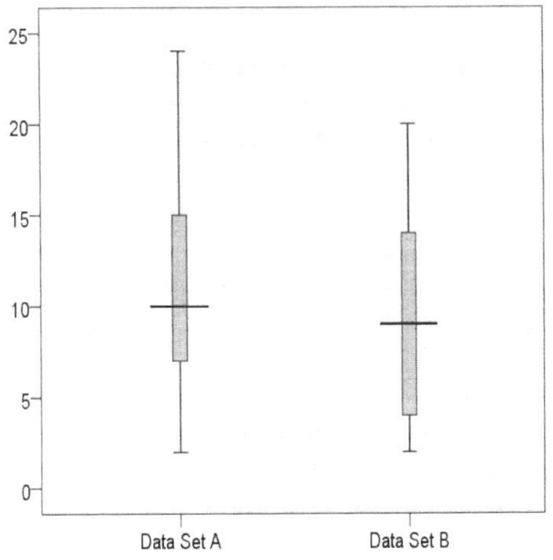

a. Data Set A has a larger range and a larger median.
b. Data Set A has a smaller range and a larger median.
c. Data Set A has a larger range and a smaller median.
d. Data Set A has a smaller range and a smaller median.

126. What is the interquartile range of the data below?
2, 4, 6, 8, 10, 12, 14, 16, 18, 20

a. 10
b. 11
c. 12
d. 13

127. According to the scatter plot below, which of the following is the *best* estimate for the earnings received for 20 hours of work?

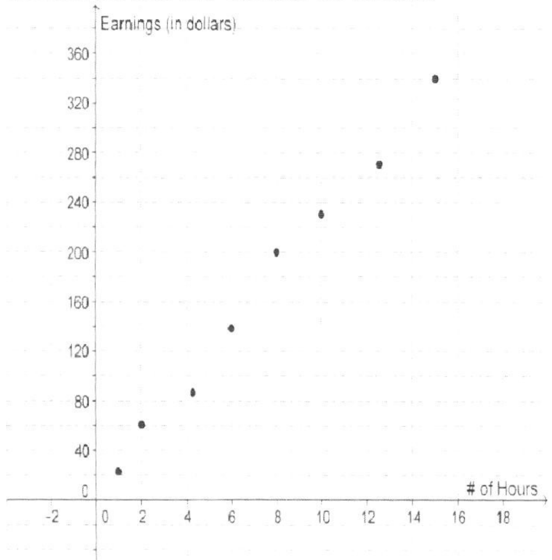

a. \$342
b. \$446
c. \$528
d. \$602

128. Which of the following statements is *not* true?

a. In a skewed distribution, the mean is pulled towards the tail.
b. In a skewed distribution, the mean is pulled towards the area with a higher frequency of scores.
c. In a normal distribution, the mean, median, and mode are the same value.
d. The area under a normal curve is 1.

129. Given the two-way frequency table below, which of the following *best* represents *P*(male or graduate)?

	Undergraduate	Graduate	Total
Male	2940	2045	4985
Female	3026	2068	5094
Total	5966	4113	10,079

a. 55%
b. 60%
c. 70%
d. 75%

130. Adam rolls a standard six-sided die. What is the probability he rolls a number greater than or equal to 5?

a. $\frac{1}{6}$
b. $\frac{1}{5}$
c. $\frac{1}{4}$
d. $\frac{1}{3}$

131. Kayla rolls a die and tosses a coin. What is the probability she gets an even number and heads?

a. $\frac{1}{6}$

b. $\frac{1}{4}$

c. $\frac{1}{3}$

d. 1

132. Eli rolls a die and tosses a coin. What is the probability he gets a prime number or tails?

a. $\frac{1}{2}$

b. $\frac{2}{3}$

c. $\frac{3}{4}$

d. $\frac{5}{6}$

133. Andrew rolls a die. What is the probability he gets a 4 or an even number?

a. $\frac{1}{4}$

b. $\frac{1}{2}$

c. $\frac{2}{3}$

d. $\frac{3}{4}$

134. The simulation of a coin toss is completed 300 times. Which of the following best represents the number of tosses you can expect to show heads?

a. 50

b. 100

c. 150

d. 200

135. How many ways can you arrange the letters below, if order does not matter?

HANNAH

a. 30

b. 60

c. 90

d. 120

136. How many ways can 1st – 3rd place winners be chosen from 6 people?

a. 120

b. 60

c. 30

d. 20

137. How many ways can the numerals 0 – 9 be arranged?

a. 36,045

b. 182,492

c. 1,048,644

d. 3,628,800

138. What is the limit of the series below?

$$1 + \frac{1}{2} + \frac{1}{4} + \frac{1}{8} + \frac{1}{16} + \cdots$$

a. 2
b. $2\frac{1}{4}$
c. $2\frac{3}{4}$
d. 3

139. What is the size of the sample space for tossing four coins?
a. 8
b. 12
c. 16
d. 20

140. 320 students are surveyed. 120 of the students like only Dallas. 150 of the students like only Houston. 48 of the students like neither city. How many students like Dallas *and* Houston?
a. 2
b. 3
c. 4
d. 5

141. $A = \{5, 9, 2, 3, -1, 8\}$ and $B = \{2, 0, 4, 5, 6, 8\}$. What is $A \cap B$?
a. $\{5, 2, 8\}$
b. $\{-1, 0, 2, 3, 4, 5, 6, 8, 9\}$
c. $\emptyset$
d. $\{5, 8\}$

142. $A = \{9, 4, -3, 8, 6, 0\}$ and $B = \{-4, 2, 8, 9, 0\}$. What is $A \cup B$?
a. $\{9, 8, 0\}$
b. $\{9, 4, -3, 8, 6, 0, -4, 2\}$
c. $\emptyset$
d. $\{9, 8, 0, 2, 4\}$

143. $A = \{3, -4, 1\}$ and $B = \{0, 5, 9, 2\}$. What is $A \cap B$?
a. $\{3, -4, 1, 0, 5, 9, 2\}$
b. $\{-4, 2, 3\}$
c. $\{0, 1, 2, 3, 5, 9\}$
d. $\emptyset$

144. What is the contrapositive of the statement below?
If I get paid, then I go to the beach.
a. If I get paid, then I do not go to the beach.
b. If I go to the beach, then I get paid.
c. If I do not get paid, then I go to the beach.
d. If I do not go to the beach, then I do not get paid.

145. What is the converse of the statement below?
If I go skiing, then it is winter.
a. If it is not winter, then I do not go skiing.
b. If it is winter, then I go skiing.
c. If it is not winter, then I go skiing.
d. If I go skiing, then it is not winter.

146. Using logic, when is $p \vee q$ false?
a. When p is true and q is true.
b. When p is true and q is false.
c. When p is false and q is true.
d. When p is false and q is false.

147. Using logic, when is $p \wedge q$ true?
a. When p is true and q is true.
b. When p is true and q is false.
c. When p is false and q is true.
d. When p is false and q is false.

148. Which of the following is logically equivalent to $p \rightarrow q$?
a. $q \rightarrow p$
b. $\sim p \rightarrow \sim q$
c. $\sim q \rightarrow \sim p$
d. $p \wedge q$

149. Eric's dietary plan consists of 4 different entrées, 5 different appetizers, and 3 different desserts. How many possible meals may he create containing one entrée, one appetizer, and one dessert?
a. 12
b. 24
c. 60
d. 120

150. Which of the following represents a tautology?
a. $p \wedge \sim p$
b. $p \vee \sim p$
c. $p \vee \sim q$
d. $p \vee q$

Constructed Response

1. A family bought a new car for a purchase price of $32,000. The car will lose 15% of its value the day it is purchased and the car will depreciate at a constant rate following that. The value of the car as a function of time can be modeled by $y = c - 0.09cx$, where y is the value of the car x years after the car was purchased and c is the value of the car after the initial 15% depreciation.

A. What is the value of the car 2 years after its purchase date? Show your work.
B. On an xy-grid, graph the value, y, of the car, as a function of x, where x represents the number of years after the purchase date, for $0 \le x \le 7$ years. Label the axes and show the scales used for the graph.
C. Use your graph to estimate the number of years, x, after the purchase date that the value of the car is $15,000. Label this point on your graph and indicate the approximate coordinates of the point.
D. Algebraically find the number of years, x, after the purchase date that the value of the car is exactly $15,000. Round your solution to the nearest tenth of a year. Show your work.

2.

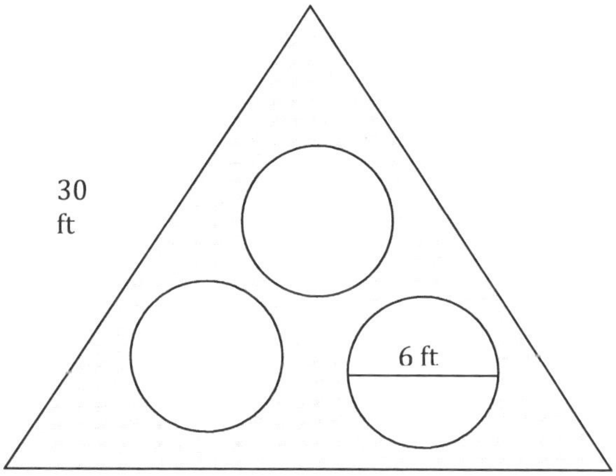

The diagram above shows the plan Berenice has for a triangular splash pad in a local city park. There will be three circles, each with a diameter of 6 feet, and the circles will be enclosed by an equilateral triangle with a side length of 30 feet. Berenice plans to have splash areas/fountains within the circles and walkways in the shaded areas of the triangle.

A. According to the diagram, what is the maximum area, in square feet, available for Berenice to have for splash/fountain areas in the triangle? Show your work.
B. According to the diagram, what percentage of the triangle will be set aside for walkways? Show your work.
C. If a ball were to fall on a random point within the triangular splash pad, what is the probability that the ball would fall where Berenice plans to have splash areas? Show your work or explain your reasoning.

3. Below are listed the heights in centimeters of the 19 students in a class.

48, 53, 53, 54, 55, 56, 59, 60, 60, 63, 63, 63, 64, 65, 66, 67, 69, 71, 73

A. For the numbers above, define and identify the median and the range.
B. Define and calculate the mean for the list of numbers above.
C. Draw a stem and leaf plot of the data using the tens digits as the stems and the units digits as the leaves.

Answers and Explanations

Number Sense and Operations

1. C: The sum is written as:

$$\begin{array}{r} 2222 \\ +\ 303 \\ \hline 3030 \end{array}$$

The sum of 2 and 3 equals 5, which must be represented as a 10. In the base-5 number system, a number cannot contain any 5's. The 1 of each 10 is carried to the next column to the left.

2. D: The percent increase is represented as $\frac{1100-800}{800}$, which equals 0.375 or 37.5%.

3. C: The set of integers is contained within the set of rational numbers, and is hence, a subset. A rational number may be written as the ratio, $\frac{a}{b}$, where a and b are integers and $b \neq 0$.

4. D: You first divide 2 into 55, recording the remainder. You then divide 2 into each resulting quotient, until the quotient is smaller than 2. Next, you put the final quotient as the first digit. You then go backwards and write the remainders and place them as digits, in order from left to right.

5. D: The original cost may be represented by the equation $45 = x - 0.25x$ or $45 = 0.75x$. Dividing both sides of the equation by 0.75 gives $x = 60$.

6. A: If a number is divisible by 2 and 3, it is also divisible by the lowest common multiple of these two factors. The lowest common multiple of 2 and 3 is their product, 6.

7. B: The decimal expansion of an irrational number does not terminate or repeat. The decimal expansion of $\sqrt{2}$ does not terminate or repeat.

8. C: The original price may be represented by the equation $24{,}210 = x - 0.10x$ or $24{,}210 = 0.9x$. Dividing both sides of the equation by 0.9 gives $x = 26{,}900$.

9. C: His monthly salary may be modeled as $\frac{1}{8}x = 320$. Multiplying both sides of the equation by 8 gives $x = 2{,}560$.

10. C: Division of a nonzero rational number by another nonzero rational number will always result in a nonzero rational number.

11. D: The set of integers is represented as $\{..., -3, -2, -1, 0, 1, 2, 3, ...\}$. The numbers 1, 2, 3, ..., are counting numbers, or natural numbers. Thus, the set contains the counting numbers, zero, and the negations of the counting numbers.

12. C: The set of irrational numbers is separate from the set of rational numbers. A rational number cannot be irrational, and an irrational number cannot be rational.

13. B: The multiplicative inverse property states that the product of a number and its reciprocal is 1.

14. A: If $a|b$ and $a|c$, it does not necessary follow that $b|c$. One counterexample is $3|6$ and $3|15$, but 6 does not divide 15.

15. A: The repeating decimal may be converted to a fraction by writing:

$$\begin{array}{r} 10x = 4.\overline{4} \\ -\quad x = 0.\overline{4} \\ \hline \end{array}$$

which simplifies as $10x - x = 4.\overline{4} - 0.\overline{4}$.

16. C: The amount he donates is equal to 0.01(45,000). Thus, he donates $450.

17. B: The amount she spends on rent and utilities is equal to 0.38(40,000), or $15,200, which is approximately $15,000.

18. D: The 8 is in the tenths place, the 6 in the hundredths place, and the 7 in the thousandths place. Thus, 0.867 is equal to the sum of the product of 8 and $\frac{1}{10}$, the product of 6 and $\frac{1}{100}$, and the product of 7 and $\frac{1}{1000}$.

19. D: The rectangular array represents the product of the side lengths of 7 and (4 + 2).

20. A: $b|a$ means that a is divisible by b: that is, that a is equal to the product of b and some quotient, q.

21. C: Subtraction of a natural number from another natural number may result in an integer that is not a natural number. For example, 1 – 2 = –1, which is not a natural number.

22. C. The original price may be modeled by the equation, $(x - 0.45x) + 0.0875(x - 0.45x) = 39.95$, which simplifies to $0.598125x = 39.95$. Dividing each side of the equation by the coefficient of x gives $x \approx 66.79$.

23. C: There are 36 months in 3 years. The following proportion may be written: $\frac{450}{3} = \frac{x}{36}$. The equation $3x = 16200$, may be solved for x. Dividing both sides of the equation by 3 gives $x = 5{,}400$.

24. D: The total rainfall is 25.38 inches. Thus, the ratio $\frac{4.5}{25.38}$, represents the percentage of rainfall received during October. $\frac{4.5}{25.38} \approx 0.177$ or 17.7%.

25. D: The decimal point is 4 places to the right of the first digit, 3. Thus, $30{,}490 = 3.049 \times 10^4$.

Algebra and Functions

26. C: The ratio between successive terms is constant (2), so this is a geometric series. A geometric sequence is represented by an exponential function.

27. A: The sum of 3 and the product of each term number and 5 equals the term value. For example, for term number 4, the value of 23 is equal to 5(4) + 3, or 23.

28. B: A vertical line will cross the graph at more than one point. Thus, it is not a function.

29. B: The graph is a straight line that passes through the origin, or point (0, 0).

30. C: This graph is shifted 4 units to the right and 3 units up from that of the parent function, $y = x^2$.

31. D: The product of $(x - 5)(2x + 6)$ equals $2x^2 + 6x - 10x - 30$, which simplifies to $2x^2 - 4x - 30$.

32. D: The constant of proportionality is equal to the slope. Using the points, (2, −8) and (5, −20), the slope may be written as $\frac{-20-(-8)}{5-2}$, which equals −4.

33. C: An inverse proportional relationship is written in the form $y = \frac{k}{x}$, thus the equation $y = \frac{3}{x}$ shows that y is inversely proportional to x.

34. D: The expression $(x - 2)^2$ may be expanded as $x^2 - 4x + 4$. Multiplication of $-3x$ by this expression gives $-3x^3 + 12x^2 - 12x$.

35. A: This graph shows a slope of 3, a y-intercept of −6, and the correct shading above the line. Using the test point (0, 0), the equation $0 \geq 0 - 6$ may be written. Since $0 \geq -6$, the solution is the shaded area above the line, which contains the point (0, 0).

36. C: Substituting 2 for each x-value gives $f(2) = \frac{2^3-2(2)+1}{3(2)}$, which simplifies to $f(2) = \frac{5}{6}$.

37. D: The table shows the y-intercept to be −5. The slope is equal to the ratio of change in y-values to change in corresponding x-values. As each x-value increases by 1, each y-value increases by 3. Thus, the slope is $\frac{3}{1}$, or 3. This graph represents the equation $y = 3x - 5$.

38. B: Each of the graphs shows the correct y-intercept of −6, but only graph B shows the correct slope. Using the points (0, −6) and (−2, 2), the slope of graph B may be written as $m = \frac{2-(-6)}{-2-0}$, which simplifies to $m = -4$.

39. B: The graph shows $f(2) = 10$. Since the y-intercept of the parabola is 2, the following equation may be written: $10 = a(2)^2 + 2$, which simplifies to $10 = 4a + 2$. Subtracting 2 from both sides gives $8 = 4a$. Dividing both sides of the equation by 4 gives $a = 2$. Thus the graph represents the function, $f(x) = 2x^2 + 2$. Evaluating this function for an x-value of 5 gives $f(5) = 2(5)^2 + 2$ or $f(5) = 52$. The average rate of change may be written as $A(x) = \frac{52-10}{5-2}$, which simplifies to $A(x) = 14$.

40. C: The slope is equal to 4, since each ticket costs $4. The y-intercept is represented by the constant fee of $30. Substituting 4 for m and 30 for b into the equation $y = mx + b$ gives $y = 4x + 30$.

41. D: The lines cross at the point with an x-value of -3 and a y-value of 2. Thus, the solution is $(-3, 2)$.

42. A: On a graph, the lines intersect at the point, $(-5, 9)$. Thus, $(-5, 9)$ is the solution to the system of linear equations.

43. A: The test point of (0, 0) indicates that shading should occur below the blue line. The same test point indicates that shading should occur above the red line. The overlapped shading occurs between these two lines, in the upper right.

44. D: A graph of the function shows the positive x-intercept to occur at approximately (2.6, 0). Thus, the ball will reach the ground after approximately 2.6 seconds.

45. D: The table represents a geometric sequence, with a common ratio of 2. Geometric sequences are modeled by exponential functions.

46. C: Using the points $(-3, 1)$ and $(1, -11)$, the slope may be written as $m = \frac{-11-1}{1-(-3)}$ or $m = -3$. Substituting the slope of -3 and the x- and y-values from the point $(-3, 1)$, into the slope-intercept form of an equation gives $1 = -3(-3) + b$, which simplifies to $1 = 9 + b$. Subtracting 9 from both sides of the equation gives $b = -8$. Thus, the linear equation that includes the data in the table is $y = -3x - 8$.

47. B: The slope of the graphed line is -2. A line perpendicular to this one will have a slope of $\frac{1}{2}$. Substituting the slope and the x- and y-values from the point (3, 2), into the slope-intercept form of an equation gives: $2 = \frac{1}{2}(3) + b$, which simplifies to $2 = \frac{3}{2} + b$. Subtracting $\frac{3}{2}$ from each side of the equation gives $b = \frac{1}{2}$. So the equation of a line perpendicular to this one and passing through the point (3, 2) is $y = \frac{1}{2}x + \frac{1}{2}$.

48. D: The slope of the graphed line is 2. A line parallel to this one will also have a slope of 2. Substituting the slope and the x- and y-values from the point $(-1, 4)$, into the slope-intercept form of an equation gives: $4 = 2(-1) + b$, which simplifies to $4 = -2 + b$. Adding 2 to both sides of the equation gives $b = 6$. So the equation of a line parallel to this one and passing through the point $(-1, 4)$ is $y = 2x + 6$.

49. B: The graph is a straight line that passes through the origin, or (0, 0). Thus, it is linear and proportional.

50. A: This situation may be modeled by a geometric sequence, with a common ratio of 2 and initial value of 0.02. Substituting the common ratio and initial value into the formula $a_n = a_1 \cdot r^{n-1}$, gives $a_n = 0.02 \cdot 2^{n-1}$.

51. D: This situation may be modeled by an arithmetic sequence, with a common difference of 4 and initial value of 3. Substituting the common difference and initial value into the formula, $a_n = a_1 + (n-1)d$, gives $a_n = 3 + (n-1)4$, which simplifies to $a_n = 4n - 1$.

52. D: If we divide both terms in the numerator by n, the expression reduces to $n + \frac{1}{n}$. Although $\frac{1}{n}$ converges to 0, n increases without bound. The expression therefore has no limit.

53. C: The limit is simply the quotient of $5n$ divided by n, or 5.

54. B: The sum of an infinite geometric series may be modeled by the formula $S = \frac{a}{1-r}$, where a represents the initial value and r represents the common ratio. Substituting the initial value of 3 and common ratio of $\frac{2}{3}$ into the formula, gives $= \frac{3}{1-\frac{2}{3}}$, which simplifies to $S = \frac{3}{\frac{1}{3}}$ or 9.

55. C: The situation may be modeled by the system $\begin{array}{c} 4x + 3y = 9.55 \\ 2x + 2y = 5.90 \end{array}$. Multiplying the bottom equation by −2 gives $\begin{array}{c} 4x + 3y = 9.55 \\ -4x - 4y = -11.80 \end{array}$. Addition of the two equations gives $-y = -2.25$ or $y = 2.25$. Thus, one box of crackers costs \$2.25.

56. C: The derivative of an equation of the form $y = ax^n$ is equal to $(n \cdot a)x^{n-1}$. So the derivative of $y = 9x^2$ is equal to $(2 \cdot 9)x^{2-1}$ or $18x$.

57. C: The limit of the expression $\frac{4x}{x}$, is 4, so the limit of the entire function is 1,004. The function converges.

58. B: The sequence $\frac{1}{5}, \frac{1}{25}, \frac{1}{125}, \frac{1}{625}, \ldots$, may be used to represent the situation. Substituting the initial value of $\frac{1}{5}$ and common ratio of $\frac{1}{5}$ into the formula $S = \frac{a}{1-r}$ gives $= \frac{\frac{1}{5}}{1-\frac{1}{5}}$, which simplifies to $S = \frac{\frac{1}{5}}{\frac{4}{5}}$ or $S = \frac{1}{4}$.

59. B: As the denominator approaches infinity, the value of the function will get smaller and smaller and converge to 0.

60. B: The derivative of an equation of the form $y = x^n$ is equal to $n \cdot x^{n-1}$. So the derivative of $g(x) = x^{ab}$ is equal to $ab \cdot x^{ab-1}$.

61. A: An inverse proportional relationship is represented by an equation in the form $y = \frac{k}{x}$, where k represents some constant of proportionality. The graph of this equation is a hyperbola with diagonal axes, symmetric about the lines $y = x$ and $y = -x$.

62. C: The value of the 50th term may be found using the formula $a_n = a_1 + (n - 1)d$. Substituting the number of terms for n, the initial value of 2 for a, and the common difference of 2 for d gives: $a_{50} = 2 + (50 - 1)(2)$, which simplifies to $a_{50} = 100$. Now, the value of the 50th term may be substituted into the formula, $S_n = \frac{n(a_1+a_n)}{2}$, which gives: $S_{50} = \frac{50(2+100)}{2}$, which simplifies to $S_{50} = 2{,}550$.

63. B: The sign of the constant, inside the squared term, is positive for a shift to the left and negative for a shift to the right. Thus, a movement of 5 units left is indicated by the expression $y = (x + 5)^2$. A shift of 4 units down is indicated by subtraction of 4 units from the squared term.

64. B: Relation B is the only one in which there is not any x-value that is mapped to more than one y-value. Thus, this relation represents a function.

65. C: The position of an accelerating car is changing according to a non-constant speed. Thus, the graph will show a curve with an increasing slope. The slope is increasing since it represents the velocity, and the velocity is increasing.

66. A: The inequality will be less than or equal to, since he may spend $100 or less on his purchase.

67. D: Since she spends at least $16, the relation of the number of packages of coffee to the minimum cost may be written as $4p \geq 16$. Alternatively, the inequality may be written as $16 \leq 4p$.

68. B: The horizontal asymptote is equal to the ratio of the coefficient of x to the coefficient of $2x$, or $\frac{1}{2}$.

69. C: The horizontal asymptote is equal to the ratio of the two coefficients of x, or $\frac{1}{1}$, which equals 1.

70. D: As x goes to positive or negative infinity, only the leading term of a polynomial function of x matters. Therefore, we can ignore the "+2" in the denominator; $\lim_{x \to -\infty} \frac{4x^2}{x+2} = \lim_{x \to -\infty} \frac{4x^2}{x} = \lim_{x \to -\infty} 4x$. As x goes to negative infinity, $4x$ decreases without bound. The expression therefore has no limit.

71. A: Evaluation of the expression for an x-value of −2 gives: $(3(-2)^3 - 6(-2)^2 + 4)$, which equals −44.

72. B: The situation may be modeled with the equation $\frac{1}{3} + \frac{1}{2} = \frac{1}{t}$, which simplifies to $\frac{5}{6} = \frac{1}{t}$. Thus, $t = \frac{6}{5}$. If working together, it will take them 1.2 hours to decorate the cake.

73. A: The situation may be modeled by the inequality $3x + 2y \geq 20$. Isolating the y-term gives $2y \geq -3x + 20$. Solving for y gives $y \geq -\frac{3}{2}x + 10$. Thus, the y-intercept will be 10, the line will be solid, and a test point of (0, 0) indicates the shading should occur above the line.

74. C: The situation may be modeled by the following system of inequalities: $\begin{matrix} 6x + 3y \leq 75 \\ x + y \leq 30 \end{matrix}$. A test point of (0, 0) indicates shading should occur below the blue line and below the red line. The overlapped shading occurs below the blue line. Thus, graph C represents the correct combinations of items that she may buy, given her budget.

75. D: The table represents part of a geometric sequence, with a common ratio of 2, so it also represents points of an exponential function.

Measurement and Geometry

76. B: The following proportion may be written and solved for x: $\frac{5{,}280}{1} = \frac{6{,}700}{x}$. Thus, $x \approx 1.27$.

77. C: The volume of a cylinder may be calculated using the formula $V = \pi r^2 h$, where r represents the radius and h represents the height. Substituting 1.5 for r and 3 for h gives $V = \pi(1.5)^2(3)$, which simplifies to $V \approx 21.2$.

78. B: The volume of a sphere may be calculated using the formula $V = \frac{4}{3}\pi r^3$, where r represents the radius. Substituting 3.5 for r gives $V = \frac{4}{3}\pi(3.5)^3$, which simplifies to $V \approx 179.6$.

79. C: The surface area of a rectangular prism may be calculated using the formula $SA = 2lw + 2wh + 2hl$. Substituting the dimensions of 14 inches, 6 inches, and 8 inches gives $SA = 2(14)(6) + 2(6)(8) + 2(8)(14)$. Thus, the surface area is 488 square inches.

80. C: The volume of a pyramid may be calculated using the formula $V = \frac{1}{3}Bh$, where B represents the area of the base and h represents the height. Since the base is a square, the area of the base is equal to 6^2, or 36 square inches. Substituting 36 for B and 9 for h gives $V = \frac{1}{3}(36)(9)$, which simplifies to $V = 108$.

81. C: The surface area of a sphere may be calculated using the formula $SA = 4\pi r^2$. Substituting 9 for r gives $SA = 4\pi(9)^2$, which simplifies to $SA \approx 1017.36$. So the surface area of the ball is approximately 1017.36 square inches. There are twelve inches in a foot, so there are $12^2 = 144$ square inches in a square foot. In order to convert this measurement to square feet, then, the following proportion may be written and solved for x: $\frac{1}{144} = \frac{x}{1017.36}$. So $x \approx 7.07$. He needs approximately 7.07 square feet of wrapping paper.

82. D: The volume of a prism may be calculated using the formula $V = Bh$, where B represents the area of the base and h represents the height of the prism. The area of each triangular base is represented by $A = \frac{1}{2}(9)(12)$. So the area of each base is equal to 54 square centimeters. Substituting 54 for the area of the base and 15 for the height of the prism gives $V = (54)(15)$ or $V = 810$. The volume of the prism is 810 cm^3.

83. B: Since the figures are similar, the following proportion may be written and solved for x: $\frac{6}{4} = \frac{8}{x}$. Thus, $x = \frac{32}{6}$ or $5\frac{1}{3}$.

84. C: Angles g and c are alternate exterior angles. Thus, they are congruent.

85. D: The corresponding angles have congruent angle measures, each measuring 44°. According to the Corresponding Angles Converse Theorem, two lines are parallel if a transversal, intersecting the lines, forms congruent corresponding angles.

86. C: The measure of the inscribed angle is half of the measure of the intercepted arc. Since the intercepted arc measures 110°, the inscribed angle is equal to $\frac{110°}{2}$ or 55°.

87. B: The following proportion may be written and solved for x: $\frac{15}{5} = \frac{6}{x}$. Solving for x gives $x = 2$. Thus, the shadow cast by the man is 2 feet in length.

88. C: The following equation may be written and solved for x: $\sin 40° = \frac{x}{6}$. Multiplying both sides of the equation by 6 gives: $6 \cdot \sin 40° = x$, or $x \approx 3.9$.

89. D: The area of the square is equal to $(30)^2$, or 900 square centimeters. The area of the circle is equal to $\pi(15)^2$, or approximately 707 square centimeters. The area of the shaded region is equal to the difference of the area of the square and the area of the circle, or 900 cm^2 – 707 cm^2, which equals 193 cm^2. So the area of the shaded region is about 193 cm^2.

90. B: Two of the angles, plus one side, not included between the angles, are congruent to the corresponding angles and side of the other triangle. Thus, the AAS (Angle-Angle-Side) Theorem may be used to prove the congruence of the triangles.

91. D: The Pythagorean Theorem may be used to find the diagonal distance from the top of his head to the base of the shadow. The following equation may be written and solved for c: $5.8^2 + 6.2^2 = c^2$. Thus, $c \approx 8.5$. The distance is approximately 8.5 ft.

92. D: The cross-section of a cylinder will never be a triangle.

93. D: The measure of an angle formed by intersecting chords inside a circle is equal to one-half of the sum of the measures of the intercepted arcs. Thus, $x = \frac{1}{2}(48° + 62°)$, or 55°.

94. D: The measure of the angle formed by the chord and the tangent is equal to one-half of the measure of the intercepted arc. Since the measure of the angle is 68°, the measure of the intercepted arc may be found by writing $68° = \frac{1}{2}x$. Dividing both sides of the equation by $\frac{1}{2}$ gives x = 136°. The measure of the intercepted arc may also be found by multiplying 68° by 2. Thus, the value of x is 136°.

95. A: The net of a triangular prism has three rectangular faces and two triangular faces. This is true of both A and C, but net C cannot be folded into a triangular prism, because the two rectangular faces on the end cannot be made to join each other. So only A can be folded into a triangular prism.

96. B: The relationship between number of faces, edges, and vertices is represented by Euler's Formula, $E = F + V - 2$. Substituting 9 for E and 6 for V gives: $9 = F + 6 - 2$, which simplifies to $9 = F + 4$. Thus, $F = 5$.

97. C: When two parallel lines are cut by a transversal, the consecutive angles formed inside the lines are supplementary.

98. B: The two triangles are similar because they each have an angle measuring 65°, and the measurement of Angle A is the same for both triangles, due to the Reflexive Property. So the two triangles are similar according to the AA (Angle-Angle) Similarity Postulate.

99. C: The original triangle was reflected across the x-axis. When reflecting across the x-axis, the x-values of each point remain the same, but the y-values of the points will be opposites. $(1, 4) \rightarrow (1, -4), (5, 4) \rightarrow (5, -4), (3, 8) \rightarrow (3, -8)$.

100. C: A reflection across the x-axis will result in a triangle with vertices at (2, −3), (4, −7), and (6, −3). A rotation of 270 degrees is denoted by the following: $(a, b) \rightarrow (b, -a)$. Thus, a rotation of the

reflected triangle by 270 degrees will result in a figure with vertices at (−3, −2), (−7, −4), and (−3, −6). The transformed triangle indeed has these coordinates as its vertices.

101. C: The midpoint may be calculated by using the formula $m = \left(\frac{x_1+x_2}{2}, \frac{y_1+y_2}{2}\right)$. Thus, the midpoint of the line segment shown may be written as $m = \left(\frac{1+8}{2}, \frac{2+8}{2}\right)$, which simplifies to m = (4.5, 5).

102. C: The distance may be calculated using the distance formula, $d = \sqrt{(x_2 - x_1)^2 + (y_2 - y_1)^2}$. Substituting the given coordinates, the following equation may be written:
$d = \sqrt{(4 - (-8))^2 + (3 - 6)^2}$, which simplifies to $d = \sqrt{153}$.

103. B: The perimeter is equal to the sum of the lengths of the two bases, 2 and 6 units, and the diagonal distances of the other two sides. Using the distance formula, each side length may be represented as $d = \sqrt{20} = 2\sqrt{5}$. Thus, the sum of the two sides is equal to $2\sqrt{20}$, or $4\sqrt{5}$. The whole perimeter is equal to $8 + 4\sqrt{5}$.

104. C: The area of a trapezoid may be calculated using the formula, $A = \frac{1}{2}(b_1 + b_2)h$. Thus, the area of the trapezoid is represented as $A = \frac{1}{2}(4 + 2)(2)$, which simplifies to A = 6. The area of the triangle is represented as $A = \frac{1}{2}(4)(3)$, which also simplifies to A = 6. Thus, the total area is 12 square units.

105. D: The larger triangle has a base length of 3 units and a height of 3 units. The smaller triangle has a base length of 2 units and a height of 2 units. Thus, the dimensions of the larger triangle were multiplied by a scale factor of $\frac{2}{3}$. Note that $3 \cdot \left(\frac{2}{3}\right) = 2$.

106. A: The vertical line of symmetry is represented by an equation of the form $x = a$. The horizontal line of symmetry is represented by an equation of the form $y = a$. One line of symmetry occurs at $x = -4$. The other line of symmetry occurs at $y = 6$.

107. C: Equilateral triangles and regular hexagons may tessellate a plane. Each triangle may be attached to each side of a hexagon, leaving no gaps in the plane.

108. A: The amount to be administered may be written as $\frac{1}{12} \cdot \frac{34}{10}$, which equals $\frac{17}{60}$. Thus, she should administer $\frac{17}{60}$ fluid ounces of medicine.

109. C: The slope may be written as $m = \frac{4-0}{-3-(-4)}$, which simplifies to m = 4.

110. D: The perimeter of the triangle is equal to the sum of the side lengths. The length of the longer diagonal side may be represented as $d = \sqrt{(4 - 1)^2 + (5 - 2)^2}$, which simplifies to $d = \sqrt{18}$. The length of the shorter diagonal side may be represented as $d = \sqrt{(6 - 4)^2 + (2 - 5)^2}$, which simplifies to $d = \sqrt{13}$. The base length is 5 units. Thus, the perimeter is equal to $5 + \sqrt{18} + \sqrt{13}$, which is approximately 12.85 units. Since each unit represents 5 miles, the total distance she will have walked is equal to the product of 12.85 and 5, or approximately 64 miles.

111. C: The following proportion may be written and solved for x: $\frac{144}{1} = \frac{2012}{x}$. $144x = 2012$. Dividing both sides of the equation by 144 gives $x \approx 13.97$. Thus, 2,012 square inches is approximately equal to 13.97 square feet.

112. D: The triangle is a 45-45-90 right triangle. Thus, if each leg is represented by x, the hypotenuse is represented by $x\sqrt{2}$. Thus, the hypotenuse is equal to $8\sqrt{2}$ cm.

Statistics, Probability, and Discrete Mathematics

113. A: Data sets B and C are asymmetrical: data set B is skewed toward lower values, and data set C is skewed toward higher values. This makes the mean a poor measure of center. Data set D is mostly symmetrical, but has a large outlier. The mean is very sensitive to outliers, and is not an appropriate measure of center for data sets that include them. Data set A is roughly symmetrical and has no outliers; the mean would be an appropriate measure of center here.

114. C: A z-score may be calculated using the formula $z = \frac{X-\mu}{\sigma}$. Substituting the score of 82, class average of 87, and class standard deviation of 2 into the formula gives: $z = \frac{82-87}{2}$, which simplifies to $z = -2.5$. Thus, the student's score is 2.5 standard deviations below the mean.

115. D: The z-score is written as $z = \frac{61-81}{10}$, which simplifies to $z = -2$. A z-score with an absolute value of 2 shows a mean to z area of 0.4772. Subtracting this area from 0.5 gives 0.0228, or 2.28%.

116. D: The z-score is written as $z = \frac{96-84}{4}$, which simplifies to $z = 3$. A z-score of 3 shows a mean to z area of 0.4987. Adding 0.5 to this area gives 0.9987, or 99.87%.

117. D: Two z-scores should be calculated, one for each student's score. The first z-score may be written as $z = \frac{68-80}{8}$, which simplifies to $z = -1.5$. The second z-score may be written as $z = \frac{84-80}{8}$, which simplifies to $z = 0.5$. The percentage of students scoring between these two scores is equal to the sum of the two mean to z areas. A z-score with an absolute value of 1.5 shows a mean to z area of 0.4332. A z-score of 0.5 shows a mean to z area of 0.1915. The sum of these two areas is 0.6247, or 62.47%.

118. D: A two-sample t-test should be used. Entering the sample mean, sample standard deviation, and sample size of each group into a graphing calculator reveals a p-value that is less than 0.05, so a significant difference between the groups may be declared.

119. C: A t-test should be used. A t-score may be calculated using the formula $t = \frac{\bar{X}-\mu}{\frac{s}{\sqrt{n}}}$. Substituting the sample mean, population mean, sample standard deviation, and sample size into the formula gives $t = \frac{19.8-20}{\frac{0.2}{\sqrt{30}}}$, which simplifies to $t \approx -5.48$. For degrees of freedom of 29, any t-value greater than 3.659 will have a p-value less than 0.001. Thus, there is a significant difference between what the manufacturer claims and the actual amount included in each bottle. The claim is likely false, due to a p-value less than 0.01.

120. B: A z-test may be used, since the population standard deviation is known. A z-score may be calculated using the formula $z = \frac{\bar{X}-\mu}{\frac{\sigma}{\sqrt{n}}}$. Substituting the sample mean, population mean, population standard deviation, and sample size into the formula gives $z = \frac{17.9-18}{\frac{0.3}{\sqrt{25}}}$, which simplifies to $z \approx -1.67$. The p-value is approximately 0.1, which is greater than 0.05. Thus, there does not appear to be a significant difference between what the manufacturer claims and the actual number of ounces found in each container. The claim is likely true, due to a p-value greater than 0.05.

121. B: A t-test should be used. A t-score may be calculated using the formula $t = \frac{\bar{X}-\mu}{\frac{s}{\sqrt{n}}}$. Substituting the sample mean, population mean, sample standard deviation, and sample size into the formula gives $t = \frac{83-82}{\frac{2}{\sqrt{30}}}$, which simplifies to $t \approx 2.74$. For degrees of freedom of 29, the p-value is approximately 0.01. Thus, there is a significant difference between what the professor claimed to be the final exam average and what the actual sample average showed. His claim is likely false, as evidenced by a p-value less than 0.05.

122. C: Use of an intact group is called a convenience sample. Such a sample increases sampling error, since randomization was not employed. The other described techniques utilize random sampling.

123. C: A z-score of 2 has a mean to z area of 0.4772, or 47.72%. Twice this percentage is about 95%.

124. D: The standard deviation is equal to the square root of the ratio of the sum of the squares of the deviation of each score from the mean to the square root of the difference of n and 1. The mean of the data set is 7.625. The deviations are −4.625, −3.625, −3.625, −2.625, −1.625, 4.375, 4.375, and 7.375. The sum of the squares of the deviations may be written as 21.39 + 13.14 + 13.14 + 6.89 + 2.64 + 19.14 + 19.14 + 54.39, which equals 149.87. Division of this sum by 7 (n – 1) gives 21.41. The square root of this quotient is approximately 4.6.

125. A: The ends of Data Set A are farther apart, indicating a larger range. The horizontal line in the middle of a boxplot represents the median, so Data Set A also has a larger median.

126. A: The median of the lower half of the scores is 6. The median of the upper half of the scores is 16. The interquartile range is equal to the difference in the first and third quartiles. Thus, the interquartile range is 10.

127. B: The points may be entered into a graphing calculator or Excel spreadsheet to find the least-squares regression line. This line is approximately $y = 22x + 6$. Substituting 20 for x gives $y = 22(20) + 6$, or $y = 446$. Thus, $446 is a good estimate for the earnings received after 20 hours of work. If a line of best fit is predicted visually, the slope between points near that line is around 20, and the line passes near the origin. Thus, another good estimate would be $400. The estimate of $446 is closer to $400 than any of the other choices.

128. B: The mean is pulled towards the tail of a skewed distribution. It is not pulled towards the area with the larger frequency of scores. Outliers pull the mean towards those outliers.

129. C: The probability may be written as $P(M \text{ or } G) = P(M) + P(G) - P(M \text{ and } G)$. Substituting the probabilities, the following may be written: $P(M \text{ or } G) = \frac{4985}{10{,}079} + \frac{4113}{10{,}079} - \frac{2045}{10{,}079}$, which simplifies to $P(M \text{ or } G) = \frac{7053}{10{,}079}$ or approximately 70%.

130. D: The number of outcomes in the event is 2 (rolling a 5 or 6), and the sample space is 6 (numbers 1 - 6). Thus, the probability may be written as $\frac{2}{6}$, which simplifies to $\frac{1}{3}$.

131. B: The probability may be written as $P(E \text{ and } H) = P(E) \cdot P(H)$. Substituting the probability of each event gives $(E \text{ and } H) = \frac{1}{2} \cdot \frac{1}{2}$, which simplifies to $\frac{1}{4}$.

132. D: Since they are not mutually exclusive events, the probability may be written as $P(P \text{ or } T) = P(P) + P(T) - P(P \text{ and } T)$. Because the events are independent, $P(P \text{ and } T) = P(P) \cdot P(T)$. Substituting the probability of each event gives $(P \text{ or } T) = \frac{1}{2} + \frac{1}{2} - \left(\frac{1}{2} \cdot \frac{1}{2}\right)$, or 3/4.

133. B: Since they are not mutually exclusive events, the probability may be written as $P(4 \text{ or } E) = P(4) + P(E) - P(4 \text{ and } E)$. Substituting the probability of each event gives $(4\ or\ E) = \frac{1}{6} + \frac{1}{2} - \frac{1}{6}$, or $\frac{1}{2}$.

134. C: The theoretical probability is $\frac{1}{2}$, and $\frac{1}{2}(300) = 150$.

135. C: The number of ways the letters can be arranged may be represented as $\frac{6!}{2!2!2!}$, which equals 90.

136. A: This situation describes a permutation, since order matters. The formula for calculating a combination is $P(n,r) = \frac{n!}{(n-r)!}$. This situation may be represented as $P(6,3) = \frac{6!}{(6-3)!}$, which equals 120.

137. D: Since there are 10 numerals, the answer is equal to 10!, or 3,628,800.

138. A: The series is an infinite geometric series. The sum may be calculated using the formula $S = \frac{a}{1-r}$, where a represents the value of the first term and r represents the common ratio. Substituting 1 for a and $\frac{1}{2}$ for r gives $S = \frac{1}{1-\frac{1}{2}}$ or 2.

139. C: The number in the sample space is equal to the number of possible outcomes for one coin toss, 2, raised to the power of the number of coin tosses, or 4. $2^4 = 16$.

140. A: A Venn diagram such as the one shown below may be drawn to assist in finding the answer.

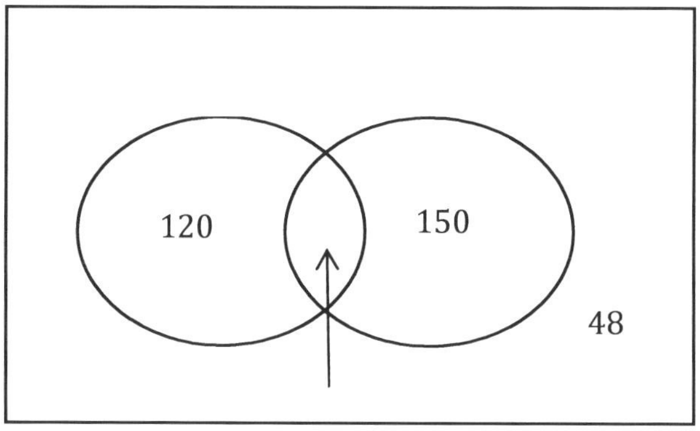

Since the set contains 320 total people, the solution is equal to $320 - (120 + 150 + 48)$ or 2 people.

141. A:$A \cap B$ means "A intersect B," or the elements that are common to both sets. "A intersect B" represents "A and B," that is, an element is in the intersection of A and B if it is in A *and* it is in B. The elements 2, 5, and 8 are common to both sets.

142. B:$A \cup B$ means "A union B," or all of the elements in either of the two sets. "A union B" represents "A or B," that is, an element is in the union of A and B if it is in A *or* it is in B. The elements in sets A and B are 9, 4, −3, 8, 6, 0, −4, and 2.

143. D: The intersection of the two sets is empty, denoted by the symbol, $\emptyset$. There are not any elements common to both sets.

144. D: If the statement is written in the form $p \rightarrow q$, then the contrapositive is represented as $\sim q \rightarrow \sim p$. Thus, the contrapositive should read, "If I do not go to the beach, then I do not get paid."

145. B: If the statement is written in the form $p \rightarrow q$, then the converse is represented as $q \rightarrow p$. Thus, the converse should read, "If it is winter, then I go skiing."

146. D: Only when both p and q are false is the union of p and q false.

147. A: Both p and q must be true in order for the intersection to be true.

148. C: A conditional statement $p \rightarrow q$ and its contrapositive $\sim q \rightarrow \sim p$ are logically equivalent because of the identical values in a truth table. See below.

p	q	$\sim p$	$\sim q$	$p \rightarrow q$	$\sim q \rightarrow \sim p$
T	T	F	F	T	T
T	F	F	T	F	F
F	T	T	F	T	T
F	F	T	T	T	T

149. C: This is a counting problem. The possible number of meals is equal to the product of the possibilities for each category. The product of 4, 5, and 3 is 60. Thus, there are 60 meals that he may create.

150. B: A tautology will shows all true values in a truth table column. Look at the table below:

p	q	$\sim p$	$\sim q$	p or $\sim p$	p and $\sim p$	p or $\sim q$	p or q
T	T	F	F	T	F	T	T
T	F	F	T	T	F	T	T
F	T	T	F	T	F	F	T
F	F	T	T	T	F	T	F

Only the statement $p \vee \sim p$ shows all T's in the column.

Science Practice Test

Practice Questions

1. A researcher is studying the response of bacteria to a certain chemical. In three experiments, the bacteria swim towards the chemical, and in one experiment the bacteria swim away from it. What would be the most appropriate next step for the researcher?
   a. Report only the first three experiments.
   b. Report all the experiments, but refrain from making any conclusions.
   c. Repeat the experiment several more times and apply a statistical analysis to the data.
   d. Repeat the experiment, adding a new chemical to determine its effect on the bacteria.

2. In a study investigating the causes of stomach ulcers, researchers observed that coffee drinkers had a higher incidence of stomach ulcers than those who didn't drink coffee. This is an example of
   a. A controlled experiment
   b. A cause and effect relationship
   c. Correlation between two variables
   d. Systematic error in sampling

3. In terms of mass, which of the following represents the greatest amount of sucrose (Molar mass = 342 grams)?
   a. 1 mole
   b. 100 grams
   c. 1 L of a 0.1 M solution
   d. 100 mL of a 1 M solution

4. In an experiment on respiration, carbon dioxide production is measured over time. Placing the data in a chart is
   a. A visual representation of the data
   b. A conclusion based on the data
   c. The raw data
   d. A comparative analysis of the data

5. In order to be included in the formation of a scientific conclusion, evidence must be
   a. Quantitative
   b. Reproducible
   c. Obvious
   d. All of the above

6. During a lesson, teachers should keep in mind that they need to demonstrate to their students how to
   a. Understand, organize, and remember information
   b. Organize, emphasize, and understand information
   c. Emphasize, understand, and remember information
   d. Organize, understand, and remember information

7. Which of the following compounds is not allowed in a school laboratory because it is a potential carcinogen?
   a. Lead
   b. Benzene
   c. Aspartame
   d. Methanol

8. A laboratory experiment requires that red blood cells be separated from the serum in whole blood. Which of the following laboratory techniques would be most appropriate for this task?
   a. Spectroscopy
   b. Sublimation
   c. Microscopy
   d. Centrifugation

9. Which of the following quantities is largest in the metric system of measurement?
   a. 10 decigrams
   b. 100 milligrams
   c. 100 grams
   d. 1 decagram

10. In a lesson on invertebrates, an instructor plans to show the students the fly eye. He has dissected a fly and mounted a sample on a slide, but the students aren't able to make out the structure. He should advise his students to
   a. Find pictures of the fly eye in a book
   b. Use a more powerful magnification on the microscope
   c. Stain the specimen
   d. Place the specimen on a dark background

11. Which of the following biological discoveries was made first?
   a. Louis Pasteur discovered the causative role of microorganisms in disease.
   b. Charles Darwin discovered the principles of natural selection.
   c. Gregor Mendel discovered that genes are the basic units of inheritance.
   d. Carl Von Linnaeus developed the binomial system of nomenclature for living things.

12. Which of the following is a constant?
   a. The freezing point of water
   b. The temperature at which iron ore will melt
   c. The human population size
   d. The time the sun rises each day

13. The volume of water in a bucket is 2.5 liters. When an object with an irregular shape and a mass of 40 grams is submerged in the water, the volume of the water is 4.5 liters. What is the density of the object?
   a. 1/10 g/L
   b. 2 g/L
   c. 20 g/L
   d. 80 g/L

14. The amount of potential energy an object has depends on all of the following except its
  a. mass.
  b. height above ground.
  c. gravitational attraction.
  d. temperature.

15. The specific heat capacity of ice is half as much as that of liquid water. What is the result of this?
  a. It takes half the amount of energy to increase the temperature of a 1 kg sample of ice by 1°C than a 1 kg sample of water.
  b. It takes twice the amount of energy to increase the temperature of a 1 kg sample of ice by 1°C than a 1 kg sample of water.
  c. It takes a quarter the amount of energy to increase the temperature of a 1 kg sample of ice by 1°C than a 1 kg sample of water.
  d. It takes the same amount of energy to increase the temperature of a 1 kg sample of ice and a 1 kg sample of water by 1°C.

16. What happens to the temperature of a substance as it is changing phase from a liquid to a solid?
  a. Its temperature increases due to the absorption of latent heat.
  b. Its temperature decreases due to the heat of vaporization.
  c. Its temperature decreases due to the latent heat of fusion.
  d. Its temperature remains the same due to the latent heat of fusion.

17. A long nail is heated at one end. After a few seconds, the other end of the nail becomes equally hot. What type of heat transfer does this represent?
  a. Radiation
  b. Conduction
  c. Convection
  d. Entropy

18. Which of the following statements about heat transfer is not true?
  a. As the energy of a system changes, its thermal energy must change or work must be done.
  b. Heat transfer from a warmer object to a cooler object can occur spontaneously.
  c. Heat transfer can never occur from a cooler object to a warmer object.
  d. If two objects reach the same temperature, energy is no longer available for work.

19. The measure of energy within a system is called ________.
  a. temperature
  b. heat
  c. entropy
  d. thermodynamics

20. Which of the following is true of an isotope?
  a. It has a different number of protons than its element.
  b. It has a different number of electrons than its element.
  c. It has a different charge as compared to its element.
  d. It has a different number of neutrons than its element.

21. If an atom's outer shell is filled, what must be true?
a. It reacts with other atoms through chemical reactions.
b. It exchanges electrons to form bonds with other atoms.
c. It has 32 electrons in its outer shell.
d. It is a stable atom.

22. Which type of nuclear process features atomic nuclei splitting apart to form smaller nuclei?
a. Fission
b. Fusion
c. Decay
d. Ionization

23. Which of the following components of an atom varies in isotopes?
a. Protons
b. Neutrons
c. Electrons
d. Leptons

24. Which of the following components of an atom is most likely to be lost or gained in a chemical reaction?
a. Protons
b. Neutrons
c. Electrons
d. Isotopes

25. Which of the following phenomena would most readily lend itself to mathematical modeling?
a. The position of an electron in orbit around the nucleus of an atom
b. The rate of blood flow through an artery
c. The force required to extend a metal spring by a certain length
d. The rate at which cells divide in an embryo

26. Without _______ applied to it, an object in motion will tend to stay in motion.
a. Force
b. Inertia
c. Gravity
d. Acceleration

27. A car trip to a point 50 miles away from home and back takes four hours. The top speed of the car was 50 miles per hour, and this speed was maintained during the second and third hours of the trip. Which of the following values represents the average velocity of the car?
a. 0 miles/hour
b. 12.5 miles/hour
c. 25 miles/hour
d. 50 miles/hour

28. Which of the following is *not* an example of one of Newton's laws of motion at work?
   a. Once in orbit, a satellite will continue moving around the earth.
   b. It takes three times as much force to move a block that has twice the mass of another.
   c. A ball rolling across the floor will continue moving across the floor.
   d. When a shotgun is fired, the gun moves sharply in the opposite direction of the bullet.

29. Which of the following does NOT contribute to an object's potential energy?
   a. Mass
   b. Gravity
   c. Height
   d. Temperature

30. Energy is measured in
   a. Joules
   b. Volts
   c. Ohms
   d. Amperes

31. If a refrigerator was running in an empty room with its door open, the temperature of the room would eventually
   a. Increase
   b. Decrease
   c. Stay the same
   d. It depends on the size of the room.

32. The human eye perceives leaves on a tree as green because of light that is
   a. Absorbed
   b. Refracted
   c. Reflected
   d. Diffracted

33. Which of the following kinds of waves require particles to propagate?
   a. Radio waves
   b. Sound waves
   c. Microwaves
   d. X-rays

34. Which of the following is a property of nonmetals?
   a. They are good conductors of electricity.
   b. They do not form isotopes.
   c. They react with metals.
   d. They are dense, hard, and have high melting points.

35. An element on the periodic table will have chemical reactivity most like the element
   a. To the right or left of it on the table
   b. Above or below it on the table
   c. Within two horizontal spaces of it on the table
   d. Placement on the table is not related to the chemical properties of an element.

36. Which of the following changes in physical properties is a chemical change?
  a. Dissolving a seltzer tablet in water
  b. Grinding pepper into powder
  c. Freezing water
  d. Churning cream into butter

37. Which of the following is an example of a chemical reaction?
  a. Heating ethanol so that it evaporates
  b. Igniting ethanol so that it burns
  c. Dissolving salt in water
  d. Making ice cubes in a freezer

38. Of the following, which is the most basic unit of matter?
  a. A helium atom
  b. A sodium ion
  c. A proton
  d. An oxygen molecule

39. Heating a liquid will most likely change its
  a. Crystal structure
  b. Density
  c. Mass
  d. Electrical conductivity

40. In an experiment, you want to measure the amount of mass a piece of wood liberates when it burns. The most accurate way of doing this would be to
  a. Measure the volume and pressure of the gases emitted by the burning wood, and then calculate the number of molecules present.
  b. Chill the gases emitted by the burning wood over liquid nitrogen so the mass of the solid carbon dioxide (dry ice) can be measured.
  c. Determine the mass of the ash after the wood burns.
  d. Measure the mass of the wood before and after it burns.

41. Which of the following substances is most likely to contain acetic acid?
  a. Cream of tartar
  b. Vinegar
  c. Baking powder
  d. Water

42. All of the following are membrane-bound organelles except
  a. Nucleoli
  b. Chromoplasts
  c. Mitochondria
  d. Endoplasmic reticulum

43. The component of blood essential for clotting is the
  a. Plasma
  b. Platelets
  c. Erythrocytes
  d. Leukocytes

44. Which of the following biomolecules is NOT a polymer?
a. Cellulose
b. DNA
c. Phospholipid
d. Protein

45. All living things have
a. Organelles
b. Cells
c. Tissues
d. Cell walls

46. Which class of hormones is most likely to be released after a serious injury?
a. Acetylcholine
b. Oxytocin
c. Luteinizing hormone
d. Endorphins

47. A purple-flowered pea plant is crossed with a white-flowered pea plant and all of the progeny are purple. The purple allele is ____________ to white.
a. Recessive
b. Dominant
c. Codominant
d. Not enough information is given to tell.

48. A color-blind woman marries a man with normal vision. What proportion of their daughters will be color blind if color blindness is a recessive sex-linked trait?
a. 100%
b. 50%
c. 33%
d. 0%

49. In order to clone a gene, what must a researcher have or know?
a. Its cDNA
b. Its expression profile
c. Its method of transcription
d. Its phenotype

50. In a lab experiment, students are presented with three types of flowers, some with stamens, some with pistils, and some with both. They conclude that all flowers have at least one kind of reproductive structure. They are engaging in
a. Deductive reasoning
b. Inductive reasoning
c. Indirect instruction
d. Causal reasoning

51. The horn of a rhinoceros and human hair are evolutionarily related. They are
   a. Ancestral characteristics
   b. Detrimental characteristics
   c. Homologous characteristics
   d. Analogous characteristics

52. In highly industrialized areas, trees used to become covered in soot. Eventually, most moths found in that area were gray rather than white. Which factor most likely contributed to the change in color of these moths?
   a. Natural selection
   b. Genetic drift
   c. Sexual selection
   d. Punctuated equilibrium

53. Which of the following is the most likely explanation for the reason finches on separate islands within an archipelago have differently shaped beaks?
   a. Each bird evolved from a pre-existing ancestor on each island.
   b. The finches spread among the islands, but in small numbers, so genetic drift caused beak shape to change.
   c. Natural selection shaped the beaks in accordance with food availability on each island.
   d. The different finches were introduced by ancient humans.

54. Which of the following is NOT a useful source of evidence with respect to the evolutionary history of an organism?
   a. Its placement in the fossil record
   b. Its anatomy
   c. Its distribution among the continents
   d. Its population size

55. A mouse that feeds on grain is a part of which trophic level?
   a. Primary producer
   b. Primary consumer
   c. Secondary consumer
   d. Decomposer

56. In an ear infection, bacteria become trapped in the middle ear and colonize it. The bacteria in the infection would be considered
   a. A population
   b. A community
   c. An ecosystem
   d. Individuals

57. In photosynthesis, what kind of chemical reaction transforms CO_2 into carbohydrates?
   a. Oxidation
   b. Chemiosmosis
   c. Reduction
   d. Hydrolysis

58. When a mimosa plant is touched on its leaves, they rapidly crumple, and then gradually relax again after the stimulus stops. This is an example of a(n)

a. Innate behavior
b. Learned behavior
c. Response to stimuli
d. Single cell response

59. Which of the following organisms is capable of undergoing asexual reproduction?

a. Ferns
b. Yeast
c. Flowering plants
d. Trees

60. Which organ system is most responsible for maintaining control of body temperature?

a. The skeletal system
b. The circulatory system
c. The immune system
d. The muscular system

61. When animals eat, insulin is released from the pancreas, stimulating glucose uptake by the liver. When glucose levels drop, the pancreas reduces insulin release. This is an example of which mechanism for maintaining homeostasis?

a. Negative feedback
b. Positive feedback
c. Stress response
d. Parasympathetic regulation

62. On the ocean floor, volcanoes can erupt, causing what are known as thermal vents. Temperatures can be very high near these vents. Which of the following types of organisms would most likely live near them?

a. Protists
b. Eukaryotes
c. Prokaryotes
d. Metazoans

63. Orchids grow on the trunks or branches of trees. They receive more light than they would on the forest floor and absorb nutrients that run down tree trunks or along branches. This ecological relationship is best described as

a. Mutualism
b. Competition
c. Parasitism
d. Commensalism

64. An ecosystem consists of

a. The abiotic environment
b. A collection of populations
c. A community of organisms and the physical environment
d. Many populations of a species interacting with one another

65. A biome contains
  a. Populations that are independent of each other
  b. Species with shared evolutionary histories
  c. At least one biosphere
  d. Independently evolving species

66. The size of a population is constrained by
  a. The carrying capacity of its habitat
  b. The size of the organism
  c. The neighboring communities
  d. The biome in which it is located

67. Which type of rock is formed by high temperatures and great pressures?
  a. Sedimentary rock
  b. Igneous rock
  c. Composite rock
  d. Metamorphic rock

68. The best-preserved animal remains are found in
  a. Tar
  b. Rock
  c. Water
  d. Solidified magma

69. A lesson on fossils incorporating a lab during which rocks are classified would most benefit
  a. Auditory learners
  b. Visual learners
  c. Kinesthetic learners
  d. Slow learners

70. Which of the following is a true statement about a caldera?
  a. It is formed when a massive explosion destroys the cone of a volcano.
  b. It is created when the rock above a fault plane moves up relative to the rock below.
  c. It is a class of volcano characterized by quiet eruptions.
  d. It is formed by cooling lava.

71. Which of the following is *not* part of the carbon cycle?
  a. Respiration
  b. Sedimentation
  c. Transpiration
  d. Decomposition

72. Nitrogen becomes available to organisms solely as a result of
  a. Photosynthesis
  b. Leaching from rocks
  c. Decomposition
  d. Nitrogen-fixing bacteria

73. Continental plates sliding sideways past each other often result in
   a. Seafloor spreading
   b. Earthquakes
   c. Rifting
   d. Subduction

74. The point at which water vapor in the air begins to condense is called the
   a. Relative humidity
   b. Barometric pressure
   c. Dew point
   d. Gulf stream

75. Given the half-life of the following radioactive isotopes, which would be most useful for dating fossils?
   a. P32 – 14.2 days
   b. H3 – 4500 days
   c. C14 – 5740 years
   d. U235 – 700 million years

76. The British Isles on the east side of the Atlantic Ocean are often warmer than the coastal parts of Canada at the same latitude. This is because ocean currents warm the atmosphere of the British Isles. This kind of heat transfer is called
   a. Radiation
   b. Convection
   c. Thermoregulation
   d. Transduction

77. Which of the following does *not* contribute to the creation of ocean currents?
   a. Wind
   b. The moon's gravitational pull
   c. Ice cap and glacial melting
   d. The sun's heat

78. The percentage of the earth's water that is saline most closely matches which figure?
   a. 98%
   b. 70%
   c. 30%
   d. 2%

79. Which of the following properties of a meteorite moving through the planet's atmosphere would change as it approached the surface of the earth?
   a. Its mass
   b. Its volume
   c. Its density
   d. Its weight

80. The factor most responsible for determining which season an area is experiencing is
  a. Elevation
  b. The position of the earth in its orbit around the sun
  c. Latitude
  d. Air masses

81. The primary chemical process in the sun that creates light is
  a. The fission of helium into hydrogen
  b. The fission of lithium into helium and hydrogen
  c. The fusion of hydrogen into helium
  d. The fusion of helium into beryllium

82. What is the main type of chemical reaction in the sun?
  a. Nuclear fusion
  b. Nuclear fission
  c. Nucleation
  d. Hydrogenation

83. When a star burns itself out, it can collapse to such a degree that light becomes trapped by its intense gravitational field. Such an instance creates
  a. A quasar
  b. A pulsar
  c. Dark matter
  d. A black hole

84. Which of the following is the best definition of a comet?
  a. A mass of gases that produces massive amounts of energy through nuclear fusion
  b. A mass of frozen gases, cosmic dust, and rocky particles
  c. Particles of rock that pass through the earth's atmosphere
  d. A massive satellite that orbits a planet

85. Which of the following is an example of a renewable resource?
  a. Trees
  b. Ore minerals
  c. Fossil fuels
  d. Cash crops

86. A student's science fair project involves studying the effects of fertilizer on grass height. After four weeks of measuring height weekly, the student was not able to tell any difference between two pots of grass he had fertilized and watered weekly. How could this experiment be improved?
  a. Measure height more frequently
  b. Only water one of the pots
  c. Use a more accurate method of measurement
  d. Only fertilize one of the pots

87. Which of the following would be most useful in providing a summative assessment?
a. Student lab reports
b. Quizzes and essays
c. Standardized entrance exams
d. Anecdotal records

88. Individual testing is appropriate when
a. Students are being tested on qualitative rather than quantitative subjects.
b. A student has linguistic barriers.
c. Time and resources are limited.
d. The student needs a re-test.

89. All of the following teacher behaviors are motivating to students except
a. Modeling positive expectations and attributes
b. Having a supply of incentives, such as rewards
c. Placing students in one-on-one competition in front of their peers
d. Goal setting, combined with self-appraisal and reinforcement

90. Which of the following was *not* a significant factor in the dramatic increase of the human population over the past few hundred years?
a. Increased availability of habitable land
b. Scientific advances in agriculture
c. Improved sanitation
d. An understanding of the causes of communicable diseases

Constructed Response

1. Several students tested a group of different soils in order to compare how much water they each can hold. First, they capped the end of a funnel with a cloth filter and placed the soil (sand, clay, garden soil, etc.) into the funnel. They placed the funnel inside a larger vessel and poured water into the funnel. They then measured how much water dripped through the funnel into the larger vessel. They repeated this exercise for all soil types.

Please describe two improvements you could make to their procedure. Please detail how each change you make would make the data and conclusion more reliable.

2. In a science class, the teacher mixed two unknown (to the students) substances together and the students observed the outcome. The students concluded that a chemical reaction had taken place. Describe how the students were able to determine that a chemical reaction had occurred. In your answer please include evidence that would support the students' conclusion.

3. A young woman plays tennis several times per week. Lately she has noticed that the tennis ball appears to bounce higher on some courts and not as high on other courts. She is curious if this is caused by the surface of the court. Design an experiment that will test if her hypothesis is correct. Your response should include the following:

- The hypothesis
- The factor that will be varied
- Two factors that should be held constant
- A description of the procedures

Answers and Explanations

1. C: By repeating the experiment, the researcher could determine whether the instance of the bacteria swimming away from the chemical was simply due to chance. Observing the same results would allow the researcher to make conclusions with more certainty, and statistical analysis would help determine the significance of the data. Researchers must report all data (A), and reaching a conclusion is a vital part of any experiment (B). Adding a new chemical would completely change the experiment, so it would not be helpful (D).

2. C: When there is a correlation, it means that variables are related. A change in one is associated with a change in the other. In this case, the variables are stomach ulcers and coffee consumption (no coffee consumption is associated with fewer stomach ulcers, and vice versa). A controlled experiment would involve controlling the exact amount of coffee consumption (A), and there is not enough data to conclude that coffee causes ulcers (B) There is nothing to suggest biases in measurement (systematic error) making (D) incorrect.

3. A: Since the molar mass of sucrose is 342 grams, one mole weighs 342 grams. This is greater than 100 grams (B). In one liter of a 0.1 M solution (C) there are 34.2 grams of sucrose. (1 ~~liter~~ × 0.1 moles/~~liter~~ = 0.1 moles; 0.1 ~~moles~~ × 342 grams/~~mole~~ = 34.2 grams) In 100 ml (0.1 liters) of a 1 M solution (D) , there are 34.2 grams of sucrose. (0.1 ~~liter~~ × 1 moles/~~liter~~ = 0.1 moles; 0.1 ~~moles~~ × 342 grams/~~mole~~ = 34.2 grams)

4. A: Creating a chart from collected data is a way to present information visually. Bar graphs, pie charts, histograms, organizational charts, and flow charts are all considered visual representations of data. Simply charting data does not involve making any conclusions (B). The raw data is what is being used to construct the chart. It doesn't need to be charted to be raw data, making (C). incorrect. Charting this data does not involve analyzing it or comparing it to anything else, making (D) incorrect.

5. B: Evidence used to make a scientific conclusion must be reproducible, meaning the same results would occur time and again if an experiment was repeated. The boiling point of water, for instance, always remains the same, regardless of where, when, or how many times it is measured. Evidence used to make scientific conclusions can be quantitative or qualitative, making (A) incorrect, and evidence doesn't have to be obvious to be valid, making (C) an incorrect choice. Since (A) and (C) are incorrect, (D) is also incorrect.

6. D: Organizing information first tells students what they will be learning and establishes how it will be covered. Then, methods are used to help students understand the topics presented. Finally, the instructor must help students remember the information by reinforcing it through practice, examples, activities, etc. Information cannot really be understood before it is organized (A), and emphasizing information is not effective if students don't understand it first or it is not taught at all (B) and (C).

7. B: Benzene, an organic compound, is classified as a carcinogen by the U.S. Department of Health and Human Services. The chemical has been linked to kidney cancer, leukemia, and other health problems. For that reason, benzene is not allowed in school laboratories. Lead (A) can harm individuals, particularly children, if ingested, but is not considered a carcinogen. Aspartame (C) is

an artificial sweetener found in many foods and beverages. Methanol (D), or methyl alcohol, can be fatal if ingested, but is not considered a potential carcinogen.

8. D: Centrifugation is a technique used in laboratories and by industries to separate mixtures, including blood. The force exerted during rotation or spinning (centrifugal force) causes mixtures to separate according to their densities. In the case of blood, the denser red blood cells will settle on the bottom of the tube, while the less dense serum will remain on top. Spectroscopy (A) involves studying matter by analyzing emissions, while sublimation (B) is a change in a state of matter. Microscopy (C) involves the use of microscopes.

9. C: 100 grams represents the largest quantity. To solve a problem like this, it is often helpful to convert all answer choices to one quantity. 10 decigrams (A) is equal to 1 gram (10 ~~decigrams~~ × 0.1 grams/~~decigram~~ = 1 gram). 100 milligrams (B) is equal to 0.1 grams (100 ~~milligrams~~ × 0.001grams/~~milligram~~ = 0.1 grams). 1 decagram (D) is equal to 10 grams (1 ~~decagram~~ × 10 grams/~~decagram~~ = 10 grams). All of these quantities are smaller than (C), 100 grams.

10. C: Many biological specimens are not visible because the cells are fairly transparent. Staining the specimen will color the cells so they can be viewed and studied more easily. Finding a picture in a book (A) is not a suitable solution since the purpose is to view the actual specimen. A more powerful magnification (B) wouldn't solve the problem since it wouldn't make the transparent specimen any more visible. Placing the specimen on a dark background (D) would not help since it would still be transparent.

11. D: The binomial system of nomenclature was developed by Carl Von Linnaeus in the mid 18th-century. This system named organisms according to their genus name and their species name. Humans, for instance, are known as *Homo sapiens*. Pasteur (A), Darwin (B), and Mendel (C), made important discoveries regarding disease, evolution, and genetics, respectively. None of these men were even born until the 19th century, making Linnaeus's contributions to science the first.

12. A: Pure water will always freeze at the same temperature: 0° Celsius, or 32° Fahrenheit. The temperature at which iron ore will melt (B) varies depending on the types of impurities that are present in the substance. The human population size (C) has been changing ever since humans first inhabited the earth. The time the sun rises (D) varies according to the time of year and the location of the observer.

13. C: 20 g/L. One way to measure the density of an irregularly shaped object is to submerge it in water and measure the displacement. This is done by taking the mass (40 grams), then finding the volume by measuring how much water it displaces. Fill a graduated cylinder with water and record the amount. Put the object in the water and record the water level. Subtract the difference in water levels to get the amount of water displaced, which is also the volume of the object. In this case, 4.5 liters minus 2.5 liters equals 2 liters. Divide mass by volume (40 grams divided by 2 liters) to get 20 g/L (grams per liter).

14. D: Temperature. The amount of potential energy an object has depends on mass, height above ground and gravitational attraction, but not temperature. The formula for potential energy is PE = mgh, or potential energy equals mass times gravity times height. Answers (A), (B), and (C) are all valid answers as they are all contained in the formula for potential energy. Potential energy is the amount of energy stored in a system particularly because of its position.

15. A: It takes half the amount of energy to increase the temperature of a 1 kg sample of ice by 1°C than a 1 kg sample of water. Heat capacity refers to the amount of heat or thermal energy required to raise the temperature of a specific substance a given unit. A substance with a higher heat capacity requires more heat to raise its temperature than a substance with a lower heat capacity. The comparison here is that the specific heat capacity of ice is half as much as that of liquid water, so it takes half the amount of energy to increase the same amount of ice one temperature unit than it would if it were liquid water.

16. D: Its temperature remains the same due to the latent heat of fusion. The temperature of a substance during the time of any phase change remains the same. In this case, the phase change was from liquid to solid, or freezing. Latent heat of fusion, in this case, is energy that is released from the substance as it reforms its solid form. This energy will be released and the liquid will turn to solid before the temperature of the substance will decrease further. If the substance were changing from solid to liquid, the heat of fusion would be the amount of heat required to break apart the attractions between the molecules in the solid form to change to the liquid form. The latent heat of fusion is exactly the same quantity of energy for a substance for either melting or freezing. Depending on the process, this amount of heat would either be absorbed by the substance (melting) or released (freezing).

17. B: Conduction. A long nail or other type of metal, substance or matter that is heated at one end and then the other end becomes equally hot is an example of conduction. Conduction is energy transfer by neighboring molecules from an area of hotter temperature to cooler temperature. Radiation (A), or thermal radiation, refers to heat being transferred through empty space by electromagnetic radiation. An example is sunlight heating the earth. Convection (C) refers to heat being transferred by molecules moving from one location in the substance to another creating a heat current, usually in a gas or a liquid. Entropy (D) relates to the second law of thermodynamics and refers to how much heat or energy is no longer available to do work in a system. It can also be stated as the amount of disorder in a system.

18. C: Heat transfer can never occur from a cooler object to a warmer object. While the second law of thermodynamics implies that heat never spontaneously transfers from a cooler object to a warmer object, it is possible for heat to be transferred to a warmer object, given the proper input of work to the system. This is the principle by which a refrigerator operates. Work is done to the system to transfer heat from the objects inside the refrigerator to the air surrounding the refrigerator. All other answer choices are true.

19. B: Heat. The measure of energy within a system is called heat. Temperature (A) is a measurement of the average kinetic energy of molecules in a substance. A higher temperature means greater kinetic energy or faster moving molecules. Entropy (C) is the amount of energy that is no longer available for work, related to the second law of thermodynamics. Thermodynamics (D) is the study of the conversion of energy into heat and work in a system.

20. D: It has a different number of neutrons than its element. An isotope is a variation of an element that has a different number of neutrons. The element and its various isotopes continue to have the same numbers of protons and electrons. For example, carbon has three naturally occurring isotopes, carbon-12, carbon-13 and carbon-14, which is radioactive. Isotopes of an element differ in mass number, which is the number of protons and neutrons added together, but have the same atomic number, or number of protons.

21. D: It is a stable atom. If an atom's outer shell is filled, it is a stable atom. The outer shell refers to one of many energy levels, or shells, that electrons occupy around a nucleus. An atom whose outer shell is not filled wants to become stable by filling the outer shell. It fills its outer shell by forming bonds. The atom can do this by gaining electrons or losing electrons in ionic compounds, or if the atom is a part of a molecule, by sharing electrons. If an atom has a full outer shell, such as the noble gases, it does not readily react with other atoms and does not exchange electrons to form bonds. These atoms are known as inert. Therefore, neither (A) nor (B) can be true. It has 32 electrons in its outer shell (C) is not necessarily true because not all elements have the fourth shell that can hold 32 electrons. Some have fewer shells that hold fewer electrons.

22. A: Fission. Fission is a nuclear process where atomic nuclei split apart to form smaller nuclei. Nuclear fission can release large amounts of energy, emit gamma rays and form daughter products. It is used in nuclear power plants and bombs. Fusion (B) refers to a nuclear process whereby atomic nuclei join to form a heavier nucleus, such as with stars. This can release or absorb energy depending upon the original elements. Decay (C) refers to an atomic nucleus spontaneously losing energy and emitting ionizing particles and radiation. Ionization (D) refers to a process by which atoms obtain a positive or negative charge because the number of electrons does not equal that of protons.

23. B: Isotopes are different configurations of the same element, and are distinguished by the number of neutrons they contain. Oxygen-16, oxygen-17, and oxygen-18 isotopes, for example, have 8 protons each and 8, 9, and 10 neutrons, respectively. The number of protons (A) and electrons (C) does not vary in an element's isotopes. Leptons (D) are the elementary particles that make up matter (electrons, neutrinos, muons, and taus). Their numbers don't vary among different isotopes.

24. C: The electrons that are present in an atom's outermost electron shell are gained or lost during a reaction. Consider the reaction between sodium and chlorine as an example. Sodium has one valence electron; chlorine has seven. When they react, sodium gives up an electron and chorine gains one. Both outermost electron shells are full. Protons (A) and neutrons (B) are in an atom's nucleus, and therefore are not exchanged during a chemical reaction. Isotopes (D) are different configurations of an atom.

25. C: A mathematical model is a depiction of a device or process that involves a number of variables. It often involves developing equations to describe a process or system. In this instance, the person developing the model is trying to determine the relationship between two variables (force and the length of the spring), and an equation could likely be developed to illustrate this relationship. The other choices involve determining position and rate. These are simple measurements, and would not require models or equations.

26. A: Newton's first law (commonly known as the law of inertia) states that an object in motion tends to stay in motion and an object at rest tends to stay at rest unless a force is applied. Inertia (B) isn't what is being applied to the object, but the name of the concept. Gravity (C) is a force that can cause an object to start or stop moving, but it is only one of many. Acceleration (D) is a measure of an object's increase in velocity.

27. A: Velocity measures not only the speed of an object, but also its displacement. Since the starting point and ending point of the car are the same, the displacement is zero. Therefore, the velocity is also zero. Answers (B) and (C) are incorrect since they don't accurately represent the displacement of the vehicle. Additionally, since 50 miles/hour (D) was the top speed of the car, it couldn't represent the average velocity.

28. B: This is related to Newton's second law of motion, expressed as $F = m \times a$. To determine whether the statement is true, let the value of a be 2. Let the mass of the first block be 1 ($F = 2$). The mass of the second block is 2. Therefore, $F = 2 \times 2$; $F = 4$. It would take twice as much force, not three times as much. (A) and (C) are examples of the law of inertia. (D) is an example of Newton's third law.

29. D: The equation used to calculate an object's potential energy is $E = m \times g \times z$. In this equation, m represents the object's mass (A), g represents the acceleration of gravity (B), and z represents the height of the object (C). The temperature of the object does not play a role in the amount of potential energy it contains, making (D) the correct answer choice.

30. A: Joules is the unit used to measure thermal, electrical, and mechanical energy, and is defined as the amount of work required to move an object 1 meter using a force of 1 Newton (1 Joule = 1 N× m). Volts (B) is used to measure voltage, ohms (C) is used to measure resistance, and amperes (D) is used to measure current. All of the choices except (A) are units related to electricity.

31. A: Heat that is removed from the air is emitted by the fridge, usually at the back. Since the process is not 100% efficient and requires electrical energy, the fridge will emit slightly more heat than it removes. The temperature will not decrease (B) since heat removed from the air is being emitted, and the temperature would only remain the same (C) if the fridge was 100% efficient. The size of the room (D) does not matter since the question is asking what would eventually happen.

32. C: The leaves on a tree appear to be green because that is the color of the light that is being reflected. All other colors are absorbed (A) and are not perceived by the human eye. Refraction (B) is when light bends slightly, usually when it enters one medium from another. Diffraction (D) is when light bends around obstacles or spreads out after it passes through a small opening.

33. B: Sound can be defined as the vibration of particles, whether those particles are present in a gas, liquid, or solid. The fact that sound requires particles is illustrated by the fact that sound cannot travel through a vacuum. Radio waves (A), microwaves (C), and X-rays (D) are all types of electromagnetic rays. They can travel in vacuums, and do not require particles to propagate.

34. C: Nonmetal ions are negatively charged, while metal ions are positively charged. Because of these opposite charges, they readily bond and react. The metal iron, for instance, reacts readily with the nonmetal oxygen to form rust. As a general rule, nonmetals are considered nonconductors (A). Nonmetals, including oxygen, can form isotopes (B). Nonmetals typically have low densities, are not hard, and have low melting points (D).

35. B: The vertical rows on the period table are known as groups. All elements in the same group will have similar electron shell configurations, which plays a key role in chemical reactivity. The horizontal rows (A) and (C) of the periodic table are known as periods. Although elements in a period may have similar atomic weights and numbers, their chemical reactivity may be quite different. Since (B) is correct, (D). is incorrect.

36. A: Dissolving a seltzer tablet in water is an example of a chemical change since a new substance is produced. In this case, carbon dioxide is produced as a result of the reaction. Grinding pepper (B) and freezing water (C) merely changes the form of these substances, not their composition. Churning butter (D) is a physical change. The globules of milk fat are broken apart so they can

clump together and form butter. Although butter looks different than cream, they are composed of the same substances.

37. B: Chemical reactions are non-reversible. In addition, the byproducts or substances that are created are not the same as the original substances. When ethanol is burned, it reacts with the surrounding oxygen to produce carbon dioxide and water, two totally different substances. Evaporation (A) is a physical change since it can be reversed. Dissolving salt in water (C) is also reversible, and nothing new is created. Freezing water (D) is also an example of a physical change. Only the water's state of matter has changed.

38. C: The most basic units of matter are protons, electrons, and neutrons. Protons are found in the nucleus, and have a positive charge. They are one of the three components of a helium atom (A). When atoms have positive or negative charges, they are known as ions (B). Molecules of oxygen, water, etc. (D). are even more complex, consisting of one or more atoms held together by bonds.

39. B: Heating a liquid is most likely to change its density, a measure of mass per unit of volume. Water, for instance, has a density of $1 g/cm^3$ at 4°C. As it is heated and molecules become more spread apart, the density decreases. In general, liquids do not have a crystal structure (A). A liquid's mass, or the amount of matter it contains (C), will not change according to temperature, nor will its electrical conductivity (D).

40. D: By measuring the mass of the wood before and after burning and then calculating the difference between the two masses, the amount of matter lost during burning can be determined. Since different types of gases with different molecular weights are released, calculating the total number of molecules would not allow the mass to be calculated (A). The gases emitted combine with oxygen in the air, making (B) an unsuitable approach. The weight of the ash alone (C) wouldn't be helpful without knowing the original mass.

41. B: Acetic acid is a weak organic acid with a chemical formula of CH_3COOH. It is characterized by its sour taste and strong smell. Vinegar is a diluted form of acetic acid. Cream of tartar (A) is a type of acid salt used in cooking. Its chemical formula is $KC_4H_5O_6$, and it does not contain acetic acid. Baking powder (C) is a mixture of a salt and an acid, but it does not contain acetic acid. Water (D) is neutral and its formula is H_2O.

42. A: The nucleolus is located in the nucleus of the cell, and is responsible for the transcription and assembly of r-RNA. Roughly spherical in shape, this organelle is not surrounded by any type of membrane. Chromoplasts (B)., mitochondria (C), and endoplasmic reticulum (D) can all be classified as membrane bound organelles. They are responsible for storing and synthesizing pigments, energy production, and the transportation of proteins, respectively.

43. B: When there is a wound, platelets travel to the injury site and gather there to block the flow of blood from the body. The platelets have a sticky surface and react with the air to form a scab. Plasma (A) is the liquid part of the blood in which cells are suspended. Erythrocytes (C), or red blood cells, transport oxygen throughout the body. Leukocytes (D) or white blood cells, help the body defend against infectious disease.

44. C: Polymers consist of repeating units that are joined together by covalent bonds. Cellulose (A) is a type of carbohydrate polymer consisting of hundreds of even thousands of glucose units. DNA (B) consists of two polymer strands composed of nucleotides. Proteins (D) are polymers composed

of amino acids. Phospholipids are part of cell membranes, and consist of a hydrophilic head and a hydrophobic tail. These lipids do not form polymers.

45. B: Cells are the basic units of life, and all organisms have them. Some organisms like bacteria have just a single cell, while complex organisms like humans have hundreds of trillions. Prokaryotes do not have organelles (A). Not all organisms have tissues (C), groups of cells that make up connective tissue, muscle tissue, etc. Finally, only some types of cells, including plant cells, have cell walls (D).

46. D. Endorphins are a special group of neurotransmitters. When an injury occurs, endorphins are released, and are capable of reducing the severity of pain. They are also released during intense exercise and periods of intense relaxation. Acetylcholine (A), also a neurotransmitter, activates muscles and plays a role in attention and sensory perception. Oxytocin (B) plays a crucial role in female reproduction. Luteinizing hormone (C) plays an important role in female ovulation and testosterone production in males.

47. B: Since all of the offspring are purple, the purple allele must be dominant, and the purple plant must be homozygous. The Punnett square would look like this (R is purple, r is white):

	R	R
r	Rr	Rr
r	Rr	Rr

If purple was recessive (A) to white (white was dominant), at least some of the plants would be white. If the alleles were codominant (C), the flowers would be light purple or contain both colors. Since (B) is correct, (D) is incorrect.

48. D. Sex-linked traits are associated with the X chromosome. Since it is recessive, the mother must have two copies of the recessive gene (X^cX^c). The father is not colorblind, and since only the X chromosome carries the allele, his genotype is X^CY. All daughters will have the genotype X^cX^C. Since colorblindness (C) is recessive, none of the daughters will be colorblind, although they will all carry the allele for color blindness.

49. A: Cloning genes involves making copies of DNA fragments. To do this successfully, researchers much have cDNA, also known as complementary DNA. It is copied from messenger RNA, and includes all of the DNA in a gene, molecule, cell, or organism. In genetics, expression profiling (B) involves measuring the activity of thousands of genes simultaneously. All DNA is transcribed in the same manner (C) and phenotypes (D) are physical traits associated with genes.

50. B: Inductive reasoning involves using direct observations to make a general conclusion. In this case, students concluded that since the flowers they observed had one or two reproductive structures, all flowers must have at least one. Deductive reasoning (A) involves using general information to make a conclusion about something more specific. Indirect instruction (C) is a method used by teachers, while causal reasoning (D) attempts to explain the cause of a particular event or phenomenon.

51. C: Rhinoceros horns and human hair are both made of compressed fibers of keratin. They are homologous characteristics, meaning they are inherited from a common ancestor, even though they may serve various functions in different species. Ancestral characteristics (A) are unmodified characteristics found in common ancestors, not the species that developed from them. Detrimental

characteristics (B) are those that interfere with normal functioning or threaten an organism's survival. Analogous characteristics (D) are not evolutionarily related, but serve similar functions in different species.

52. A: According to natural selection, organisms with traits that are well suited to their environments are the ones that survive. In this instance, gray moths were able to blend in with soot-covered trees better than white moths. Therefore, the gray moths survived and reproduced. Genetic drift (B) refers to the random changes in gene frequencies over time. Sexual selection (C) refers to the fact that organisms compete for or choose mates. Punctuated equilibrium (D) states that evolution occurs quickly after long periods of little change.

53. C: Finches with beaks well-suited for the types of food available on an island had an evolutionary advantage. As a result, these finches survived and reproduced, a phenomenon known as natural selection. The finches share a common ancestor, regardless of the island on which they now live (A). Genetic drift refers to genetic changes that occur due to random chance; this would not account for different beaks on different islands (B). Introduction by humans would not account for different beaks (D), since phenotypes change over time.

54. D: Population size is not relevant when determining an organism's evolutionary history. Population sizes vary over time according to many factors, so no real conclusions can be drawn from this information. Fossil record placement (A) can help determine when species developed and how they are related to other organisms. Studying an organism's anatomy (B) is useful because ancestors can be identified by looking at physical characteristics like bone structure and appendages. Studying distribution among continents (D) can help determine where an organism originated.

55. B: A primary consumer is an organism that feeds on plants. Herbivores (plant eaters) like mice are considered primary consumers. Primary producers (A) are at the bottom of the food chain, and include plants. They are a food source for primary consumers. A secondary consumer (C) relies on primary consumers for food. If a fox ate the mouse, the fox would be a secondary consumer. Decomposers (D) rely on dead organisms for food, and include bacteria and fungi.

56. A: The term population is used to refer to a collection of a single species. In this case, the bacteria in the middle ear would be classified as a population. For a community (B) to be formed, there would have to be more than one type of species present. An ecosystem (C) would require a community of organisms living in a natural environment on land or in the water. All of the bacteria would not form individuals (D). Instead, the individuals form a population.

57. C: Photosynthesis can be represented by the following equation: $6CO_2 + 6H_2O \rightarrow C_6H_{12}O_6 + 6O_2$. A reduction reaction transforms CO_2 into glucose ($C_6H_{12}O_6$), a type of carbohydrate. An oxidation reaction (A) is what transforms the water into oxygen. Chemiosmosis (B) describes the movement of ions across cell membranes, and hydrolysis (D) is a type of reaction in which water is separated into hydrogen and hydroxide ions.

58. C: In this example, the stimulus is the touching of the leaves. The response is the plant's rapid crumpling of its leaves. If the stimulus is absent, the response does not occur. Innate behaviors (A) are ones an animal is born with. They are not learned. The term is not used in relation to plants. Learned behaviors (B) are acquired through observation, practice, and instruction. Plants are not capable of learning. A single cell response (D) involves just one cell; a plant's leaves consist of many.

59. B: Asexual reproduction means that offspring are produced by a single parent. Yeast cells reproduce asexually through budding. The genetic material of the cell is copied, and a small bud forms on the outside of the yeast cell. It grows and eventually breaks away, forming a new yeast cell. Most organisms, including ferns (A), flowering plants (C), and trees (D) require two parents to produce seeds, spores, etc. In other words, they are not capable of asexual reproduction.

60. B: The circulatory system carries blood throughout the body, and plays an important role in controlling body temperature. Capillaries below the skin contract or expand to release or contain body heat. Heat is also transported from hotter parts to colder parts to ensure an even body temperature. The skeletal system (A) protects organs and provides the body with its structure and shape. The immune system (C) helps fight off illnesses and infections. The muscular system (D) is what allows the body to move.

61. A: Maintaining homeostasis means that conditions are kept stable and relatively constant. Negative feedback is a mechanism used to reverse or minimize changes in a system. In this example, negative feedback is used to keep the body's glucose and insulin levels stable. Positive feedback (B) is a mechanism that increases changes in a system. A stress response (C) describes the body's reaction to threats or pressures. Parasympathetic regulation (D) refers to activities of the nervous system, including slowing the heart rate and boosting intestinal activity.

62. C: Organisms that thrive in environments where other living things could not survive – such as around hot thermal vents found under the sea – are often known as extremophiles. These organisms are typically microorganisms like bacteria, which are prokaryotes. Protists (A) are classified as eukaryotes (B), which are not typically found in extreme environments. Metazoans (D) are multi-cellular, eukaryotic organisms. Like all eukaryotes, metazoans do not thrive near thermal vents or in other extreme environments.

63. D: Commensalism describes a relationship in which one organism benefits while the other is not affected. In this instance, the orchid benefits from the extra sunlight and nutrients, but the tree is neither helped nor harmed. Mutualism (A) describes a relationship in which both organisms benefit. The organisms are not in competition (B), since the leaves of the trees receive sunlight and the roots collect nutrients from the soil. In a parasitic relationship (C), one organism is harmed.

64. C: An ecosystem is an environment that includes both the physical environment and the plants, animals, and other organisms that reside within it. By definition, an ecosystem consists of both the abiotic (A) and biotic environment. An ecosystem does not need to contain a collection of population (B); it could consist of an environment with only one population. Ecosystems can (and often do) contain more than a single species (D).

65. B: Biome is a term often used interchangeably with ecosystem. It is a community of plants and animals. Some types of biomes are oceans, deserts, and forests. Organisms in a biome will be evolutionarily related since they thrive in the same environment. Biome populations are interconnected, and species depend on each other for survival (A). The biosphere is defined as all of the earth's ecosystems (C). Species in a biome are interdependent; they don't evolve independently (D).

66. A: Carrying capacity is defined as the size of a population an environment can support indefinitely. Food, water, and suitable habitat are all needed. Once any of these resources is exhausted, a population can no longer increase. An organism's size (B) does not determine the size of the population. In suitable conditions, numbers of organisms (regardless of size) will increase.

Neighboring communities (C) are not important; only the organism's environment is. The type of biome (D) doesn't matter if conditions are suitable for a species.

67. D: Metamorphic rock is found deep beneath the surface of the earth, and is an important component of the earth's crust. This type of rock is formed at temperatures of up to 200°C. The formation also requires great amounts of pressure, which is often exerted by layers above the metamorphic rock. Sedimentary rock (A) is formed by particles that settle on land or in water. Igneous rock (B) is cooled, solidified magma, and the term composite (C) does not describe a type of rock.

68. A: Tar can preserve the teeth and bones of animals, as well as the outer bodies of insects. The preserved bones of many animals have been found in numerous tar pits, including the famous La Brea tar pit in California. Fossils that form on rock (B) are simply impressions left by plants and animals. They are not actual remains. Animal remains would not be preserved in water (C), and magma (D) would completely destroy animal remains before it solidified.

69. C: Kinesthetic learners benefit most from hands-on activities during which they can touch and manipulate objects. Therefore, an activity in the lab would be quite beneficial. Auditory learners learn best by listening to information (A), while visual learners (B) benefit when information is presented in the form of pictures, graphs, and other visual representations. Slow learners (D) perform at a lower than average level. There is nothing about the lab activity that would benefit this group in particular.

70. A: During volcanic eruptions, magma is expelled. As a result, the emptied area is not able to support the rock above it. It collapses, creating a crater-like formation known as a caldera. Calderas are created when rocks move down, not up (B) A caldera is not a class of volcano (C); it is a volcanic feature that occasionally forms after eruptions. It is not the cooling of lava (D) that accounts for calderas, but rather the expulsion of magma.

71. C: The carbon cycle is defined as the movement of the earth's carbon through organisms, oceans, air, rocks, and soil. Animals breathe out carbon dioxide during respiration (A), which deposits carbon into the air. Carbon from the atmosphere is dissolved in sea water, and can settle on the ocean floor. This collected matter is known as sedimentation (B). When organisms die, the carbon in their bodies is returned to the soil through decomposition (D). Transpiration, the process by which plants lose water, does not transport carbon.

72. D: Nitrogen is abundant in the earth's atmosphere, but is not in a form that organisms can use. Nitrogen fixing refers to the conversion of nitrogen in the atmosphere to ammonia. Organisms require this form of nitrogen to synthesize DNA and proteins, and only nitrogen-fixing bacteria are capable of carrying out this conversion. Photosynthesis (A) produces glucose and oxygen, and rocks do not leach (B) nitrogen that can be used. Nitrogen is essential to decomposition (C), but the process doesn't provide a usable source of the element.

73. B: Continental plates have irregular boundaries. When they move past each other, the edges can lock together. The rest of the plates still move somewhat, though, which creates stress and stored energy. When the plates do finally become unlocked, energy is released, creating an earthquake. Seafloor spreading (A) is the formation of new ocean crust via earthquakes. Rifting (C) is a split in the earth's surface caused by continental plates separating. Subduction (D) is when one continental plate moves under another.

74. C: Dew is condensed water from the air. The point at which vapor in the air transforms into liquid is known as the dew point. Relative humidity (A) is a measurement used to express the amount of water vapor in the air. Barometric pressure (B) is the amount of pressure exerted by the atmosphere as a result of its weight. The Gulf Stream (D) is an ocean current that warms the climate of some countries.

75. D: A half-life of a radioactive isotope is the length of time it takes for the amount of an isotope present to decline by half. Some animal fossils are hundreds of millions of years old. Therefore, a U235 isotope would be most useful since it has the greatest half-life. If one gram was present initially, half a gram would still be present after 700 million years. The half-lives of (A), (B), and (C). are too short to date very old fossils.

76. B: The water at the surface of the ocean will usually be slightly warmer than the air. It evaporates, enters the air, and then rises, making the atmosphere slightly warmer. Radiation (A) is the active emitting of energy from an object. Thermoregulation (C) is the ability of an organism to control its body temperature. Transduction (D) is the transfer of DNA among different bacteria by viruses.

77. C: Currents are basically the horizontal movement of water in the earth's oceans. Numerous forces act on the oceans to produce currents. Wind (A) blowing on the surface causes movement because it pushes the water. Water heated by the sun expands (D), which causes movement, and the moon is responsible for the ocean's tides and the resulting tidal currents. Ice cap and glacial melting (C) causes ocean levels to rise vertically, but does not influence the horizontal movement of ocean water.

78. A: The vast majority of the earth (approximately 70%) (B) is covered in water. Therefore, approximately 30% of the earth (C) is solid land. Of all the water on earth, only about 2% of that (D) is fresh water, and most of that is present in glaciers and the polar ice caps. Therefore 98% (100% - 2%) of the earth's water is the salt water (saline) found in the oceans.

79. D: An object's weight is actually a measure of the gravitational force acting on that object. In this case, as the meteorite moves towards earth's surface, the gravitational force on it would be greater. In other words, it would weigh more. The mass of the meteorite (A) refers to the amount of matter it contains, which remains the same regardless of its location. Volume (B) (the amount of space the meteorite occupies) and density (C) (mass per unit of volume) would also stay the same.

80. B: As the earth travels around the sun, it tilts towards the sun or away from it, depending on where it is in its orbit. This tilt is what determines the seasons. The earth is tilted towards the sun in summer and away from it in winter. Elevation (A) and latitude (C) of an area remain constant throughout the year, so they cannot account for the changing of the seasons. Air masses (D) can influence the weather, but don't determine the seasons.

81. C: The sun is mainly composed of hydrogen and helium. During nuclear fusion reactions, hydrogen is transformed into helium and energy that is released in the form of visible light. This reaction produces 85% of the sun's energy. Hydrogen is transformed into helium, not the other way around (A). Lithium produces helium only, and is not the primary process that creates sunlight (B). Helium does form beryllium and a gamma ray (D), but that is not how most of the sun's light is produced.

82. A: Most of the sun's energy is produced by a nuclear fusion reaction. During these reactions, hydrogen atoms react to produce helium and energy, which we perceive as visible light. Nuclear fission occurs when atoms are broken apart (B). Nucleation (C) is a process that occurs during the formation of crystals, and hydrogenation (D) is the reaction that results when H_2 is added to a solution.

83. D: When a star begins running out of fuel and its temperature decreases, it cannot resist its own gravity, and collapses in on itself. This is known as a black hole. Nothing, not even light, can escape from black holes. Quasars (A) are observed in the center of very young galaxies and emit energy. Pulsars (B), like black holes, are the remnants of stars. Unlike black holes, however, they emit light. Dark matter (C) is matter that is thought to exist, but is not readily detectable.

84. B: A comet is an irregularly-shaped solar system body that has a large nucleus and a tail that appears to trail behind. Comets are composed of rock, ice, cosmic dust, and frozen gases such as methane and carbon dioxide. (A) would be an accurate description of the sun. (C) is a description of a meteoroid. Massive satellites that orbit planets are also commonly known as moons (D).

85. D: A renewable resource is one that can be replaced at a rate that is similar to or equal to its rate of consumption by humans. Cash crops can be grown in a reasonable amount of time, and fields can be replenished with bananas, corn, coffee, etc. to meet demand. Trees (A) that are cut down take many years to grow back, and cannot really be considered a renewable resource. Ore minerals (B) and fossil fuels (C) would take thousands or millions of years to be replenished.

86. D: In order to investigate the effects of fertilizer on grass height, the student needs to have a control sample. He should only fertilize one pot so he can compare the differences in growth between the two. Measuring more frequently (A) and accurately (C) would still not allow him to make any conclusions since there is no control sample. The student is investigating the effect of fertilizer, not water (B), so both plants must be given equal amounts of water.

87. B: A summative assessment is conducted after a certain amount of learning takes place. These types of assessments are used to measure whether a student possesses the knowledge and skills taught during a unit or course. Periodic quizzes and essays are useful for conducting summative assessments. Lab reports (A) are formative assessments, which are completed during a course or specific unit. Entrance exams (C) and anecdotal records (D) would be completed before any learning took place.

88. B: Individual testing typically involves one-on-one interaction with the student. This would be a good approach for a student whose first language is not English, since questions could be read to the student and explained. Group testing is an equally appropriate approach to assess knowledge of qualitative and quantitative information (A). A teacher would need extra time and resources (C) to conduct individual testing, and a re-test (D) would typically be completed in the same way as the original.

89. C: Making students compete in front of others will likely be more harmful than helpful, particularly for students who are shy or struggling academically. Most students would not be motivated by this approach. Having positive expectations and modeling desirable attributes (A) , offering incentives for meeting certain goals (B) , and setting attainable goals for students (D) are all approaches that can motivate students at all grade levels.

90. A: A shortage of habitable land was never a factor that stopped the human population from increasing. Even today, North America has only about 32 people per square mile, so land availability has never been a huge problem. Advances in agriculture (B) allowed more food to be produced on the same amount of land. Better food availability was a factor in population growth, as was improved sanitation (C), which resulted in less sickness and disease. Understanding the causes of communicable diseases (D) resulted in fewer deaths.

Secret Key #1 - Time is Your Greatest Enemy

Pace Yourself

Wear a watch. At the beginning of the test, check the time (or start a chronometer on your watch to count the minutes), and check the time after every few questions to make sure you are "on schedule."

If you are forced to speed up, do it efficiently. Usually one or more answer choices can be eliminated without too much difficulty. Above all, don't panic. Don't speed up and just begin guessing at random choices. By pacing yourself, and continually monitoring your progress against your watch, you will always know exactly how far ahead or behind you are with your available time. If you find that you are one minute behind on the test, don't skip one question without spending any time on it, just to catch back up. Take 15 fewer seconds on the next four questions, and after four questions you'll have caught back up. Once you catch back up, you can continue working each problem at your normal pace.

Furthermore, don't dwell on the problems that you were rushed on. If a problem was taking up too much time and you made a hurried guess, it must be difficult. The difficult questions are the ones you are most likely to miss anyway, so it isn't a big loss. It is better to end with more time than you need than to run out of time.

Lastly, sometimes it is beneficial to slow down if you are constantly getting ahead of time. You are always more likely to catch a careless mistake by working more slowly than quickly, and among very high-scoring test takers (those who are likely to have lots of time left over), careless errors affect the score more than mastery of material.

Secret Key #2 - Guessing is not Guesswork

You probably know that guessing is a good idea - unlike other standardized tests, there is no penalty for getting a wrong answer. Even if you have no idea about a question, you still have a 20-25% chance of getting it right.

Most test takers do not understand the impact that proper guessing can have on their score. Unless you score extremely high, guessing will significantly contribute to your final score.

Monkeys Take the Test

What most test takers don't realize is that to insure that 20-25% chance, you have to guess randomly. If you put 20 monkeys in a room to take this test, assuming they answered once per question and behaved themselves, on average they would get 20-25% of the questions correct. Put 20 test takers in the room, and the average will be much lower among guessed questions. Why?

1. The test writers intentionally write deceptive answer choices that "look" right. A test taker has no idea about a question, so picks the "best looking" answer, which is often wrong. The

monkey has no idea what looks good and what doesn't, so will consistently be lucky about 20-25% of the time.

2. Test takers will eliminate answer choices from the guessing pool based on a hunch or intuition. Simple but correct answers often get excluded, leaving a 0% chance of being correct. The monkey has no clue, and often gets lucky with the best choice.

This is why the process of elimination endorsed by most test courses is flawed and detrimental to your performance- test takers don't guess, they make an ignorant stab in the dark that is usually worse than random.

$5 Challenge

Let me introduce one of the most valuable ideas of this course- the $5 challenge:

You only mark your "best guess" if you are willing to bet $5 on it.
You only eliminate choices from guessing if you are willing to bet $5 on it.

Why $5? Five dollars is an amount of money that is small yet not insignificant, and can really add up fast (20 questions could cost you $100). Likewise, each answer choice on one question of the test will have a small impact on your overall score, but it can really add up to a lot of points in the end.

The process of elimination IS valuable. The following shows your chance of guessing it right:

If you eliminate wrong answer choices until only this many remain:	Chance of getting it correct:
1	100%
2	50%
3	33%

However, if you accidentally eliminate the right answer or go on a hunch for an incorrect answer, your chances drop dramatically: to 0%. By guessing among all the answer choices, you are GUARANTEED to have a shot at the right answer.

That's why the $5 test is so valuable- if you give up the advantage and safety of a pure guess, it had better be worth the risk.

What we still haven't covered is how to be sure that whatever guess you make is truly random. Here's the easiest way:

Always pick the first answer choice among those remaining.

Such a technique means that you have decided, **before you see a single test question**, exactly how you are going to guess- and since the order of choices tells you nothing about which one is correct, this guessing technique is perfectly random.

This section is not meant to scare you away from making educated guesses or eliminating choices- you just need to define when a choice is worth eliminating. The $5 test, along with a pre-defined random guessing strategy, is the best way to make sure you reap all of the benefits of guessing.

Secret Key #3 - Practice Smarter, Not Harder

Many test takers delay the test preparation process because they dread the awful amounts of practice time they think necessary to succeed on the test. We have refined an effective method that will take you only a fraction of the time.

There are a number of "obstacles" in your way to succeed. Among these are answering questions, finishing in time, and mastering test-taking strategies. All must be executed on the day of the test at peak performance, or your score will suffer. The test is a mental marathon that has a large impact on your future.

Just like a marathon runner, it is important to work your way up to the full challenge. So first you just worry about questions, and then time, and finally strategy:

Success Strategy

1. Find a good source for practice tests.
2. If you are willing to make a larger time investment, consider using more than one study guide- often the different approaches of multiple authors will help you "get" difficult concepts.
3. Take a practice test with no time constraints, with all study helps "open book." Take your time with questions and focus on applying strategies.
4. Take a practice test with time constraints, with all guides "open book."
5. Take a final practice test with no open material and time limits

If you have time to take more practice tests, just repeat step 5. By gradually exposing yourself to the full rigors of the test environment, you will condition your mind to the stress of test day and maximize your success.

Secret Key #4 - Prepare, Don't Procrastinate

Let me state an obvious fact: if you take the test three times, you will get three different scores. This is due to the way you feel on test day, the level of preparedness you have, and, despite the test writers' claims to the contrary, some tests WILL be easier for you than others.

Since your future depends so much on your score, you should maximize your chances of success. In order to maximize the likelihood of success, you've got to prepare in advance. This means taking practice tests and spending time learning the information and test taking strategies you will need to succeed.

Never take the test as a "practice" test, expecting that you can just take it again if you need to. Feel free to take sample tests on your own, but when you go to take the official test, be prepared, be focused, and do your best the first time!

Secret Key #5 - Test Yourself

Everyone knows that time is money. There is no need to spend too much of your time or too little of your time preparing for the test. You should only spend as much of your precious time preparing as is necessary for you to get the score you need.

Once you have taken a practice test under real conditions of time constraints, then you will know if you are ready for the test or not.

If you have scored extremely high the first time that you take the practice test, then there is not much point in spending countless hours studying. You are already there.

Benchmark your abilities by retaking practice tests and seeing how much you have improved. Once you score high enough to guarantee success, then you are ready.

If you have scored well below where you need, then knuckle down and begin studying in earnest. Check your improvement regularly through the use of practice tests under real conditions. Above all, don't worry, panic, or give up. The key is perseverance!

Then, when you go to take the test, remain confident and remember how well you did on the practice tests. If you can score high enough on a practice test, then you can do the same on the real thing.

General Strategies

The most important thing you can do is to ignore your fears and jump into the test immediately- do not be overwhelmed by any strange-sounding terms. You have to jump into the test like jumping into a pool- all at once is the easiest way.

Make Predictions

As you read and understand the question, try to guess what the answer will be. Remember that several of the answer choices are wrong, and once you begin reading them, your mind will immediately become cluttered with answer choices designed to throw you off. Your mind is typically the most focused immediately after you have read the question and digested its contents. If you can, try to predict what the correct answer will be. You may be surprised at what you can predict.

Quickly scan the choices and see if your prediction is in the listed answer choices. If it is, then you can be quite confident that you have the right answer. It still won't hurt to check the other answer choices, but most of the time, you've got it!

Answer the Question

It may seem obvious to only pick answer choices that answer the question, but the test writers can create some excellent answer choices that are wrong. Don't pick an answer just because it sounds right, or you believe it to be true. It MUST answer the question. Once you've made your selection, always go back and check it against the question and make sure that you didn't misread the question, and the answer choice does answer the question posed.

Benchmark

After you read the first answer choice, decide if you think it sounds correct or not. If it doesn't, move on to the next answer choice. If it does, mentally mark that answer choice. This doesn't mean that you've definitely selected it as your answer choice, it just means that it's the best you've seen thus far. Go ahead and read the next choice. If the next choice is worse than the one you've already selected, keep going to the next answer choice. If the next choice is better than the choice you've already selected, mentally mark the new answer choice as your best guess.

The first answer choice that you select becomes your standard. Every other answer choice must be benchmarked against that standard. That choice is correct until proven otherwise by another answer choice beating it out. Once you've decided that no other answer choice seems as good, do one final check to ensure that your answer choice answers the question posed.

Valid Information

Don't discount any of the information provided in the question. Every piece of information may be necessary to determine the correct answer. None of the information in the question is there to throw you off (while the answer choices will certainly have information to throw you off). If two seemingly unrelated topics are discussed, don't ignore either. You can be confident there is a relationship, or it wouldn't be included in the question, and you are probably going to have to determine what is that relationship to find the answer.

Avoid "Fact Traps"

Don't get distracted by a choice that is factually true. Your search is for the answer that answers the question. Stay focused and don't fall for an answer that is true but incorrect. Always go back to the question and make sure you're choosing an answer that actually answers the question and is not just a true statement. An answer can be factually correct, but it MUST answer the question asked. Additionally, two answers can both be seemingly correct, so be sure to read all of the answer choices, and make sure that you get the one that BEST answers the question.

Milk the Question

Some of the questions may throw you completely off. They might deal with a subject you have not been exposed to, or one that you haven't reviewed in years. While your lack of knowledge about the subject will be a hindrance, the question itself can give you many clues that will help you find the correct answer. Read the question carefully and look for clues. Watch particularly for adjectives and nouns describing difficult terms or words that you don't recognize. Regardless of if you completely understand a word or not, replacing it with a synonym either provided or one you more familiar with may help you to understand what the questions are asking. Rather than wracking your mind about specific detailed information concerning a difficult term or word, try to use mental substitutes that are easier to understand.

The Trap of Familiarity

Don't just choose a word because you recognize it. On difficult questions, you may not recognize a number of words in the answer choices. The test writers don't put "make-believe" words on the test; so don't think that just because you only recognize all the words in one answer choice means that answer choice must be correct. If you only recognize words in one answer choice, then focus on that one. Is it correct? Try your best to determine if it is correct. If it is, that is great, but if it doesn't, eliminate it. Each word and answer choice you eliminate increases your chances of getting the question correct, even if you then have to guess among the unfamiliar choices.

Eliminate Answers

Eliminate choices as soon as you realize they are wrong. But be careful! Make sure you consider all of the possible answer choices. Just because one appears right, doesn't mean that the next one won't be even better! The test writers will usually put more than one good answer choice for every question, so read all of them. Don't worry if you are stuck between two that seem right. By getting down to just two remaining possible choices, your odds are now 50/50. Rather than wasting too much time, play the odds. You are guessing, but guessing wisely, because you've been able to knock out some of the answer choices that you know are wrong. If you are eliminating choices and realize that the last answer choice you are left with is also obviously wrong, don't panic. Start over and consider each choice again. There may easily be something that you missed the first time and will realize on the second pass.

Tough Questions

If you are stumped on a problem or it appears too hard or too difficult, don't waste time. Move on! Remember though, if you can quickly check for obviously incorrect answer choices, your chances of guessing correctly are greatly improved. Before you completely give up, at least try to knock out a couple of possible answers. Eliminate what you can and then guess at the remaining answer choices before moving on.

Brainstorm

If you get stuck on a difficult question, spend a few seconds quickly brainstorming. Run through the complete list of possible answer choices. Look at each choice and ask yourself, "Could this answer the question satisfactorily?" Go through each answer choice and consider it independently of the other. By systematically going through all possibilities, you may find something that you would otherwise overlook. Remember that when you get stuck, it's important to try to keep moving.

Read Carefully

Understand the problem. Read the question and answer choices carefully. Don't miss the question because you misread the terms. You have plenty of time to read each question thoroughly and make sure you understand what is being asked. Yet a happy medium must be attained, so don't waste too much time. You must read carefully, but efficiently.

Face Value

When in doubt, use common sense. Always accept the situation in the problem at face value. Don't read too much into it. These problems will not require you to make huge leaps of logic. The test writers aren't trying to throw you off with a cheap trick. If you have to go beyond creativity and make a leap of logic in order to have an answer choice answer the question, then you should look at the other answer choices. Don't overcomplicate the problem by creating theoretical relationships or explanations that will warp time or space. These are normal problems rooted in reality. It's just that the applicable relationship or explanation may not be readily apparent and you have to figure things out. Use your common sense to interpret anything that isn't clear.

Prefixes

If you're having trouble with a word in the question or answer choices, try dissecting it. Take advantage of every clue that the word might include. Prefixes and suffixes can be a huge help. Usually they allow you to determine a basic meaning. Pre- means before, post- means after, pro - is positive, de- is negative. From these prefixes and suffixes, you can get an idea of the general meaning of the word and try to put it into context. Beware though of any traps. Just because con is the opposite of pro, doesn't necessarily mean congress is the opposite of progress!

Hedge Phrases

Watch out for critical "hedge" phrases, such as likely, may, can, will often, sometimes, often, almost, mostly, usually, generally, rarely, sometimes. Question writers insert these hedge phrases to cover every possibility. Often an answer choice will be wrong simply because it leaves no room for exception. Avoid answer choices that have definitive words like "exactly," and "always".

Switchback Words

Stay alert for "switchbacks". These are the words and phrases frequently used to alert you to shifts in thought. The most common switchback word is "but". Others include although, however, nevertheless, on the other hand, even though, while, in spite of, despite, regardless of.

New Information

Correct answer choices will rarely have completely new information included. Answer choices typically are straightforward reflections of the material asked about and will directly relate to the question. If a new piece of information is included in an answer choice that doesn't even seem to relate to the topic being asked about, then that answer choice is likely incorrect. All of the information needed to answer the question is usually provided for you, and so you should not have to make guesses that are unsupported or choose answer choices that require unknown information that cannot be reasoned on its own.

Time Management

On technical questions, don't get lost on the technical terms. Don't spend too much time on any one question. If you don't know what a term means, then since you don't have a dictionary, odds are you aren't going to get much further. You should immediately recognize terms as whether or not you know them. If you don't, work with the other clues that you have, the other answer choices and terms provided, but don't waste too much time trying to figure out a difficult term.

Contextual Clues

Look for contextual clues. An answer can be right but not correct. The contextual clues will help you find the answer that is most right and is correct. Understand the context in which a phrase or statement is made. This will help you make important distinctions.

Don't Panic

Panicking will not answer any questions for you. Therefore, it isn't helpful. When you first see the question, if your mind goes blank, take a deep breath. Force yourself to mechanically go through the steps of solving the problem and using the strategies you've learned.

Pace Yourself

Don't get clock fever. It's easy to be overwhelmed when you're looking at a page full of questions, your mind is full of random thoughts and feeling confused, and the clock is ticking down faster than you would like. Calm down and maintain the pace that you have set for yourself. As long as you are on track by monitoring your pace, you are guaranteed to have enough time for yourself. When you get to the last few minutes of the test, it may seem like you won't have enough time left, but if you only have as many questions as you should have left at that point, then you're right on track!

Answer Selection

The best way to pick an answer choice is to eliminate all of those that are wrong, until only one is left and confirm that is the correct answer. Sometimes though, an answer choice may immediately look right. Be careful! Take a second to make sure that the other choices are not equally obvious. Don't make a hasty mistake. There are only two times that you should stop before checking other answers. First is when you are positive that the answer choice you have selected is correct. Second is when time is almost out and you have to make a quick guess!

Check Your Work

Since you will probably not know every term listed and the answer to every question, it is important that you get credit for the ones that you do know. Don't miss any questions through careless mistakes. If at all possible, try to take a second to look back over your answer selection and make sure you've selected the correct answer choice and haven't made a costly careless mistake (such as marking an answer choice that you didn't mean to mark). This quick double check should more than pay for itself in caught mistakes for the time it costs.

Beware of Directly Quoted Answers

Sometimes an answer choice will repeat word for word a portion of the question or reference section. However, beware of such exact duplication – it may be a trap! More than likely, the correct choice will paraphrase or summarize a point, rather than being exactly the same wording.

Slang

Scientific sounding answers are better than slang ones. An answer choice that begins "To compare the outcomes..." is much more likely to be correct than one that begins "Because some people insisted..."

Extreme Statements

Avoid wild answers that throw out highly controversial ideas that are proclaimed as established fact. An answer choice that states the "process should be used in certain situations, if..." is much more likely to be correct than one that states the "process should be discontinued completely." The first is a calm rational statement and doesn't even make a definitive, uncompromising stance, using a hedge word "if" to provide wiggle room, whereas the second choice is a radical idea and far more extreme.

Answer Choice Families

When you have two or more answer choices that are direct opposites or parallels, one of them is usually the correct answer. For instance, if one answer choice states "x increases" and another answer choice states "x decreases" or "y increases," then those two or three answer choices are very similar in construction and fall into the same family of answer choices. A family of answer choices is when two or three answer choices are very similar in construction, and yet often have a directly opposite meaning. Usually the correct answer choice will be in that family of answer choices. The "odd man out" or answer choice that doesn't seem to fit the parallel construction of the other answer choices is more likely to be incorrect.

Special Report: How to Overcome Test Anxiety

The very nature of tests caters to some level of anxiety, nervousness or tension, just as we feel for any important event that occurs in our lives. A little bit of anxiety or nervousness can be a good thing. It helps us with motivation, and makes achievement just that much sweeter. However, too much anxiety can be a problem; especially if it hinders our ability to function and perform.

"Test anxiety," is the term that refers to the emotional reactions that some test-takers experience when faced with a test or exam. Having a fear of testing and exams is based upon a rational fear, since the test-taker's performance can shape the course of an academic career. Nevertheless, experiencing excessive fear of examinations will only interfere with the test-takers ability to perform, and his/her chances to be successful.

There are a large variety of causes that can contribute to the development and sensation of test anxiety. These include, but are not limited to lack of performance and worrying about issues surrounding the test.

Lack of Preparation

Lack of preparation can be identified by the following behaviors or situations:

Not scheduling enough time to study, and therefore cramming the night before the test or exam
Managing time poorly, to create the sensation that there is not enough time to do everything
Failing to organize the text information in advance, so that the study material consists of the entire text and not simply the pertinent information
Poor overall studying habits

Worrying, on the other hand, can be related to both the test taker, or many other factors around him/her that will be affected by the results of the test. These include worrying about:

Previous performances on similar exams, or exams in general
How friends and other students are achieving
The negative consequences that will result from a poor grade or failure

There are three primary elements to test anxiety. Physical components, which involve the same typical bodily reactions as those to acute anxiety (to be discussed below). Emotional factors have to do with fear or panic. Mental or cognitive issues concerning attention spans and memory abilities.

Physical Signals

There are many different symptoms of test anxiety, and these are not limited to mental and emotional strain. Frequently there are a range of physical signals that will let a test taker know that he/she is suffering from test anxiety. These bodily changes can include the following:

Perspiring
Sweaty palms
Wet, trembling hands
Nausea
Dry mouth
A knot in the stomach
Headache
Faintness
Muscle tension
Aching shoulders, back and neck
Rapid heart beat
Feeling too hot/cold

To recognize the sensation of test anxiety, a test-taker should monitor him/herself for the following sensations:

The physical distress symptoms as listed above
Emotional sensitivity, expressing emotional feelings such as the need to cry or laugh too much, or a sensation of anger or helplessness
A decreased ability to think, causing the test-taker to blank out or have racing thoughts that are hard to organize or control.

Though most students will feel some level of anxiety when faced with a test or exam, the majority can cope with that anxiety and maintain it at a manageable level. However, those who cannot are faced with a very real and very serious condition, which can and should be controlled for the immeasurable benefit of this sufferer.

Naturally, these sensations lead to negative results for the testing experience. The most common effects of test anxiety have to do with nervousness and mental blocking.

Nervousness

Nervousness can appear in several different levels:

The test-taker's difficulty, or even inability to read and understand the questions on the test
The difficulty or inability to organize thoughts to a coherent form
The difficulty or inability to recall key words and concepts relating to the testing questions (especially essays)
The receipt of poor grades on a test, though the test material was well known by the test taker

Conversely, a person may also experience mental blocking, which involves:

Blanking out on test questions
Only remembering the correct answers to the questions when the test has already finished.

Fortunately for test anxiety sufferers, beating these feelings, to a large degree, has to do with proper preparation. When a test taker has a feeling of preparedness, then anxiety will be dramatically lessened.

The first step to resolving anxiety issues is to distinguish which of the two types of anxiety are being suffered. If the anxiety is a direct result of a lack of preparation, this should be considered a normal reaction, and the anxiety level (as opposed to the test results) shouldn't be anything to worry about. However, if, when adequately prepared, the test-taker still panics, blanks out, or seems to overreact, this is not a fully rational reaction. While this can be considered normal too, there are many ways to combat and overcome these effects.

Remember that anxiety cannot be entirely eliminated, however, there are ways to minimize it, to make the anxiety easier to manage. Preparation is one of the best ways to minimize test anxiety. Therefore the following techniques are wise in order to best fight off any anxiety that may want to build.

To begin with, try to avoid cramming before a test, whenever it is possible. By trying to memorize an entire term's worth of information in one day, you'll be shocking your system, and not giving yourself a very good chance to absorb the information. This is an easy path to anxiety, so for those who suffer from test anxiety, cramming should not even be considered an option.

Instead of cramming, work throughout the semester to combine all of the material which is presented throughout the semester, and work on it gradually as the course goes by, making sure to master the main concepts first, leaving minor details for a week or so before the test.

To study for the upcoming exam, be sure to pose questions that may be on the examination, to gauge the ability to answer them by integrating the ideas from your texts, notes and lectures, as well as any supplementary readings.

If it is truly impossible to cover all of the information that was covered in that particular term, concentrate on the most important portions, that can be covered very well. Learn these concepts as best as possible, so that when the test comes, a goal can be made to use these concepts as presentations of your knowledge.

In addition to study habits, changes in attitude are critical to beating a struggle with test anxiety. In fact, an improvement of the perspective over the entire test-taking experience can actually help a test taker to enjoy studying and therefore improve the overall experience. Be certain not to overemphasize the significance of the grade - know that the result of the test is neither a reflection of self worth, nor is it a measure of intelligence; one grade will not predict a person's future success.

To improve an overall testing outlook, the following steps should be tried:

Keeping in mind that the most reasonable expectation for taking a test is to expect to try to demonstrate as much of what you know as you possibly can.
Reminding ourselves that a test is only one test; this is not the only one, and there will be others.
The thought of thinking of oneself in an irrational, all-or-nothing term should be avoided at all costs.
A reward should be designated for after the test, so there's something to look forward to. Whether it be going to a movie, going out to eat, or simply visiting friends, schedule it in advance, and do it no matter what result is expected on the exam.

Test-takers should also keep in mind that the basics are some of the most important things, even beyond anti-anxiety techniques and studying. Never neglect the basic social, emotional and biological needs, in order to try to absorb information. In order to best achieve, these three factors must be held as just as important as the studying itself.

Study Steps

Remember the following important steps for studying:

Maintain healthy nutrition and exercise habits. Continue both your recreational activities and social pass times. These both contribute to your physical and emotional well being.
Be certain to get a good amount of sleep, especially the night before the test, because when you're overtired you are not able to perform to the best of your best ability.
Keep the studying pace to a moderate level by taking breaks when they are needed, and varying the work whenever possible, to keep the mind fresh instead of getting bored.
When enough studying has been done that all the material that can be learned has been learned, and the test taker is prepared for the test, stop studying and do something relaxing such as listening to music, watching a movie, or taking a warm bubble bath.

There are also many other techniques to minimize the uneasiness or apprehension that is experienced along with test anxiety before, during, or even after the examination. In fact, there are a great deal of things that can be done to stop anxiety from interfering with lifestyle and performance. Again, remember that anxiety will not be eliminated entirely, and it shouldn't be. Otherwise that "up" feeling for exams would not exist, and most of us depend on that sensation to perform better than usual. However, this anxiety has to be at a level that is manageable.

Of course, as we have just discussed, being prepared for the exam is half the battle right away. Attending all classes, finding out what knowledge will be expected on the exam, and knowing the exam schedules are easy steps to lowering anxiety. Keeping up with work will remove the need to cram, and efficient study habits will eliminate wasted time. Studying should be done in an ideal location for concentration, so that it is simple to become interested in the material and give it complete attention. A method such as SQ3R (Survey, Question, Read, Recite, Review) is a wonderful key to follow to make sure that the study habits are as effective as possible, especially in the case of learning from a textbook. Flashcards are great techniques for memorization. Learning to take good notes will mean that notes will be full of useful information, so that less sifting will need to be done to seek out what is pertinent for studying. Reviewing notes after class and then again on occasion will keep the information fresh in the mind. From notes that have been taken summary sheets and outlines can be made for simpler reviewing.

A study group can also be a very motivational and helpful place to study, as there will be a sharing of ideas, all of the minds can work together, to make sure that everyone understands, and the studying will be made more interesting because it will be a social occasion.

Basically, though, as long as the test-taker remains organized and self confident, with efficient study habits, less time will need to be spent studying, and higher grades will be achieved.

To become self confident, there are many useful steps. The first of these is "self talk." It has been shown through extensive research, that self-talk for students who suffer from test anxiety, should be well monitored, in order to make sure that it contributes to self confidence as opposed to sinking the student. Frequently the self talk of test-anxious students is negative or self-defeating, thinking that everyone else is smarter and faster, that they always mess up, and that if they don't do well, they'll fail the entire course. It is important to decreasing anxiety that awareness is made of self talk. Try writing any negative self thoughts and then disputing them with a positive statement instead. Begin self-encouragement as though it was a friend speaking. Repeat positive statements to help reprogram the mind to believing in successes instead of failures.

Helpful Techniques

Other extremely helpful techniques include:

Self-visualization of doing well and reaching goals
While aiming for an "A" level of understanding, don't try to "overprotect" by setting your expectations lower. This will only convince the mind to stop studying in order to meet the lower expectations.
Don't make comparisons with the results or habits of other students. These are individual factors, and different things work for different people, causing different results.
Strive to become an expert in learning what works well, and what can be done in order to improve. Consider collecting this data in a journal.
Create rewards for after studying instead of doing things before studying that will only turn into avoidance behaviors.
Make a practice of relaxing - by using methods such as progressive relaxation, self-hypnosis, guided imagery, etc - in order to make relaxation an automatic sensation.
Work on creating a state of relaxed concentration so that concentrating will take on the focus of the mind, so that none will be wasted on worrying.
Take good care of the physical self by eating well and getting enough sleep.
Plan in time for exercise and stick to this plan.

Beyond these techniques, there are other methods to be used before, during and after the test that will help the test-taker perform well in addition to overcoming anxiety.
Before the exam comes the academic preparation. This involves establishing a study schedule and beginning at least one week before the actual date of the test. By doing this, the anxiety of not having enough time to study for the test will be automatically eliminated. Moreover, this will make the studying a much more effective experience, ensuring that the learning will be an easier process. This relieves much undue pressure on the test-taker.

Summary sheets, note cards, and flash cards with the main concepts and examples of these main concepts should be prepared in advance of the actual studying time. A topic should never be eliminated from this process. By omitting a topic because it isn't expected to be on the test is only setting up the test-taker for anxiety should it actually appear on the exam. Utilize the course syllabus for laying out the topics that should be studied. Carefully go over the notes that were made in class, paying special attention to any of the issues that the professor took special care to emphasize while lecturing in class. In the textbooks, use the chapter review, or if possible, the chapter tests, to begin your review.

It may even be possible to ask the instructor what information will be covered on the exam, or what the format of the exam will be (for example, multiple choice, essay, free form, true-false).

Additionally, see if it is possible to find out how many questions will be on the test. If a review sheet or sample test has been offered by the professor, make good use of it, above anything else, for the preparation for the test. Another great resource for getting to know the examination is reviewing tests from previous semesters. Use these tests to review, and aim to achieve a 100% score on each of the possible topics. With a few exceptions, the goal that you set for yourself is the highest one that you will reach.

Take all of the questions that were assigned as homework, and rework them to any other possible course material. The more problems reworked, the more skill and confidence will form as a result. When forming the solution to a problem, write out each of the steps. Don't simply do head work. By doing as many steps on paper as possible, much clarification and therefore confidence will be formed. Do this with as many homework problems as possible, before checking the answers. By checking the answer after each problem, a reinforcement will exist, that will not be on the exam. Study situations should be as exam-like as possible, to prime the test-taker's system for the experience. By waiting to check the answers at the end, a psychological advantage will be formed, to decrease the stress factor.

Another fantastic reason for not cramming is the avoidance of confusion in concepts, especially when it comes to mathematics. 8-10 hours of study will become one hundred percent more effective if it is spread out over a week or at least several days, instead of doing it all in one sitting. Recognize that the human brain requires time in order to assimilate new material, so frequent breaks and a span of study time over several days will be much more beneficial.

Additionally, don't study right up until the point of the exam. Studying should stop a minimum of one hour before the exam begins. This allows the brain to rest and put things in their proper order. This will also provide the time to become as relaxed as possible when going into the examination room. The test-taker will also have time to eat well and eat sensibly. Know that the brain needs food as much as the rest of the body. With enough food and enough sleep, as well as a relaxed attitude, the body and the mind are primed for success.

Avoid any anxious classmates who are talking about the exam. These students only spread anxiety, and are not worth sharing the anxious sentimentalities.

Before the test also involves creating a positive attitude, so mental preparation should also be a point of concentration. There are many keys to creating a positive attitude. Should fears become rushing in, make a visualization of taking the exam, doing well, and seeing an A written on the paper. Write out a list of affirmations that will bring a feeling of confidence, such as "I am doing well in my English class," "I studied well and know my material," "I enjoy this class." Even if the affirmations aren't believed at first, it sends a positive message to the subconscious which will result in an alteration of the overall belief system, which is the system that creates reality.

If a sensation of panic begins, work with the fear and imagine the very worst! Work through the entire scenario of not passing the test, failing the entire course, and dropping out of school, followed by not getting a job, and pushing a shopping cart through the dark alley where you'll live. This will place things into perspective! Then, practice deep breathing and create a visualization of the opposite situation - achieving an "A" on the exam, passing the entire course, receiving the degree at a graduation ceremony.

On the day of the test, there are many things to be done to ensure the best results, as well as the most calm outlook. The following stages are suggested in order to maximize test-taking potential:

Begin the examination day with a moderate breakfast, and avoid any coffee or beverages with caffeine if the test taker is prone to jitters. Even people who are used to managing caffeine can feel jittery or light-headed when it is taken on a test day.
Attempt to do something that is relaxing before the examination begins. As last minute cramming clouds the mastering of overall concepts, it is better to use this time to create a calming outlook.
Be certain to arrive at the test location well in advance, in order to provide time to select a location that is away from doors, windows and other distractions, as well as giving enough time to relax before the test begins.
Keep away from anxiety generating classmates who will upset the sensation of stability and relaxation that is being attempted before the exam.
Should the waiting period before the exam begins cause anxiety, create a self-distraction by reading a light magazine or something else that is relaxing and simple.

During the exam itself, read the entire exam from beginning to end, and find out how much time should be allotted to each individual problem. Once writing the exam, should more time be taken for a problem, it should be abandoned, in order to begin another problem. If there is time at the end, the unfinished problem can always be returned to and completed.

Read the instructions very carefully - twice - so that unpleasant surprises won't follow during or after the exam has ended.

When writing the exam, pretend that the situation is actually simply the completion of homework within a library, or at home. This will assist in forming a relaxed atmosphere, and will allow the brain extra focus for the complex thinking function.

Begin the exam with all of the questions with which the most confidence is felt. This will build the confidence level regarding the entire exam and will begin a quality momentum. This will also create encouragement for trying the problems where uncertainty resides.

Going with the "gut instinct" is always the way to go when solving a problem. Second guessing should be avoided at all costs. Have confidence in the ability to do well.

For essay questions, create an outline in advance that will keep the mind organized and make certain that all of the points are remembered. For multiple choice, read every answer, even if the correct one has been spotted - a better one may exist.

Continue at a pace that is reasonable and not rushed, in order to be able to work carefully. Provide enough time to go over the answers at the end, to check for small errors that can be corrected.

Should a feeling of panic begin, breathe deeply, and think of the feeling of the body releasing sand through its pores. Visualize a calm, peaceful place, and include all of the sights, sounds and sensations of this image. Continue the deep breathing, and take a few minutes to continue this with closed eyes. When all is well again, return to the test.

If a "blanking" occurs for a certain question, skip it and move on to the next question. There will be time to return to the other question later. Get everything done that can be done, first, to guarantee all the grades that can be compiled, and to build all of the confidence possible. Then return to the weaker questions to build the marks from there.

Remember, one's own reality can be created, so as long as the belief is there, success will follow. And remember: anxiety can happen later, right now, there's an exam to be written!

After the examination is complete, whether there is a feeling for a good grade or a bad grade, don't dwell on the exam, and be certain to follow through on the reward that was promised...and enjoy it! Don't dwell on any mistakes that have been made, as there is nothing that can be done at this point anyway.

Additionally, don't begin to study for the next test right away. Do something relaxing for a while, and let the mind relax and prepare itself to begin absorbing information again.

From the results of the exam - both the grade and the entire experience, be certain to learn from what has gone on. Perfect studying habits and work some more on confidence in order to make the next examination experience even better than the last one.

Learn to avoid places where openings occurred for laziness, procrastination and day dreaming. Use the time between this exam and the next one to better learn to relax, even learning to relax on cue, so that any anxiety can be controlled during the next exam. Learn how to relax the body. Slouch in your chair if that helps. Tighten and then relax all of the different muscle groups, one group at a time, beginning with the feet and then working all the way up to the neck and face. This will ultimately relax the muscles more than they were to begin with. Learn how to breathe deeply and comfortably, and focus on this breathing going in and out as a relaxing thought. With every exhale, repeat the word "relax."

As common as test anxiety is, it is very possible to overcome it. Make yourself one of the test-takers who overcome this frustrating hindrance.

Additional Bonus Material

Due to our efforts to try to keep this book to a manageable length, we've created a link that will give you access to all of your additional bonus material.

Please visit http://www.mometrix.com/bonus948/priipacams4-8 to access the information.